The Alhambra and the Generalife

OFFICIAL GUIDE

JUNTA DE ANDALUCIA

Patronato de la Alhambra y Generalife
CONSEJERÍA DE CULTURA

TF. EDITORES

Introduction

As it did in the past, this ancient Nasrid palatial city continues to reign over the horizon of Granada's urban landscape, setting it apart from all other historical sites in the south of Spain. It so happens that it is the only property declared a World Heritage Site (in 1984) that is directly managed by the Andalusian government's Department of Culture; this is done through the Council of the Alhambra and Generalife, an agency specialising in the conservation and restoration of the site's heritage elements.

For years, it has been and continues to be the destination of choice for millions of travellers worldwide who share a lifelong aspiration of visiting the Alhambra and the Generalife. A programme of sustainable management ensures that these visitors can enjoy their right to take part in this gratifying cultural experience. This new official guide has been produced in order to help visitors to fully take advantage of this experience. It includes important new features and shares some of the recent scientific advances that have been made regarding the site, fruit of the continued work of the technical team of the Council of the Alhambra and Generalife and a large, multi-disciplinary group of professionals who collaborate with it on a regular basis.

Along with some always-useful practical tips to consider when preparing for a visit, the guide also includes a set of detailed maps to orient visitors, both on their tour through the different areas in the main compound and on the various routes that connect the city to the monument.

An assessment of the monument's historical value and its artistic significance is given in detail in the commentaries on the different areas making up the main itinerary. This has been enriched with splendid photographic images accompanying the text, the majority of which were previously unpublished or were taken especially for this publication. Also for the first time, a balanced explanation is offered of the heritage-related dimension of the complex as an authentic urban system woven into an area that uses a remarkable hydraulic system to capture and channel water from the Darro River. This water now shapes a cultural landscape in an exceptional state of conservation.

It is with great pleasure that the Department of Culture presents this new guide which, as its primary means of sharing information about the Alhambra and the Generalife, will certainly become a required reference for all those who wish to acquire the knowledge needed to fully enjoy this monumental complex.

Paulino Plata
Minister of Culture of the Andalusian Regional Government

The Alhambra, with the Alcazaba to the left, the Palacio de Carlos V to the right and the Generalife in the background

The Alhambra and the Generalife Monumental Complex: from Nasrid Palace-City to World Heritage Site

The monumental complex of the Alhambra and the Generalife is one of the world's most-visited heritage sites. It is, without a doubt, the city's most important landmark and the hallmark of its identity. Its historical value as a palace-city of the Nasrid dynasty (13th–15th centuries) and the last redoubt of the power of al-Andalus lies not only in its artistic excellence and refined aesthetics but, above all, in its unique and remarkable location with views of the Sierra Nevada mountain range framed by the plains of the Vega. The land became a true earthly paradise thanks to the water that was channelled from the Darro River, making its way through the rough terrain by means of a sophisticated hydraulic system of *acequias* (water channels), canals, wells, water wheels, ponds, reservoirs, *aljibes* (cisterns) and fountains. Almost all of this system has been preserved and maintained over the centuries and, even today, one can see traces of it in the surrounding environment.

Perhaps it is because the landscape helps to create a whole from its many parts that one can state with assurance that the Alhambra and its surroundings were purposely conceived as a cultural construction. It is impossible to explain the existence of this palace-city without also considering the beginnings of the new dynasty that emerged at the end of the Nasrid rule over

Granada. This dynasty aspired to legitimise a new line and a new symbol with which it could be identified — the palace-city of the Alhambra. This would gradually be joined by other royal palaces and *almunias* (country estates), such as the Generalife and its meadows and the Alijares or Dar al-Arusa palaces, to create a truly different urban system separate from the city of Granada, to which it contributes elements of exceptional beauty.

Here, the experience of enjoying its cultural heritage — part and parcel of any cultural visit — is further enriched by sensory and emotional components that know no national borders or religious or historical conventionalisms. Though its origins were based on conflict, it is now a place of meditation, where memories can be uplifted to the goal of peaceful coexistence among all peoples. If a refined and exquisite culture such as that of the Nasrids was capable of conceiving and developing this place over a period of some two hundred and fifty years, another, quite different culture — the Spanish — has been able to maintain and preserve it, thus enabling its existence as the sole remaining example of medieval Muslim palaces and gardens of its time. Not only have its architecture and decoration been widely admired and imitated, they have also been the basis for the creation of other

Side room of the Salón del Trono in the Palacio de Comares

artistic expressions, from literature to music, from painting and sculpture to the creation of designs and craftwork, from architecture to gardening, and from photography to audiovisual creations. Accompanying these historical and material realities is its transcendental intellectual reality, so that today its present is filled with a wide variety of contents that reveal and enrich its social and cultural dimensions.

Included on the list of World Heritage Sites since 1984, its declaration file stated that "The Alhambra and the Generalife are representative of an exceptional architectural and urban category combining defensive, residential, recreational and palace-related functions." To this exceptional universal value we must add the criteria of authenticity and integrity, both of which are closely related to its conservation, and through its conservation we can analyse the way in which architectural restoration was conceived and accepted in our country. The Alhambra compound maintains the essence of its heritage despite the transformations to which it has been subjected, and it always stirs the emotions of those who visit it. This is a constant, regardless of the visitor's home country, language or culture. The universality of the Alhambra touches all who enter it, filling them with the desire to remain forever in this place that so closely resembles our idea of Paradise.

It is also probably the only group of buildings whose walls hold precise messages that help us to better understand the aesthetics of Nasrid art. The epigraphs in the Alhambra are utopian codes encrypted by the vizier-poets of the Royal Chancellery of the Court and were created in order to perpetuate the glory of the monarchs responsible for its construction. These writings reflect the rhythms of the spiritual litanies on which they are based, creating a tapestry of amazing colours, rhythms and textures that are widespread throughout the palace. There are also stylised plant motifs and latticework designs, displayed in a diverse variety of forms and delicate compositions requiring the most meticulous visual study in order to fully enjoy the essence of their aesthetic possibilities. In addition to its function as a lookout point surveying the lower part of the city,

the Vega, the Albaicín and the Darro River valley, one can also appreciate its contrasts of light, the harmony of its courtyards, its architectural design, the contrast of its towers with defensive bastions built at different times throughout its history, the formal richness of its fountains, the skilful architecture reflected in its majestic water tanks, the fragrant perfume of its plants and flowers and its symphony of sounds.

The Palacio del Generalife is also the only royal *almunia* of its time that has been preserved, filled with flower and vegetable gardens that have been continuously cultivated and cared for over the years. Its extraordinary value as a heritage site has been complemented with new spaces added at different moments in its history, currently serving the visitor as an open book on gardens and floral decorations, as well as a model for understanding the household-related purpose of these agricultural holdings owned by the Nasrid kings that were designed as much for relaxation and pleasure as for farming purposes.

Included in this unmatched complex of palatial grounds is another exceptional example of architectural design, the Palacio de Carlos V. Its design — a circular courtyard enclosed by a square building — is symbolic of the humanistic culture admired by the Emperor, who dreamed of one day converting Granada into the capital of the Spanish empire. It currently houses the Alhambra Museum on the ground floor and the Fine Arts Museum on the main floor. The chapel and crypt in the same building are used for different cultural activities, especially temporary exhibitions. The palace also houses the meeting rooms of the Council of the Alhambra as well as a small auditorium.

For the residents of Granada, the Alhambra is the most precious treasure their city has to offer and they do not hesitate to serve as proud interpreters of its history, art and legend to visiting friends and family. They enjoy the Bosque de Gomérez, the fountains, but most of all they enjoy the Granada International Festival of Music and Dance, held every summer to launch the music season in the Alhambra. They also make sure to visit during the traditional Fiesta de la Toma celebration, every 2nd January, to ring the bell in the Torre de la Vela. This is a part of a secular ritual for single women — and, nowadays, men as well — so that they can find the love of their life in the coming year, or get married soon if they already have a partner. During Holy Week, the procession of Santa María de la Alhambra on Holy Saturday has become the main event of the day for locals and astonished visitors, with the procession passing through the Alhambra's compound and woods.

In order that visitors may thoroughly enjoy this heritage site, we have written this new official guide whose aim is to orient, enhance and increase scientific awareness regarding the monument and its surroundings. Its contents have been updated and valuable graphic material has been added, including new maps that will doubtlessly help to guide visitors as they tour the site, and at the same time provide information on the different sights. Those visitors who wish to know more about the Alhambra have not been forgotten: the final section of this guide is dedicated to them and offers additional information about significant aspects of the monument's history and art, particularly about the numerous individuals who are linked to its history. We did not want to miss the opportunity to recommend other routes and spirit-calming visits that include the complex's urban and scenic areas: these itineraries will encourage you to contemplate it from the nearby area of the Albaicín, from which the splendour of its architecture and scenery will delight your eyes. Federico García Lorca said that the Alhambra was the aesthetic focus of the city and described a summer sunrise there in the following words: "[...] and all of the softness and pallor of the wavering blues change into a splendid lightness and the ancient towers of the Alhambra are bright stars of red light..., the houses blind with their whiteness and the shadows take on a brilliant green" (from *Impressions and Landscapes*). This is the Alhambra as poetry in the voice of its most distinguished poet. Without a doubt, the monumental complex of the Alhambra and the Generalife has received its best letter of introduction through this official guide. I hope that you will enjoy it.

María del Mar Villafranca Jiménez
Director-General of the Council of the Alhambra and Generalife

New Official Guide to the Alhambra

This guide is intended to offer visitors a broad but detailed view of the Alhambra monumental complex.

The Alhambra is more than just a monument: it also includes an extensive territory of some 3,455,000 square metres, of which 655,000 square metres may be visited, including buildings from different eras built for diverse purposes, gardens, walls, forests, vegetable gardens, virgin land, water channels, and archaeological remains.

This handbook has been divided into various chapters that describe not only the Alhambra itself, but also the monument's geographical environment and the history that shaped it.

In each chapter, some elements that are unique to the area being highlighted are explained, with special information boxes that include an image and a short explanation in addition to the general description. The beginning of each chapter includes a two-page summary and a site map.

The guide is abundantly illustrated with numerous images. All maps, reproductions and old photographs are the property of the Council of the Alhambra and Generalife, unless otherwise specified below the image. The guide begins with an explanation of the Alhambra's geographical environment and its relationship with the city of Granada, and it includes several different ways to reach the gates to the Alhambra. While we recommend that visitors follow the itinerary presented in this book, you may visit the monument in any order you wish.

The guide continues with an explanation for each of the unique areas found within the walled compound, whether visitors have access to them or not (due to their special conservation status or condition, some of these areas are excluded from the standard Alhambra tour). The Generalife — the rural estate of the Nasrid sultans outside but adjacent to the Alhambra and nestled in gardens and orchards — deserves and has been given its own chapter, while another chapter is dedicated to the archaeological remains found in the north-eastern part of the complex, which is the most mountainous and distant from the city.

Lastly, we have included two theoretical chapters. In the first, some important key concepts regarding architecture and decoration are explained so that visitors may better understand the Alhambra of the Nasrids. In the second, we present some of the historical events that took place in the Alhambra over the centuries, as well as a series of charts showing the Nasrid and other kingdoms of the era.

The Appendix offers additional useful information, including a selection of historical figures linked to the Alhambra, an index containing all of the names found in the guide, a glossary of technical or unusual words and another with Spanish names, and a small bibliography. At the end of the guide, a series of blank pages has been included for those wishing to take notes.

he Torre de Comares, site of the 14th-century Nasrid Alhambra's main hall, the Salón del Trono

Index

Carved plaster and tile detailing on the Torre de la Cautiva

1 Granada and the Alhambra

Located on one of the three hills to the north of Granada, the Alhambra dominates the city from a height of 100 metres. The historic relationship between both has been very close since the Alhambra is a visible reference point from nearly everywhere in the city. The metropolitan complex consisting of Granada, the Alhambra and the surrounding natural spaces — the Darro and Genil Rivers, the Vega and the Sierra Nevada — is one of the most renowned, worldwide.

The Alhambra dominates the city of Granada from atop Sabika Hill, some 100 metres above the city.

The relationship between the elevated area of Sabika Hill and the Alhambra is similar to that of other historically important cities with their geographical surroundings, such as Athens, Jerusalem, Rome, Fez, Istanbul, Salzburg, Toledo, etc. — which travellers everywhere have traditionally compared to Granada. As occurs in these cities, a mutually dependent relationship exists between the Alhambra and its "lower city" — a relationship that is at times idyllic, at times illusive, often chaotic, and, always, of inevitable urban symbiosis.

For these reasons, the Alhambra is considered to be one of the city's historical districts: the city centre with its cathedral compound, the Albaicín, the Sacromonte and the Realejo. It is also considered, together with the natural area that surrounds it – the Darro and Genil Rivers, the Vega and Sierra Nevada mountain range – to be one of the most famous and well-recognised metropolitan compounds in the world.

Geographical Environment

The city of Granada is located at 37° 10' 18" latitude North and 03° 35' 56" longitude West (of the Prime Meridian), and 683 metres above sea level.

Granada enjoys a typical Mediterranean climate: its summers are warm but its winters are remarkably chilly, with daily temperatures fluctuating as much as 20°C. What little precipitation there is generally occurs over the autumn and spring seasons.

Anton van den Wyngaerde, *View of Granada* (1571), wash drawing, ÖNB, Vienna
Granada as seen from the south, with the Alhambra and the mountain range in the background, has been represented repeatedly over the past four hundred years. Anton van den Wyngaerde, a Renaissance artist who travelled Europe to illustrate its cities, visited Granada in 1567, and his work is essential to understanding what the city and many others he drew in the mid-16th century were like at that time.

Panoramic view of the Albaicín, with the Alhambra, Granada and the Vega in the foreground
Overleaf: **Aerial view of the Alhambra with the Realejo neighbourhood in the foreground**

It occasionally snows in the winter, while summer often brings severe droughts.

Granada is somewhat different from other Andalusian cities, having strong contrasts both in terms of its physical characteristics and its inhabitants. It is located in the geographical centre of the eastern side of the region – in what is known as "Upper Andalusia" – where the Baetic mountain range (part of the so-called Surco Intrabético, a series of longitudinal depressions) links the Levante and the Mediterranean from Ronda to the Hoyas (trough-shaped geological depressions) of Baza and Vera, in contrast with the Guadalquivir plain and the edge of the Sierra Morena mountains to the north (the other two major geographical units in Andalusia).

Granada's location has been instrumental in its peculiar history, and in both the positive and the negative phases of its economic development.

The Nasrid kingdom was located mostly within the Andalusia framed by this large mountain range. The Baetic range – which came about as the result of geological folds in the Alps south of the ancient Hercynian massif in Germany (the origin of the current plateau adjacent to the Pyrenees and the Cantabrian Mountains) – is the youngest and tallest of the mountain ranges on the Iberian Peninsula. Though not the steepest of its mountains, they are the Peninsula's highest, soaring to nearly 3,500 metres at the Mulhacén and Veleta mountain peaks. Another peculiarity of this mountain system is its geological and geographical complexity, as it comprises two large alignments: the northern Baetic running adjacent to the lower depression of the Guadalquivir, and the Penibaetic mountain range, which runs along the Mediterranean coast. In its interior, it is outlined by a series of depressions that gradually increase in height from southeast to northeast.

The Granada Depression – the largest and most central of the depressions inside the Baetic range – is a naturally delimited area inside of which is located the city of the Alhambra. Granada benefits from being located in the middle of the essential transport routes created as the result of this depression.

The greatest difficulty – except in times of defence – is the north-south route, putting

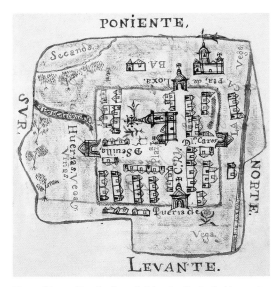

Map of Santa Fe, city founded by the Catholic Monarchs at the close of the 15th century. The Provincial Historical Archives of Granada. Cadastre of the Marquis of Ensenada

Granada at a clear disadvantage in comparison with other cities such as Málaga or Almería, due to its great distance from the two corridors – the Guadalhorce to the west and the Guadiana Menor to the east – that cross the region.

On the other hand, it is the most extensive depression, stretching more than 50 kilometres from Loja. Despite its depth (of 500 to 600 metres) its land is highly fertile and, as a result, the most widely inhabited. From the times of the first settlers, this fertility has proved to be a great advantage. Surrounded by a ring of mountains, with the great bluff of the Sierra Nevada enclosing it to the east, it has but one way out; the difficult exit where the Genil River flows out towards the Guadalquivir River through Loja. The sunken depression is composed of sedimentary soils resulting from the continual erosion of the surrounding massifs.

The first settlers of this mountain-ringed plain – known as the "Vega de Granada" – took advantage of the fertile soil rich in conglomerates, sand, silt and clay – an excellent base for planting crops – with its guaranteed water supply from the thawed waters flowing down from the Sierra Nevada replenishing the aquifer.

This natural richness — besides ensuring the existence of settlements — undoubtedly also defined the type and layout of the settlements that were established. All the urban clusters were located at the edge of the depression in the mountainous foothills or ridges, while the site of the city itself was located on the land between the Beiro, Darro and Genil Rivers, atop three hills on the skirts of the Sierra Nevada composed of large masses of red-coloured Quaternary conglomerates known as "Alhambra conglomerate." The rivers originating from the high mountains have cut into and eroded the hills, resulting in the original barrier of conglomerates taking on its current topographic characteristics.

The three hills are all approximately 750 metres high. San Cristóbal Hill, which is extremely steep, reaches some 760 metres at its highest point, while the middle hill — Albaicín Hill — less steep and somewhat flatter, has been subjected to greater urban development, particularly around the Darro River.

To the south of the Darro is the steeply sloped hill on which the city of the Alhambra sits. Reaching a height of some 790 metres, Sabika Hill is the highest and largest of the three. This hill, separated from the 980-metre high Cerro del Sol to the east by the steep ravine of the Rey Chico or of the Chinos, is virtually isolated from the Vega and the mountains that protect it by steep escarpments and ravines. In turn, the hill is divided into two sides — the higher Sabika side, and the less steep Mauror side (760 metres), home to the Torres Bermejas — by a stream crossing through Alhambra Woods.

Most of the city has been built and shaped around these hills, especially the hill on which the Alhambra is located. Initially, this development took place around the nearby foothills located between the three rivers, and this is where the first Arab *medina* (quarter) was built — both in contrast with and complementary to the more elevated *alcazabas* (citadels) — along with a

Grenade à vol d'oisseau (1853), with a view of the Generalife, the Alhambra and the city in the background. Lithograph by M. Aumont

The Alhambra seen from Granada in the early 19th century. In the background, on the left, the Torre de la Vela, and on the right, the Torres Bermejas. Coloured engraving by Alexandre Laborde (1812)

multipurpose, labyrinthine road. Later, during the Christian era, the city expanded slowly towards the plains, always giving priority to the view of the hills, particularly the hill on which the Alhambra is built, with its main visual landmarks including the Torre de la Vela, the Torres Bermejas, the Torre de Comares, etc.

As a result of recent demographic growth and urban development, Granada has spread out over the entire plain – particularly to the north and south – turning its back on this view and replacing it with others, such as that of the mountain range. In recent decades, as major access roads have been built and the ancient towns of the Vega have grown, the metropolitan area has also expanded. So much so that today Granada is a mid-sized city with some 300,000 inhabitants and over 600,000 people living in its metropolitan area.

Due to this urban expansion, the palace-city of the Alhambra has lost its important role in

organising and balancing the city's urban fabric. It is also less of a visual reference point, as there are now several neighbourhoods from which it cannot be seen. Despite these changes, however, the Alhambra continues to be the principal landmark of the city's urban scenery.

Surrounding Areas
The Alhambra monumental complex consists of the enclosed compound and a defined area surrounding it in which certain architectural elements – inseparable from the compound are found. As it climbs upwards in a clockwise direction to the north, the valley of the Darro River serves as backbone to both cities, which are located at different levels. Opposite the Albaicín, the outside of the Alhambra looks out over the river in what is today known as the "Bosque de San Pedro"; its 60,000 square metres were surely used for falconry and other similar activities in

The Alhambra seen from the south. In the foreground, the Torres Bermejas. In the background, to the right, the Generalife

medieval times, judging from the small water channels, ovens and water wheels that make use of the river passing through it, all of which are of great value as heritage elements.

Elevated above the Darro River's left bank — the bank closest to the Alhambra — is a large area of some 330,000 square metres, including the Cerro del Sol and the Generalife meadow. From above, it encircles and protects the rear of the fortress, the part furthest from Granada.

Various water-related structures were distributed throughout this area during medieval times as if they were oases designed to contain residential spaces. These were scattered among vast pastures used for grazing flocks of livestock and breeding horses, as well as extensive orchards spread across rough terrain, separated by large retaining walls or by walls erected for security purposes. All of these were used to supply provisions to the palace-city. Over time, these

hydraulic structures and various settlements colonised the southern slopes that descend gently from where the Qasr al-Disar — the mythical Palacio de los Alijares — once facing Mauror Hill. The distribution of water was managed from this slope, the site of the last of the Nasrid military parades. It also served for keeping watch over the mountain passes in the direction of the large river to the south — the Genil — which had *alquerías* (farm workers' cottages) located on its banks, and which was also the route connecting the mountain range and the gorges with the valley and the sea.

Lastly, to the southwest lies Antequeruela, the ancient neighbourhood that protected the Garnata al-Yahud (Granada's Jewish quarter) via the Torres Bermejas, the authentic observatory of Granada that is connected to the Alhambra by means of a stepped wall that runs across the Almanzora, Sabika and Churra ravine.

How to Reach the Alhambra

There are three ways to reach the Alhambra: by public transport (bus or taxi), private vehicle or on foot. The most appropriate entrance is through the Puerta de la Justicia, which may be reached via any of these three options. The three pedestrian accesses — the Cuesta de Gomérez, the Cuesta del Realejo and the Cuesta del Rey Chico —, which are accessed from three different neighbourhoods — the city centre, the Realejo and the Albaicín —, are historic routes that pass through the wooded area, home to unique elements outside of the Alhambra's walls.

Due to its geographic configuration, access from Granada to the Alhambra has traditionally been quite varied, adapting to the urban development of the time. Today, there are three different ways to access the monument: by public transport, private vehicle or on foot following the historic pedestrian routes. The most appropriate entrance to the Alhambra, in terms of practicality and symbolism, is through the Puerta de la Justicia which is accessed via the Entrance Pavilion (where tickets may be bought), either from the path running along the outside of the wall or from inside the compound.

Public Transport

There is a city-run minibus service connecting the monument to the city centre and the Albaicín; detailed information is available at bus stops.

In addition, the city offers a taxi service with stops near the Alhambra's entrances.

Access Roads for Vehicles and Parking

One can also access the complex by car or other vehicle using the city's bypass motorway, which connects Granada to the Sierra Nevada ski station and the coast. The car park covers nearly 10,000 square metres and is spread out over several terraces. With space for 600 cars and 70 buses, it is open and guarded twenty-four hours a day. Parking fees are separate from the visit to the complex.

Historic Routes to the Alhambra

Three historic pedestrian routes link the Alhambra with Granada and its traditional

neighbourhoods: the Cuesta de Gomérez (the usual route from the city centre), the Cuesta del Realejo (from the traditional neighbourhood of the same name) and the Cuesta del Rey Chico (connecting directly with the Albaicín and the Sacromonte).

The three routes — which can also be followed on the return trip — begin in three different areas of the city, but they all meet up at the spot where the visit to the monumental complex begins. Their paths run through an expansive space between the two cities known generically as "Alhambra Woods." These woods are home to unique elements including the Torres Bermejas, the Villa of Peñapartida, the Pilar de Carlos V, the Puerta de Bibrambla and the Ángel Ganivet and Washington Irving Monuments. (These latter may be visited separately, thus their descriptions appear after those of the access routes.)

Cuesta de Gomérez

This route travels from the Plaza Nueva de Granada to the Puerta de las Granadas, the opening in the wall linking the Torres Bermejas to the Alcazaba (Citadel).

It gets its name from a dynasty with roots in North Africa that settled here and created this neighbourhood— according to 16th-century historian Mármol Carvajal. In medieval times, it was a rain gully separating Sabika Hill — the site of the Alhambra — from Mauror Hill, presided over by the Torres Bermejas. The two constructions were joined by a wall that served

The Cuesta del Rey Chico as it passes by the Torre del Qadí

Access to the Alhambra

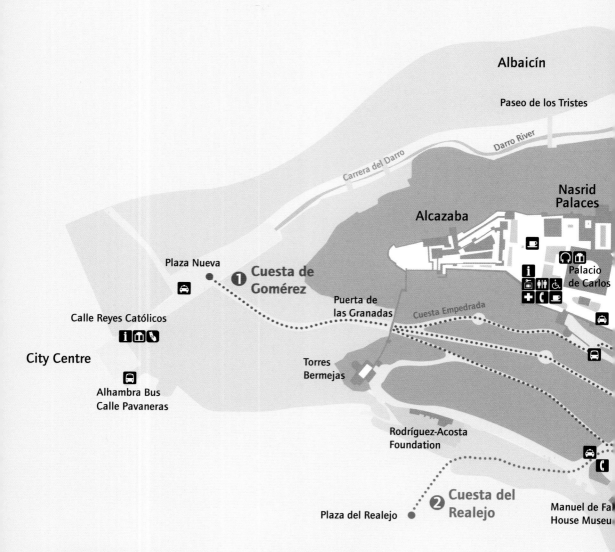

Historic pedestrian routes

❶ **Cuesta de Gomérez**
1,150 metres from the Plaza Nueva
in the centre of Granada

❷ **Cuesta del Realejo**
890 metres from the Plaza del Realejo
in the Realejo district

❸ **Cuesta del Rey Chico**
860 metres from the Paseo de
los Tristes in the Albaicín

Access by car or bus

Cars and buses: 🅿
Access via the Ronda Sur. Parking

Taxis: Tel. 958 280 654 🚕
Stops at the Alhambra, in front of the Church of
Santa María of the Alhambra, the Alhambra Palace
Hotel and the Gate of the Generalife

Alhambra minibus: 🚌
Connection to the city centre, the Alhambra and the
Albaicín, Sacromonte and Realejo neighbourhoods

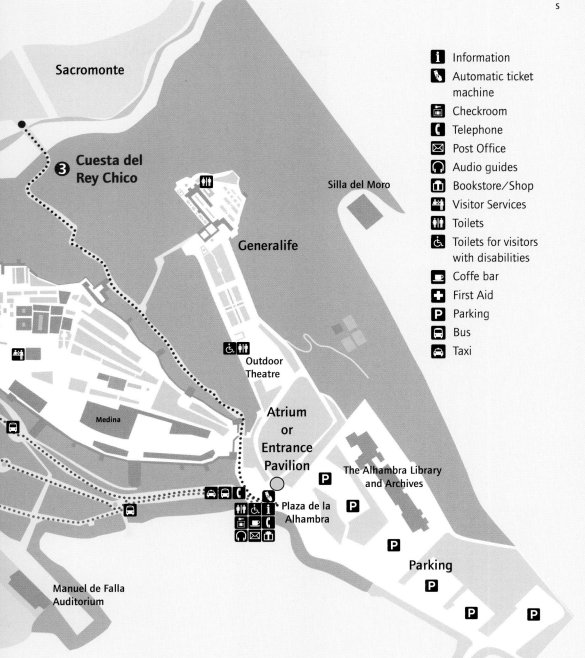

Sacromonte

③ Cuesta del Rey Chico

Silla del Moro

Generalife

Outdoor
Theatre

**Atrium
or
Entrance
Pavilion**

Medina

The Alhambra Library
and Archives

Plaza de la
Alhambra

Parking

Manuel de Falla
Auditorium

Ronda Sur
Vehicle access

	Information
	Automatic ticket machine
	Checkroom
	Telephone
	Post Office
	Audio guides
	Bookstore/Shop
	Visitor Services
	Toilets
	Toilets for visitors with disabilities
	Coffe bar
	First Aid
P	Parking
	Bus
	Taxi

0   50   100   150   200   250 m

Puerta de las Granadas

This is one of the gates located in the ancient wall surrounding Granada and is a replacement for the original medieval gate.

Attributed to Pedro Machuca — the same architect who designed the Palacio de Carlos V — this gate was built around 1536 as a triumphant entranceway following the Emperor's decision to have a residence built in the Alhambra. Constructed of rusticated stone, its pediment displays the imperial coat of arms; above this can be seen the allegorical figures of Peace and Abundance and three large pomegranates, the symbol of the city. Recently restored, it leads to Alhambra Woods — the great "green lung" of the city — and serves as an antechamber to the Alhambra fortress.

in the past — as it still does to this day — to mark the boundary between the urban area of Granada and the Alhambra compound. The Puerta de las Granadas was built around 1536, by Pedro Machuca, the same architect who designed the Palacio de Carlos V, for use as a solemn entrance to the Alhambra. The gate is built from rusticated stone similar to that of the palace. The tympanum shows the imperial coat of arms with the allegorical figures of Peace and Abundance, crowned by the three large pomegranates which give it its name. This Renaissance gate replaced an original Muslim gate, some of whose archaeological remains can be found next to it.

Detail of *Platform* by Ambrosio Vico (ca. 1614) with the Cuesta de Gomérez and the wall separating Granada from the Alhambra. Alhambra Library

Beyond the gate stretch the Alhambra Woods, home to hundreds of elms, poplars, horse chestnut trees, etc., planted over the 19th century. From this point, there are three routes passing through the woods; the two side routes are exclusively for pedestrians. The right-hand path leads to the Torres Bermejas, the Manuel de Falla Auditorium and the Carmen de los Mártires, among other sites, while the left-hand path — which used to be known as "Cobblestone Hill" — leads to the southern side of the Alhambra's wall, to the Puerta de la Justicia, also called the Puerta de la Explanada. Historically, it was also known as the "Promenade of the Crosses," as prayer crosses were installed throughout the area over the years. Recently, traffic has been prohibited on the middle path, limiting it to pedestrians only.

The Cuesta de Gomérez is the usual route taken from the centre of Granada to the Alhambra. Since the late 19th century, various businesses producing traditional Granada-style handcrafted items have set up shop here, including guitars, ceramics, marquetry and precious metal work; today, they offer a wide variety of souvenirs that are typical of the city.

There are 1,150 metres from the Plaza Nueva, where the Cuesta de Gomérez begins, to the Alhambra's Entrance Pavilion or Atrium, 660 metres to the inside of the monument and 1,000 metres to the Manuel de Falla Cultural Centre and the Carmen de los Mártires.

Cuesta del Realejo

This is the shortest but steepest route between Granada and the Alhambra, and the most direct access from the Realejo neighbourhood, one of the best-known areas of the city. According to Granada-born professor Manuel Gómez-Moreno, the name "Realejo" comes from the royal truck gardens found in this area visited by Nasrid sultans for recreation and relaxation. In the late 15th century, it was called the Campo del Rey. It was traditionally considered to have been the home of the city's Jewish quarter, perhaps because the 10th-century geographer and historian al-Razi referred to it as Garnata al-Yahud or the Jewish Granada.

In any event, the neighbourhood nowadays revolves around two very different *plazas* or squares: the Plaza de Fortuny — once known as the Plaza del Realejo Bajo, and the Campo del Príncipe. The former was named in honour of Catalonian painter Mariano Fortuny, who resided here between 1870 and 1871 and to whom Granada City Council dedicated a commemorative plaque in 1874. This square was the site of the *Bab al-Fajjarín* (Potter's Gate), which was torn down in 1551 having previously given access and a name to the neighbourhood. Next to this square is the Plaza del Realejo, previously known as the Plaza del Realejo Alto, where the route in direction of the Alhambra begins. The square was built next to a pillar of carved stone in 1616 — repaired in the mid-19th century —

whose decoration includes the sculpture of a pomegranate, eternal symbol of the city.

The first part of the slope runs alongside the Convent of Santa Catalina de Siena, built here around 1530.

The second part makes its way among the *tapias* (rammed earth walls) of the numerous *cármenes* (country houses with gardens and orchards typical of Granada), similar to those in the Albaicín. At the top of the slope the visitor is surprised by a "neo-Arabic" building, the Alhambra Palace Hotel. It was built in 1910 as a luxury hotel by Modesto Cendoya, the former architectural curator of the Alhambra, under the sponsorship of the Duke of San Pedro de Galatino. This establishment, a symbol of the boom in tourism that Granada experienced in the early 20th century, led to the 1910 installation of a tramway that ascended the Cuesta del Caidero, today reserved for vehicular traffic.

The Cuesta del Realejo ends at the country estate known as Peñapartida adjacent to an narrow street called Niño del Rollo, an area of the city where various cultural establishments are located. This is the site of the museum that was once a house inhabited by universal musician Manuel de Falla, a native of Cádiz adopted by the city of Granada. Next to this house museum is the Manuel de Falla Auditorium — one of the best in the country — which also houses the Archives and the Foundation dedicated to this composer; it was built in 1978 by architect García de Paredes. Nearby is the Carmen de los Mártires, site

View of the Upper Realejo and the Alhambra Palace Hotel (under construction) from the Belén orchard, ca. 1908. Alhambra Archives

of diverse cultural encounters and surrounded by beautiful gardens with excellent views of the city.

Niño del Rollo Street is also the location of the headquarters of the Rodríguez-Acosta Foundation. Built in 1920 under the patronage of painter and patron of the arts José María Rodríguez-Acosta, it is one of Granada's most dynamic cultural spaces. It also houses the Gómez-Moreno Foundation, site of the family archives of these Granada-based researchers from the 19th and 20th centuries. Opposite is the historic Carmen de Peñapartida country estate, with theTorres Bermejas located at the end of the street.

The Alhambra Woods begin here and their paths lead to different parts of the monumental compound.

There are 890 metres from where the Cuesta del Realejo begins to the Alhambra's Entrance Pavilion or Atrium, 800 metres to the inside of the monument and 620 metres to the Manuel de Falla Cultural Centre and the Carmen de los Mártires.

Cuesta del Rey Chico

Of the three routes to the Alhambra, this runs closest to the neighbourhoods considered most representative of the essence of Granada — the Albaicín and the Sacromonte. The route begins at the Darro River, at the end of the Paseo de los Tristes, in the area near the Cuesta del Chapiz — a kind of "umbilical cord" connecting the two neighbourhoods — overlooked by the impressive northern facades of the Alhambra wall, which can be seen from the Albaicín.

Its name came from the famous historic legend in which Aisha, the mother of Boabdil the Rey Chico (Young King), helped her son flee in order to lead the rebels waiting in the Albaicín in an attack

Manuel de Falla Auditorium, work of architect José María García de Paredes. It is the home of the City of Granada Orchestra, inaugurated in 1978 close to the musician's villa

The Rodríguez-Acosta Foundation, created from the endowment of Granada painter and patron of the arts José María Rodríguez-Acosta

against his father. Among the numerous names that it has received is the traditional Cuesta de los Molinos (Hill of the Mills), the name given to the ravine that separates the hill of the Generalife from the hill of the Alhambra. In the beginning there were several watermills along the route, and some of their remains may be seen today. They used the water flowing from the Darro River and the various channels that flowed from there towards the centre of the city. Towards the end of the 19th century it was also referred to as the Cuesta de los Muertos (Hill of the Dead), as it formed part of the route of funeral processions from the city to the recently opened cemetery located on the highest part of Sabika Hill. Finally, it is commonly referred to as the Cuesta de los Chinos since its first section was paved with pebbles at the beginning of the 20th century. The route begins at the Puente del Aljibillo and provides access to another late 19th-century emblematic site, the Fuente del Avellano (Hazelnut Tree Fountain). It gave its name to a group of Granada-based Romantic-era intellectuals headed by writer Ángel Ganivet.

After the first, very steep, section — bordered by a few houses — the city is left behind as the path heads into the ravine separating the Alhambra from the Generalife. To the right are the wall and the towers of the compound, overlooked by the Torre de las Damas in the Partal and, to the le ft, the lower part of the Generalife's orchards. About halfway along the path, we find a bastion from the Christian era with the striking Puerta de Hierro, a structure designed to defend one of the Alhambra's exterior gates, the Puerta de Arrabal at the foot of the Torre de los Picos.

Opposite and some metres above is the medieval entrance to the Generalife.

Continuing up the now somewhat gentler slope of the hill, the path passes along the outside of the Alhambra's wall next to the Torre del Qadí, the Torre de la Cautiva, the Torre de las Infantas and the Torre del Cabo de la Carrera, before crossing under the bridge and aqueduct linking the Alhambra and the Generalife and coming to the area known as La Mimbre (Wicker). Today, this erstwhile tavern is one of the city's most

The Cuesta del Rey Chico with the turret that controlled those travelling on it and closed off the bastion in front of the Torre de los Picos

The Cuesta del Rey Chico was also called the Cuesta de los Muertos as it was the traditional route for funeral processions to the cemetery located on the peak of Sabika Hill. Lithograph by J. F. Lewis (1835)

representative restaurants. Located at the foot of the reconstructed Torre del Agua and adjacent to the old entrance to the Generalife, one can see the gate that still bears the coat of arms of the Granada-Venegas family which owns the restaurant.

Next to La Mimbre we find the Entrance Pavilion to the monumental compound of the Alhambra and the Generalife.

It is 860 metres from where the Cuesta del Rey Chico begins to the Alhambra's Entrance Pavilion or Atrium, 1,200 metres to the inside of the monument and 970 metres to the Manuel de Falla Cultural Centre and the Carmen de los Mártires.

The Alhambra Woods

The historic routes connecting Granada to the Alhambra pass through the extensive and varied area known generically as the "Alhambra Woods." Today, this "green lung" — one of the city's natural heritage elements — contrasts with and enriches the monument's artistic and historic heritage and serves as its entrance hall.

In addition to their natural resources, the woods offer a richly creative natural space that is home to some unique elements of historic interest for the city: the Puerta de Bibrambla, the Pilar de Carlos V and the Ángel Ganivet and Washington Irving Monuments.

Dense trees surround the monumental compound, covering its sides as they descend to the Darro River and towards the centre of the city of Granada. Though its origins are recent, beginning in he early 16th century there are numerous accounts of elm trees taken from the Jesús del Valle area near the headwaters of the Darro River to be planted to beautify and visually unify the new pedestrian and carriage paths coming from the Cuesta de Gomérez.

It is assumed that — due to the military nature of the city of the Alhambra and the military context in which the kingdom of Granada found itself because of the Christian threat — the fortress was not surrounded by such a dense forest during medieval times, at least not on the southern and western sides, whose descent into the city and the Vega of Granada is relatively gentle. However, the steep side where the Albaicín overlooks the Darro River — facing north and supplied with abundant water — probably was home to woody shrubs and even some moderately sized trees, including Holm oaks and Portuguese oaks, hawthorns, buckthorns, butcher's broom and honeysuckle.

The gradual reforestation undertaken by the successive Christian rulers of the Alhambra probably meant that the slope was fully covered by the 17th century, though it was not until the beginning of the 19th century — with the introduction of garden species from the rest of Europe, such as the London plane or the horse chestnut — that this area would be called "Alhambra Woods."

The wooded area in the Sabika Hill valley is called the Bosque de Gomérez; it can be crossed either on foot or by car. There is another wood — known as the Bosque de San Pedro — on the hillside descending to the Darro River, opposite a church bearing the same name. As a result of their different geographical characteristics and relationship with the city, each of these areas has its own peculiar characteristics. In the Bosque de Gomérez, we find a greater number of large-sized species, with a lower density as a result of the area being open to public access. On the other hand, in the Bosque de San Pedro — access to which is restricted — the vegetation is denser, although not as tall, because the purpose of the plant cover here is to provide protection against erosion and landslides.

These wooded areas are populated mostly by deciduous trees. The elm *(Ulmus minor)*

View of Alhambra Woods on the slope of Sabika Hill, with the Palacio de los Alijares and the Sierra Nevada in the background

played an important role in their structure, dynamics and scenic value, until a fungus caused the decline of this species throughout Europe in the late 1990s. As a result, the number of elms in the Alhambra has dwindled to a few dozen.

Today, some one hundred species of trees and shrubs can be found in these forests, the most common being the European hackberry, horse chestnut, London plane, bay, European privet, hazel, lime, maple and ash.

The historic significance of the vegetation in the Alhambra and the landscape of Granada resulted in it being considered an inseparable part of the culture and heritage of the Nasrid-era constructions, receiving full legal protection following the complex's declaration as a National Monument in 1870.

The Alhambra Woods

The slopes of Sabika Hill that face Granada create a natural space that complements and enriches the monumental complex's artistic and cultural value and serves as a "green lung" between the city and the Alhambra. Its design has varied over the centuries: the woods that we know today are a recent creation, though that will not prevent us from finding a wide variety of plant species of great ecological value, some of which were brought from elsewhere in Europe.

Torres Bermejas

The earliest Torres Bermejas were part of a series of watchtowers located at the highest, most strategic points surrounding the Vega of Granada; they may have also existed at the time of the first constructions on Sabika Hill that would eventually become the Alhambra. The history of the Torres Bermejas has paralleled that of the Alhambra's Alcazaba. It is believed that it was first inhabited by Muhammad I, founder of the Nasrid dynasty, although the construction elements used to build its oldest walls — very similar to those of the Alcazaba — may date back to far earlier times.

Currently the compound consists of three towers — the middle tower is the tallest — and a prominent artillery bastion. There is evidence throughout the compound of a series of modifications carried out after the Christian conquest, particularly in the 16th century. Its interior walls hold numerous Muslim tombstones, proof that the towers — especially the middle tower — were reinforced on the inside during the Christian era. It was also after 1492 that the space inside was partitioned: one of the three floors into which the tower was divided contains a large circular dome dated around 1540. A cistern has been preserved inside, possibly modified from

The Torres Bermejas is a strategic fortification that was once part of the structure of the wall linking the southern part of the Alhambra with Granada

View from the Alhambra's Alcazaba of the Torres Bermejas, the woods and the Carmen de Peñapartida

an earlier hydraulic structure dating from the Muslim period.

The Torres Bermejas compound connects directly with the Alcazaba of the Alhambra through a wall — most of which still exists — running at a right angle to both buildings and demonstrating the important role that the towers played in the defence system of the palace-city.

The Torre Bermejas fortification was used as a prison and military barracks for many years — until almost the middle of the 20th century – which resulted in its original layout undergoing a number of changes. A Muslim cemetery is known to be nearby, further evidence of which are the numerous gravestones found in the towers' walls which — as in other parts of the Alhambra — surely were not transported from very far away. Mauror Hill — site of the towers — was traditionally known for its Jewish population, and came to be known as the Garnata al-Yahud. A magnificent panoramic view of the city and a less known architectural profile of the Alhambra's Alcazaba can be seen from these towers.

Peñapartida

This walled country house is also known as the Carmen de los Catalanes (Catalonians' Villa) due to the origin of its owners, the Miralles family, which acquired the property in the early 20th century

from the heirs of Isabel de los Cobos and Antonio Porcel (1775–1832), a well-known judge, academic and liberal politician from Granada, who served as State Councillor and parliamentary member of the Legislative Assembly of Cádiz. Influenced by 19th-century tastes, they embellished the villa — in particular the garden — with water-based elements and devices, paths, pergolas and watch towers, leaving an idiosyncratic stamp upon it that remains to this day.

The property — also known as "Paradise Villa" or the "Villa of Columbus's Folly" — measures some 20,000 square metres that are incorporated into its surroundings and the Alhambra Woods. Located on a hill parallel to and south of the Alhambra adjacent to the Torres Bermejas, both are within the fortress's system of defence. The villa is located in the area known as *Ahabul* in Arabic, within what must have been the *Maqbarat al-Sabika,* one of the cemeteries in the city. During the Nasrid era, many underground silos were built here for storing provisions while the dynasty was establishing itself in the city. A military camp was most likely situated on its wide esplanade, so the gently sloped hill would have been the occasional site of marches and parades. During the 15th century, many of the silos were also used to hold Christian prisoners so they could be exchanged for Muslim captives.

Carmen de Peñapartida

After more than 20 years of court battles, in 2002 the Council of the Alhambra, acquired the so-called Catalonians' Villa or Peñapartida — at nearly 20,000 square metres, the largest private property in the area around the monumental compound and site of important archaeological remains. There are two medieval turrets on the property, as well as a medieval hydraulic network which descends to the ancient district of Antequeruela (currently the Realejo), a large part of a *maqbarat* or cemetery, and a "corral of captives" consisting of silos dug into the ground that were used to hold prisoners. All of these elements make the property a heritage site with great potential for archaeological research.

According to tradition, the troops of the Catholic Monarchs marched from their base in Santa Fe into these hills on the morning of 2 January 1492, heading in the direction of the Puerta de los Siete Suelos to take control of the Alhambra and to later free the captives held in the dungeons. Since then, this site on the side of the hill has been called the "Field of the Martyrs" and, in memory of their captivity, the Peñapartida compound is also known as the "Corral of the Captives." Atop the hill sits a hermitage, later converted into a Carmelite monastery in which Saint John of the Cross served as prior, subsequently becoming what is today known as the "Carmen de los Mártires," or "Villa of the Martyrs." The interior of the Peñapartida country estate has survived over time with few major transformations in its enclosed compound and this, together with the silos and the *maqbarat* (cemetery), lends it great archaeological potential.

The layout of the different landscaped spaces is impressive, with the strategically placed miradors blending into their surroundings and

The Carmen de los Mártires or Peñapartida — in the past a Carmelite convent — is today the site of a small 19th-century palace and a landscaped area with paths and vantage points above the city

offering a sense of intimacy that is characteristic of the 19th-century Granada *carmen*.

Pilar de Carlos V

This Renaissance fountain is located next to the Alhambra's wall, under the Puerta de la Justicia. Its purpose was threefold: to provide water for the Emperor's cavalries; as an ingenious retaining wall joining the upper esplanade of the Nasrid gate with the fountain's small *plaza;* and as a means of symbolically glorifying the imperial greatness of Charles V. Commissioned by the Count of Tendilla, it was built in 1545 by Nicolás de Corte based on a design by Pedro Machuca. In 1624 it underwent alterations by Granada-born sculptor Alonso de Mena in preparation for King Phillip IV's visit to the city, and was subsequently known as the "Fountain of the Cornets."

Two vertical panels are positioned over an elongated rectangular basin more than eleven metres wide. Four decorated pilasters divide the first panel into three sections; the two outer pilasters bear the coat of arms of the House of Tendilla while the two in the centre are decorated with the coat of arms of Granada; each of the three areas framed by the pilasters has a central *mascarón* (decorative mask) with a tap that spouts water from its mouth (symbolising Granada's three rivers) and from the decorations on their heads. These consist of allegorical representations of summer (the Genil, with a sheaf of ears of wheat), spring (the Beiro, with flowers and bunches of fruit), and autumn (the Darro, with grapevines and clusters of grapes).

In the middle of the fountain is a cartouche with the Latin inscription "IMPERATORI CÆSARI KAROLO QUINTO HISPANIARUM REGI" between two pilasters: the one on the right depicts the Golden Fleece while the one the left is decorated with the Pillars of Hercules. On both sides are cartouches decorated with volutes, placed at an angle so as to create a triangular composition. Over the two outside pilasters there is a child holding on his shoulder a conch shell from which water spouts. The entire composition is finished with a large semicircle enclosing the imperial coat of arms bearing a two-headed eagle and surrounded by banners inscribed with the motto "PLUS ULTRA." This semicircle is flanked on each side by a sculpture of a cherub holding up a dolphin with a spout in its mouth

Pilar de Carlos V, designed by Pedro Machuca and constructed in 1545 by Italian sculptor Nicolás de Corte, one of the masterpieces of the Spanish Renaissance, located in the woods next to the Alhambra's wall

The Puerta de Bibrambla, which formed a part of the wall of Granada until 1873 and is currently found, reconstructed, in the Alhambra Woods

from which water falls to the basin below; all of this is crowned by another cherub in the centre.

The fountain is built against a wall some seven metres high, framed by six Doric-style pilasters finished with a cornice as though it were an entablature; the pilasters are decorated with small lion's heads similar to those in the imperial palace. Between the pilasters there are four medallions decorated with reliefs from classical mythology, in allegorical representation of the Emperor and the Order of the Golden Fleece.

Puerta de Bibrambla

The Bab al-Ramla or the Puerta del Arenal, commonly known as "Bibrambla" or "Bibarrambla," and also as the "Arch of the Ears," was demolished between 1873 and 1884 at its original site in the wall encircling Granada. An example of the purest of Nasrid traditional construction, it was basically made of *tapial* (rammed earth walls) with certain formal and structural elements made of stone. When it was torn down, some of its remains were stored in the Archaeological Museum of Granada until 1933, when the Alhambra's architectural curator, Leopoldo Torres Balbás, had the remains reconstructed on the path in the Alhambra Woods.

Today, the gate is a unique element in the Alhambra's compound, although only a few parts of its original structure remain. Arches, springers and voussoirs — some of which are incomplete — as well as some of the ashlars from the foundation and exterior façade are all integrated into an architectural structure designed by Torres Balbás expressly for the site. This unique architectural-museographic installation is now a part of the Alhambra Woods and formalises them it as an archaeological garden. The installation of the gate as a "ruin" gives it unique value as a late example of the architectural taste for the "poetry of ruins" that developed in European culture beginning in the 17th century.

Ángel Ganivet Monument

Ángel Ganivet (Granada, 1865–Riga, 1898) was one of Granada's most influential intellectuals from the literary movement known as the Generation of '98. Holding degrees in Philosophy and Law, he was a diplomat who was appointed to the position of consul and sent to Helsinki in 1895, beginning the period in which he wrote some of his best-known works, including *Granada la bella (Granada the Beautiful), Idearium español (Spain, an Interpretation)* and *Cartas finlandesas (Finnish Letters),* which he combined with literary articles for the Granada press. Ganivet always maintained his ties to Granada, where he founded the Cofradía del Avellano (Hazelnut Tree Brotherhood), an intellectually fertile literary group defined as a "kind of Greek academy of friends from Granada," with whom he wrote *El libro de Granada (The Book of Granada),* a reference of the time with great influence among the intelligentsia. In 1898 he was appointed consul in Riga, the city in which, on 29 November — true to his Romantic spirit — he committed suicide by drowning himself in the Dvina River.

This sculptural composition — financed by public subscription — is the work of Juan Cristóbal González Quesada (Ohanes, Almería, 1898) and was inaugurated in the Alhambra Woods on 3 October 1921. The self-taught sculptor, trained in the studio of Mariano Benlliure, received several awards at the National Fine Arts Exhibitions. For the Ángel Ganivet Monument, he created a mythological composition that symbolises the tensions between reason and instinct, rule and spontaneity, tradition and innovation. This group of sculptures is a metaphorical expression of many of Gavinet's ideas and attitudes about life.

Washington Irving Monument

The Council of the Alhambra wished to dedicate a tribute to New York native writer Washington Irving (1783–1859) by placing a statue of his image in the compound's woods on the 150th anniversary of his death. This writer — the epitome of a Romantic traveller — was perhaps the person who first and best brought the 19th-century Alhambra to the attention of the world. He went so far as to live inside the Alhambra's walls, walking through its rooms and experiencing the feelings and restlessness that shaped his *Tales of the Alhambra,* a literary recreation of popular legends about the complex based on stories from the local inhabitants of the time. In its pages, he brings together oral tradition with his own unique qualities and creativity as a writer imbued with the popular Orientalist and Romantic thought of the time.

The sculpture, inaugurated on 29 December 2009, represents the writer, who is holding in his left hand the notebook in which he wrote his impressions. Made of cast bronze, the realistic sculpture stands on a symbolic pedestal with an inverted Nasrid capital, a traveller's bag and a sketchbook.

Sculptor Julio López Hernández (Madrid, 1930) opted early on in his career for a particular style: Realism. Having an extensive professional background of individual exhibitions and public works, he has served as Professor of Sculpture at the Escuela de Artes y Oficios de Madrid since 1970; in 1986 he became a member of the Royal Academy of Fine Arts of San Fernando.

Inauguration of the Ángel Ganivet Monument in the Plaza del Tomate of the Alhambra. Alhambra Library

The Washington Irving Monument, the work of Julio López Hernández, in the Alhambra Woods

3 The Alhambra

Alhambra in Arabic means "the red one." The palace-city of the Alhambra was built by the Nasrid dynasty, which declared its independence from Almohad rule in 1232 and established its capital in Granada. They were the last Muslims to rule over the Iberian Peninsula, reigning until 1492, when they turned over their last possession — the Alhambra of Granada — to the Catholic Monarchs. To build their home and the location from which they would rule, they chose the site that fulfilled all the required conditions. This place was Sabika Hill.

An ancient Arabic tale relates that one day, in the year 1238, Sultan Muhammad I Ibn Nasr, al-Ahmar, climbed "[...] to a place known as al-Hamra'. He examined it, marked the foundations of the castle and left someone in charge of directing the work, and before the year had passed, the construction of the ramparts was completed; water was brought in from the river and a channel carrying water was built [...]" (*Anónimo de Madrid y Copenhague*, English translation based on the Arabic to Spanish translation by A. Huici Miranda, Madrid, 1917).

The Alhambra Palace-City

The best definition of the Alhambra may be the one expressed in this single compound word: palace-city. The Alhambra is, in fact, a city. It was designed as such, being conceived, planned and built, as well as developing and evolving, in accordance with certain laws, the laws of urban development, and one kind of city growth in particular: Islamic and Hispano-Muslim. The city of the Alhambra is also a palace, as it was conceived as the official seat of a government, the court of a power that extended across a defined territory with boundaries that delimited the existence of a cultural environment known as Andalusi. The Nasrid dynasty under which the Alhambra was created — known as the Banu-l-Ahmar — were from the city of Arjona, in what is now the province of Jaén. They declared their independence from Almohad rule in 1232 and established their new capital in Granada in 1238.

Decorative detail from the Sala de la Barca, in the *Palacio de Comares,* with the inscription reading "Glory to our lord the sultan," repeated often throughout the Alhambra

The Nasrids were the last link in the chain of Islam in the Iberian Peninsula, a chain that began with the *walíes*, governors under the Umayyad Caliphate of Damascus (711–756). They were followed by the Independent Emirate (756–929), the Caliphate of Córdoba (929–1031), whose fall led to the first *fitna* or civil war that gave rise to the reign of the *taifas* (independent Muslim-ruled principalities) from 1031–1090. The atmosphere of uncertainty in the Peninsula led to the successive invasion of the North African dynasties of the Almoravids (1056–1147) and the Almohads (ca. 1121–1269), both of which were fought against not only by Christian troops, but by the Andalusi population itself. Despite being of the same religion, these latter viewed the invaders as foreigners. The Nasrids fought against

Figure painted on the wall of the Sala de los Reyes in the Palacio de los Leones

Map of Spain with the general borders of the Nasrid kingdom of Granada

a truce was declared in the geographic triangle occupied by what are now the provinces of eastern Andalusi, in a corner of the western Mediterranean located on the route between Africa and Europe, the same route that in ancient times served as a bridge between so many cultures and civilisations. Time froze and this territory enclosed itself within weak and unstable borders, maintaining a still-feudal society that tried by all possible means to prolong the Middle Ages, retreating within itself and striving to consolidate an idyllic oasis outside what was occurring in the world around it. To that end, the Nasrids based their survival on frequent agreements, sometimes with their fellow Muslims from the south, other times with the Christian kings in the north, and almost always in exchange for heavy taxes or concessions of land that frequently included the exchange of prisoners. As a result, one of the Nasrids' tools for survival was negotiation, so that diplomacy, speech, the command of language as the means of communication were essential; so much so, that viziers or prime ministers were chosen through poetic competitions whose winner – besides fulfilling the requirement of expressing an exaggerated praise to their lord – was the subject with the best command of the language in the kingdom. The Alhambra is filled with poems and praises "to our lord the sultan" written by poets who at the same time held the title of prime minister, most notably Ibn al-Yayyab, Ibn al-Khatib, Ibn Zamrak and Ibn Furkun, who formed the Royal Chancellery or *Diwán al-Insá'*.

The palace-city of the Alhambra, like many other Hispano-Muslim cities, was most certainly created with the Madinat al-Zahra' – the devastated and mystical caliphate city on the outskirts of Córdoba, the 10th-century capital of the Western world – in mind. Despite its distance in time, its memory served, perhaps almost unconsciously, as the model that brought together the necessary premises for the creation of a new dynasty: the surrounding area, that is, the relationship between the site chosen and its environment, including the strategic conditions for controlling both military and trade transport routes for supplying raw materials and the

them in important cities; an example of this is the assistance offered to King Ferdinand III, the Saint, in his conquest of Seville.

History has preserved an anecdote that, upon his death, the Sultan of Granada sent a select battalion to keep vigil over the cadaver of his friend King Ferdinand.

For approximately 250 years, the Nasrids of Granada spread – sometimes more successfully than others – from Algeciras to Murcia, with the northern border in Jaén, the capital of the Holy Kingdom, and the southern border extending to the Mediterranean. With bases in the large ports of Málaga and Almería, they maintained a flourishing commercial exchange with other coastal countries. Their strong relations with Egypt, Tunisia, Venice and Genoa encouraged large artisan and commercial communities to settle in Granada; these settlers had considerable influence on the local customs and habits.

Important events that were decisive to the Western world took place as the 13th century became the 14th; in the artistic realm, the European Gothic style gave way to the Renaissance and the ideas of Humanism spread from the heart of the continent and took root. Nevertheless, for over two and a half centuries

Partial panoramic view of Sabika Hill, where the Alhambra was built, from the Albaicín

availability of natural resources (especially water); secondly, a structural organisation of the new settlement that ensured an indispensable military defence and the basic services for the court and for the needs of the bureaucracy; and, finally, plans had to be made for the new feudal lord's royal residence, taking into account both its public and private aspects.

All these needs were satisfied by Sabika Hill — a gently sloping knoll bordered by two rivers whose waters flowed almost continuously thanks to the gullies, ravines and snowfields of the mountain ranges — which is located on a fertile plain of crop fields with a prehistoric underground lake of enormous hydraulic potential. Its soil contains a very strong component "that by itself serves as material for foundations" and is referred to by geologists precisely as "Alhambra conglomerate." Its irregular veins of a reddish clay — iron oxide easily extracted for use in masonry — is known locally as *alpañata*.

Human settlements have existed from very early times in this idyllic setting in the shadow of the Sierra Nevada, bordering the Vega where the Darro and Genil Rivers meet. The Albaicín neighbourhood facing the Alhambra — also declared a UNESCO World Heritage Site in 1994 — was the capital of the Zirid dynasty of Granada in the 11th century. Its ancient fort, the Qadima alcazaba or citadel, was built over an ancient Roman forum, under which lie hidden stone walls dating from the era of the Iberians, in a thousand-year long stratification of colonies built one atop another.

The view seen today from the Plaza de San Nicolás in the Albaicín must be similar to that seen by al-Ahmar — Muhammad I — founder of the Nasrid dynasty, and may have been the reason he chose this site to establish his new fortress, the Yadida citadel — the Alhambra — as a space set apart to establish a new lineage that would dominate the existing urban fabric.

Towers, gates and streets of the Alhambra

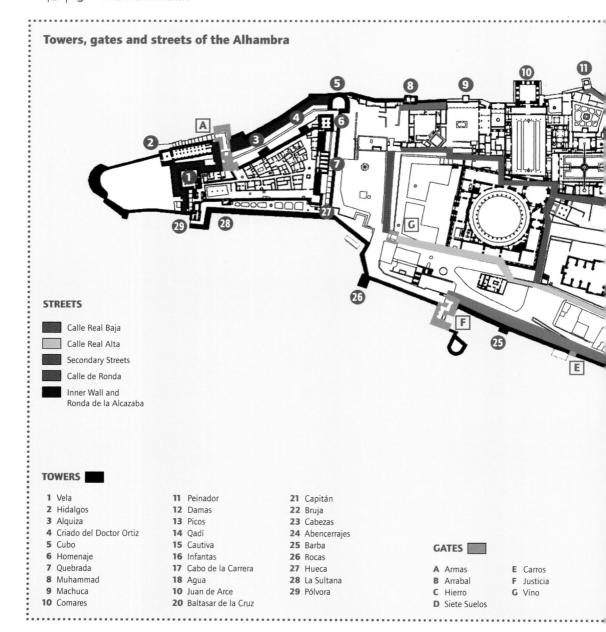

STREETS

- Calle Real Baja
- Calle Real Alta
- Secondary Streets
- Calle de Ronda
- Inner Wall and Ronda de la Alcazaba

TOWERS

1 Vela	11 Peinador	21 Capitán
2 Hidalgos	12 Damas	22 Bruja
3 Alquiza	13 Picos	23 Cabezas
4 Criado del Doctor Ortiz	14 Qadí	24 Abencerrajes
5 Cubo	15 Cautiva	25 Barba
6 Homenaje	16 Infantas	26 Rocas
7 Quebrada	17 Cabo de la Carrera	27 Hueca
8 Muhammad	18 Agua	28 La Sultana
9 Machuca	19 Juan de Arce	29 Pólvora
10 Comares	20 Baltasar de la Cruz	

GATES

A Armas	E Carros
B Arrabal	F Justicia
C Hierro	G Vino
D Siete Suelos	

The Organisation of the Complex

The Alhambra palace-city extends over some 100,000 square metres of land. It was deliberately built adjacent to another city, Granada, which is why it is protected by a surrounding wall some 2,000 metres long. Though directly connected, the two cities are independent of one another.

The area inside the Alhambra is laid out around three main spaces:

The Alcazaba: the *qasbah* (kasbah) or military residential area
The *Qasr al-Sultán:* the palaces and the Alcázar
The Medina: the court city at the service of the sultan

These spaces are connected by three basic elements: towers, streets and gates.

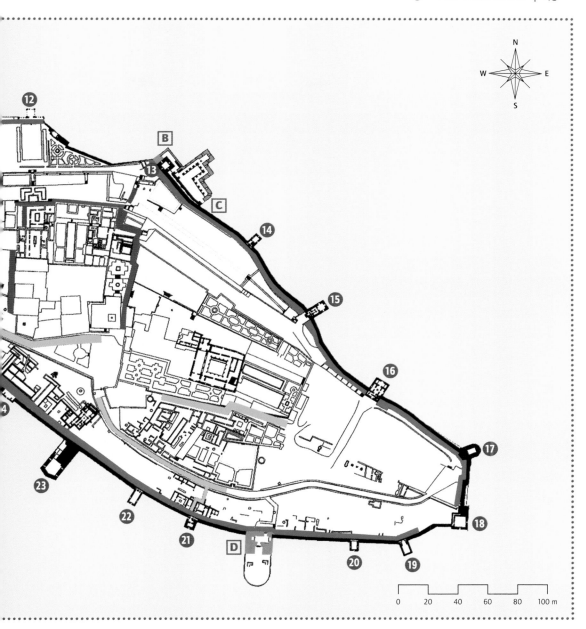

The Towers

The towers had different functions which may have complemented one another. Currently, there are thirty known towers; they usually face outwards and are distributed at irregular intervals along the wall. The majority of them date back to Nasrid times, although some are Christian and others were reconstructed during the numerous restorations of the past two centuries. A few have been destroyed or have disappeared. In general, the Muslim towers have a square design, while the circular ones are from the Christian era. These circular towers are better prepared than the square-shaped towers for receiving impacts from artillery; their use for military purposes became widespread throughout the West beginning in

Street of the inner road of the Alcazaba, with superimposed walls and the Torre de la Vela in the background

the 15th century. Although towers located along the wall in all fortifications suggest they were used for defence, in the Nasrid Alhambra three archetypes or patterns can be distinguished: the *atalaya* (watchtower) — generally smaller — whose function was military, interrupting the path of the ramparts on the wall and forcing the guards to report any new occurrences; the tower that contains a house within the palace — sometimes poetically referred to as *qalahurra* — with the rampart having a tunnel or gallery used as a passageway in order to maintain the dwelling's privacy; and the tower-pavilion — *bahw* or *mirador* — that is part of the structure of the palace, though not its most distinguished space.

The Streets

The urban design of the Alhambra was organised around three main routes and several secondary ones, with alleys, outbuildings and small *plazas* making up the urban fabric. Most of these streets were buried underground until a series of excavations, rubble-clearing and repair activities over the past century led to the discovery of most of the Nasrid Alhambra's network of streets. As a result, their current names are not the original ones, which are unknown.

The main street is the Calle de Ronda which runs along the inside of the wall of the compound; in the past, it served as a moat in the event of a siege, and for this reason it is also known as Calle del Foso. Calle Real Alta — or Calle Mayor — bordered the Medina, running from west to east in gentle ascent, and homes, public buildings (mosques, baths), workshops and small industries were hierarchically built along its route. Calle Real Baja both connected and delimited the different residential areas within the palace and had mechanisms that allowed it

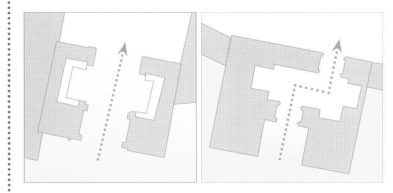

Diagram of the two basic types of access through the gates of the Alhambra
In the diagram on the left, the access is direct or in a straight line – typical of interior gates, such as the Puerta del Vino.
In the diagram on the right, the access has a bend in it, typical of exterior gates such as the Puerta de la Justicia.

to be closed in order to prevent access or isolate some areas from others.

The Gates

The gates served to control the entrance into both the walled compound and the different spaces within. There are two basic types of gate: interior and exterior. The former, like floodgates, open and close the passage to the different sectors of the city; they offer direct access, that is, via a straight line, and generally have *mastabas* (bench-shaped structures) in their interior for use by the guards who controlled the gates and who probably resided in the building; the best example is the Puerta del Vino, at the beginning of Calle Real Alta and the Medina. The exterior gates were built into the wall itself and, though necessary, they were a weak point in its defence and were therefore strongly fortified; they feature a bent entrance.

There are four defensive gates in the perimeter of the large wall that encloses and protects the Nasrid Alhambra. Almost equidistant from one another, two are located at the north and two at the south. The northern gates are the Bab al-Silah or Puerta de las Armas and what is now called the Puerta del Arrabal, while on the southern side are the Bab al-Gudur or Puerta de los Siete Suelos and the Bab al-Sharía or Puerta de la Justicia; these gates also form a part of the towers bearing the same names and used for security purposes.

Following is a description of the Alhambra's exterior gates as found when travelling in a clockwise direction (regardless of the order in which they may be visited).

Puerta de los Siete Suelos
On the southern side of the wall, to the east, is located the Puerta de los Siete Suelos, built with its current design around the middle of the 14th century on top of another, smaller gate. It is the gate closest to the Medina and was probably used for ceremonial purposes, as there are accounts that tell of military tournaments and parades being held here.

This gate is one of the most enigmatic sites of the Alhambra, probably due to the

Detail of the engraving by Hoefnagel (1575) representing the Puerta de los Siete Suelos with the inscription "Porta Castri Granatensis semper clausa."
Alhambra Library

The Puerta de los Siete Suelos — or Bab al-Gudur — in the southern of the wall

number of legends surrounding it — including Washington Irving's "Legend of the Moor's Legacy" in his famous *Tales of the Alhambra* — and to which it owes its current name. Its original name — *Bab al-Gudur* — means Puerta de los Pozos or Puerta de las Albercas.

The first Castilian troops entered through this gate in the pre-dawn morning of 2 January 1492 as the result of an agreement between the Catholic Monarchs and Boabdil. An engraving from the late 16th century bears the inscription "Porta Castri Granatensis semper clausa," leading to a mystery that lasted until recently. However, according to records, it was blocked off and closed only in 1747 and was not reopened until 1812, when Napoleonic troops unfortunately destroyed it almost completely during their retreat.

During the first restorations of the Alhambra at the end of the 19th century it was cleared

of rubble and some marble decorative pieces were carved. Over the first quarter of the 20th century, the paths and gardens were created in its surroundings, weeds and other vegetation were removed, as were some modern constructions that hid its exterior.

Thanks to old engravings that have been preserveed, it was possible to reconstruct the gate with considerable accuracy in the mid 1970s. The mirrored interior cloister vault of the door's middle chamber was completed. The northern façade — almost completely preserved up to the line of the imposts — was strengthened and reinforced with bricks. The Puerta de la Justicia was used as a reference during this reconstruction since — though they are different — they do share many details that allowed for information to be compared between the two, for example, the distance between the jambs, the layout of the entrance door, etc.

The Puerta de los Carros, built in the southern side of the wall between 1526 and 1536 in order to bring construction materials into the Alhambra to build the Palacio de Carlos V

Puerta de los Carros

The Puerta de los Carros was not an original opening in the Nasrid wall of the Alhambra; it was built between 1526 and 1536 as part of the project to build the Palacio de Carlos V.

It was necessary to modify the entire area around this Renaissance building. The ground had to be levelled in order to build a large Plaza de Armas and the corresponding adjacent smaller *plazas* in front of the façades. Although the project was never completed and the building works remained unfinished, a large part of the fill was used in building the esplanades; as a result, this entire sector of the Alhambra is called Las Placetas.

In order to transport the fill for the esplanade and the stone used for building the palace, a ramp was constructed on the slope that rises towards the wall and this gate was opened in it. In 17th-century documents, it was also referred to as the Puerta del Carril. Later, it underwent several adaptations and expansions, the last of which occurred in 1792. The threshold of the door is slightly elevated with respect to Calle de Ronda, which runs along the inside of the Alhambra's wall. Over time, this became the only gate allowing easy access for vehicles; currently, its use is restricted to guests at the compound's hotel, public or special transport and maintenance vehicles belonging to the monumental compound.

Puerta de la Justicia

Of the four exterior gates in the Alhambra's walled compound, without a doubt this is the gate that best fits the definition of "monument." Its majestic presence has converted it into one of the symbols of the Alhambra. Also known as the Puerta de la Explanada due to the wide plain that once spread before it and that is today covered in part by thick woods. Its Arabic name — *Bab al-Sharía* — has a double meaning: "esplanade" and "justice" (the name which was adopted by the Christians). The symbolic importance of Boabdil's and his troops' withdrawal from the Alhambra was immortalised in a scene in front of this gate created for the main altar of the Royal Chapel in Granada.

Symbolic elements in the Puerta de la Justicia
In addition to their practical function in connecting and protecting the walled enclosure, the gates of the Alhambra possess a symbolic value and display decorative elements representative of the world of Muslim culture, as is the case with the Puerta de la Justicia, with its key and the hand in the keystone of its portal. The key was a symbol of faith and the hand represented the five pillars of the Muslim faith; in other words, it symbolised perfection. There has been much speculation regarding the representation of these elements on one gate, and it has been seen as a metaphor for power.

Sultan Yusuf I ordered this gate to be built in 1348 and, in fact, it formally contains a compendium of meanings. In addition to its structural function, it bears one of the most important symbolic images in the Alhambra: the hand, represented on the keystone of the large exterior arch, and the key reproduced in the interior entrance arch, both of which are Islamic symbols. They sharply contrast with the Gothic figures of the Virgin and the Christ child – the work of sculptor Roberto Alemán – that the Catholic Monarchs had placed over the large stone tablet with inscriptions in Arabic made when the tower was originally built and which is located above the key.

Four attached columns with the Muslim profession of faith in their capitals frame the entrance gate, which has retained its original iron-plated leaves and other original ironware. Between the large exterior arch and the entrance gate is an open space or embrasure that originally served to harass potential attackers.

In the interior – as is characteristic of these defensive constructions – there is a double bend and a steep ramp. Still visible in the upper part of the walls are the supports or hangers used to hold the guards' weapons (pikes or spears). The use of different kinds of roofs is typical of Nasrid architecture: double

barrel vaults, barrel vaults with lunettes and cloister vaults, and domes painted to imitate red brick, also characteristic of the decorative and constructive tradition of the Almohades, predecessors of the Nasrids. Upon entering the compound, one can see an altar built against the right hand wall at the request of local residents in 1588. The work of Diego de Navas the Younger, it was built in commemoration of the first mass celebrated after the conquest.

The façade of the door facing the interior of the wall maintains some of the original decoration in the spandrels of the horseshoe arch, with a polychromatic design of ceramic rhombi. Opposite the gate is a wide street – reconstructed in Christian times by reusing gravestone slabs – running along the edge of the wall.

Puerta de las Armas

This is the gate that was historically used by the people of Granada to enter the administrative headquarters of the court from the city centre.

It was the only gate directly connecting the city of Granada with the Alhambra until the 15th century, when – as a consequence of the Christian conquest – the city grew and

Interior dome of the Puerta de las Armas
The gate has a bent entrance, just like the Alhambra's other exterior gates. Divided into three spaces by pointed horseshoe arches, there are benches for the guards to rest on.
The middle section is covered by a cloister vault, and on the sides there are umbrella vaults painted to simulate brick, typical of Nasrid decoration.
The semi-circular umbrella vaults in the side rooms are totally covered with this imitation brickwork, painted in red with white joints to accentuate the effect of depth of the wedge-shaped segments of the vaults. This characteristic is derived from Almohad architectural decoration.

The Puerta and the Torre de la Justicia

extended its boundaries, changing the habits and customs of its inhabitants. Until then, they had climbed the slope of the hill, crossing the Darro River via some of the existing bridges located along its length before finally reaching the Puerta de las Armas.

This gate was one of the first structures built by the Nasrids in the Alhambra towards the end of the 13th century, and it is the construction with the greatest influence from the Almohad tradition — both in terms of building techniques as well as decoration — inherited by the inhabitants of Granada. Being an exterior gate in a fortified compound, its interior has bent passageways which made entering difficult, so they could be used as defensive parapets. The portal stands out, with its pointed horseshoe arch made of brick embellished with pieces of coloured glazed tiles and framed by an *alfiz* (Arab style arch) with bands that intersect and enclose the spandrels, which have lost virtually all their ornamentation; the imposts that support the arch are made of stone.

Inside, the gate is divided into three separate areas under pointed horseshoe arches, with umbrella vaults at the far ends and a cloister vault in the middle, decorated with paint simulating red brick. Benches are found on the sides and in the back for use by the guards.

At the edge of the gate is a cube-shaped space in the form of an *iwán* (pavilion) from which the front entrance was controlled. Flanking this are two gates with horseshoe arches that allow access inside: the right-hand access leads to the interior of the Alcazaba and the left-hand access leads to a courtyard containing circular stones used to assist riders in dismounting from their horses. A cobblestone street — the street inside the wall, protected by the three superimposed walls of the Alcazaba — begins here and leads to the entrance to the Alhambra.

Detail of an *alambor* (sloped reinforcement) in the Alcazaba on the street running inside the wall. To the right, the inside portal of the Puerta de las Armas

The Puerta del Arrabal, located at the base of the Torre de los Picos on the northern section of the wall

The Puerta de Hierro, in the bastion of the Torre de los Picos, seen in the background

Puerta del Arrabal

This gate is located at the foot of the Torre de los Picos. Together with the Puerta de las Armas in the Alcazaba, it was one of the northern accesses connecting the city with the Alhambra. Probably built at the command of Muhammad II, it was the main entrance to the first palaces in the Alhambra, and it was the closest to the Generalife.

It has a pointed horseshoe arch, made of stone, with imposts; the keystone — no longer in existence — was probably made of marble with the traditional sculpted key. A domed walkway crosses through it, leading to a bastion with quarters and stables, defended by a detached watchtower that had been used as housing for Alhambra personnel until not long ago.

The bastion contains a gallery with segmented arches, barrel vaults and splayed windows for the artillery, probably a modification made in the 15th century.

Puerta de Hierro

The so-called Iron Gate was renovated during the era of the Catholic Monarchs; their emblems — the yoke and the arrows — can still be seen in the worn basket arch. It connects directly to the Palace of the Generalife by crossing the Cuesta del Rey Chico.

This gate formed a part of the defensive bastion of the Puerta del Arrabal found at the base of the Torre de los Picos.

Visiting the Alhambra Compound

The Alhambra is a compound surrounded by thirty towers and some 2,000 metres of wall. In order to see the Alhambra as a fortified compound, we recommend you enter through the Puerta de la Justicia. From the Atrium or Entrance Pavilion — where you can purchase tickets and obtain visitor information — continue along a path that runs along the outside of the wall, the Puerta de los Siete Suelos and several of its towers (including the Torre de las Cabezas) until reaching the esplanade of the Puerta de la Justicia where the Pilar de Carlos V can be seen.

The Itinerary Presented in this Guide

We have created a suggested itinerary so that your visit to the monumental compound of the Alhambra and the Generalife will be as enjoyable as possible. It includes the three important areas you will want to visit: the Alcazaba, the Palaces and the Generalife.

This guide's Table of Contents is listed in the same order as the suggested itinerary; however, feel free to change the order in which you visit the main areas to best suit your inclinations. When organising a visit, the only essential condition to consider is the timetable established on your ticket for entering the Nasrid Palaces; the rest of the compound may be visited in any order you wish.

Exterior and main façade of the Puerta de las Armas

Recommended Route

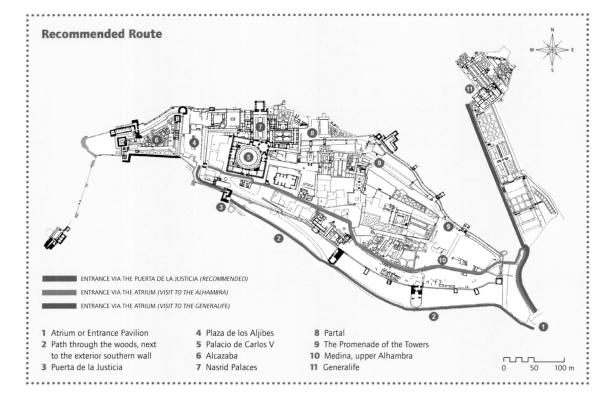

ENTRANCE VIA THE PUERTA DE LA JUSTICIA *(RECOMMENDED)*

ENTRANCE VIA THE ATRIUM *(VISIT TO THE ALHAMBRA)*

ENTRANCE VIA THE ATRIUM *(VISIT TO THE GENERALIFE)*

1 Atrium or Entrance Pavilion	4 Plaza de los Aljibes	8 Partal
2 Path through the woods, next to the exterior southern wall	5 Palacio de Carlos V	9 The Promenade of the Towers
	6 Alcazaba	10 Medina, upper Alhambra
3 Puerta de la Justicia	7 Nasrid Palaces	11 Generalife

0   50   100 m

In order to gain a better overall understanding of the monument, we recommend the following route:

1 Atrium or Entrance Pavilion
2 Path through the woods, along the exterior southern wall
3 Puerta de la Justicia
4 Plaza de los Aljibes
5 Palacio de Carlos V
6 Alcazaba
7 Nasrid Palaces
8 Partal
9 Paseo de las Torres
10 Medina, upper Alhambra and Calle Real
11 Generalife

Above the area belonging to Alhambra is the Parque Periurbano de la Dehesa del Generalife (Generalife Meadow Peri-Urban Park), a large natural space with significant archaeological remains, trails and areas for open air sports. It boasts some incredible views of the mountainous profile of the city, and Granada's Municipal Cemetery of Granada is located in its foothills.

The pedestrian accesses and public transport and vehicle roads all end together in a wide reception area where the complex's main ticket office is located. Nearby, there is a carpark for private vehicles and a variety of lodging and eating establishments.

The Alhambra Atrium

This atrium is located at the southern end of the monumental compound. In the Alhambra's Atrium — or Entrance Pavilion — you may obtain information about your visit to the compound, purchase tickets and begin your visit.

The Council of the Alhambra is committed to recovering this area, and an international call for tender has been issued to gather ideas to improve and modify this service.

You may begin your visit to the walled compound from the atrium via two main routes: through the Puerta de la Justicia or by crossing the bridge to the Generalife.

Entrance via the Puerta de la Justicia

The decision to enter the Alhambra through the Puerta de la Justicia, a 675 metres walk from the Entrance Pavilion allows the visitor to view the

Esplanade of the Puerta de la Justicia, the recommended entrance to the Alhambra

Access to the entrance of the walled compound via the new bridge to the Generalife

fortification of the city from the outside, as well as its geographical position, despite the considerable transformation caused by the growth of the woods. This route begins at La Mimbre, accessed from the city via the Cuesta del Rey Chico and continuing past the Puerta de los Siete Suelos — one of the compound's four exterior gates — then following the southern side of the wall and its towers. One of the largest of these towers is that of the Torre de las Cabezas, whose purpose was purely military, as it protected the sides of the great southern gates of the Alhambra, with its large protruding artillery bastion. In documents from the late 15th century, it was referred to as the Baluarte del Olivo (Olive Tree Bastion).

In the 16th century, a ramp was built on the side of the wall to make it easier to transport construction materials for the Palacio de Carlos V. A gate — the Puerta de los Carros — was also built, and is today the only entrance route to the compound open to vehicular traffic. It continues on to an esplanade situated in front of the Puerta de la Justicia, currently the main entrance to the Alhambra.

Entrance via the Atrium

The second option for entering the Alhambra is parallel to the option described above, but runs along the inside of the wall, covering a distance of 740 metres. This route crosses the Alhambra's upper Medina, the location of residences and cottage industries serving the court. Today, it is an archaeological path and Calle Real is the Alhambra's main road.

This route begins at the atrium or Entrance Pavilion in the Paseo de los Cipreses (Promenade of the Cypress Trees), created for the visit by Queen Isabella II in 1862. After an initial climb, a fork in the path offers a choice of two different routes: continuing straight on to visit the Generalife, or turning left towards the entrance to the Alhambra, crossing a modern bridge connecting the wall at its eastern end to the Generalife; the bridge crosses over the natural ravine of the Cuesta del Rey Chico, one of the routes coming up from the city.

From here the route runs parallel to the Acequia Real, which supplied water to the entire Alhambra. The entrance to the Alhambra — guarded by the Torre del Agua — can be seen over the bridge to the left. In addition to seeing where the Acequia Real begins at the aqueduct, the remains of buildings with pottery kilns, tanneries and houses, along with the inside of the wall and its towers (partially destroyed upon the retreat of the Napoleonic troops in 1812), are also visible.

4 Access to the Walled Compound

After entering the walled compound, the first site reached by the visitor is a wide esplanade named after the Palacio de Carlos V, which was built of stone. The original design included plans for a large, Renaissance-style porticoed Plaza de Armas in front of the palace's entrance, but it was never built. What remains today are several esplanades known as Las Placetas. From here, the visitor can access the Alcazaba, the Nasrid Palaces and the Palacio de Carlos V.

Once they have passed through the Alhambra's wall, visitors enter a city with a complex fabric of buildings, streets, squares, gardens, etc. Regardless of the direction from which they have entered the city, their steps will lead them to a wide open space where the first thing they will see is the Palacio de Carlos V, built of stone and which – as Manfredo Tafuri said – looks like a "meteor stuck by chance into the inside of the Alhambra."

Las Placetas

The original plans for this 16th-century building included a large, porticoed Plaza de Armas in front of the entrance to the palace, but it was never built. Nevertheless, some esplanades were built in front of the palace's façades. These have been traditionally known as Las Placetas.

This site – located virtually in the centre of the Alhambra – is currently where the visit to the different areas in the compound is organised.

GRANADA. 1105. Vista general de la Alhambra desde la torre del Homenaje. J. Laurent Madrid

The Palacio de Carlos V dominates the area where Las Placetas and the Plaza de los Aljibes are located.
Photograph by J. Laurent (ca. 1872)

The Plaza de los Aljibes inside the Alhambra compound, overlooked by the Torre Quebrada and the Torre del Homenaje

Access to the Walled Compound

When visitors enter the Alhambra, they discover they are inside a city surrounded by a great wall and filled with buildings, streets, squares and gardens. After passing through the Puerta de la Justicia, they arrive at a wide open space bordering the Palacio de Carlos V, the Nasrid Palaces and the Alcazaba. This large *plaza* or square was built during the construction of the Palacio de Carlos V. A large, porticoed Plaza de Armas designed to serve as an antechamber to the Renaissance palace was to be built here. Currently, this is where the visit to the Alhambra begins.

❶ Las Placetas

In front of the southern façade of the Palacio de Carlos V, in the space known as Las Placetas, archaeological excavations have been carried out and the remains of Nasrid era walls have been found. These walls belonged to a house built round a courtyard with a central *aljibe* (cistern) surrounded by rooms. It serves as an important testimonial of the urban design of the Nasrid era, marking the border of the main street.

❸ Plaza de los Aljibes

Named for the large cistern found underneath, this Plaza "of the Cisterns" was commissioned by the Count of Tendilla, the first governor of the Alhambra after the Christian conquest. It is a large esplanade from which visitors may access the different spaces in the palace-city, and it has often been the site of important cultural events. Excavations carried out in the area adjacent to the wall have uncovered remains of buildings.

❷ Puerta del Vino

Access to the residential area was through this gate. The corps of guards in charge of its security probably lived on its top floor. A key — a symbol of the power that permits the gates to be opened and closed — is reproduced on its western exterior façade. The eastern portal is notable for its tiles decorated with the dry string technique and carved plaster framing the upper window.

❹ Aljibe de Tendilla

Traveller Hieronymus Münzer referred to its construction in 1494, in other words immediately after the Alhambra was conquered by the Catholic Monarchs. The Count of Tendilla directed construction works for reinforcing the gates, walls and towers and for building bastions, but his most important work — and the one that carries his name — was the *aljibe* located on a ravine between the Alcazaba and the Nasrid Palaces, underneath the Plaza de los Aljibes.

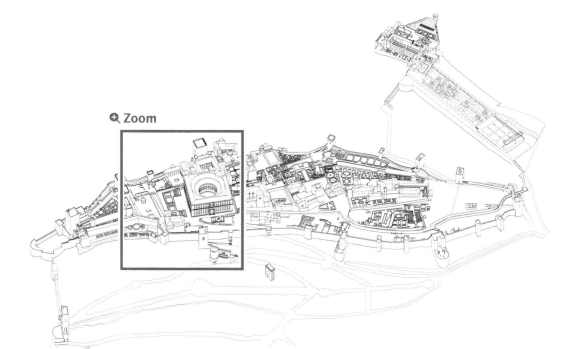

🔍 **Zoom**

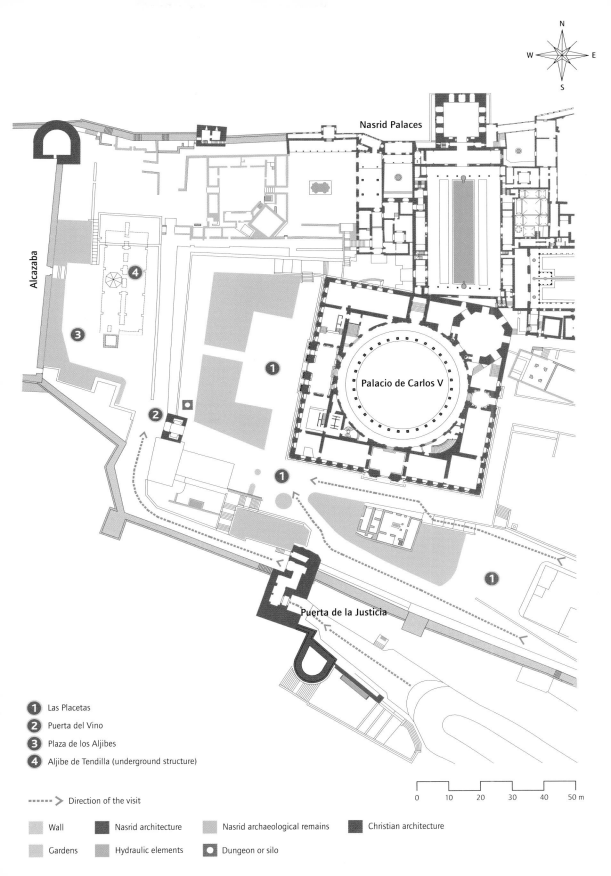

N
W — E
S

Nasrid Palaces

Alcazaba

④

③

① Palacio de Carlos V

②

①

①

①

Puerta de la Justicia

① Las Placetas

② Puerta del Vino

③ Plaza de los Aljibes

④ Aljibe de Tendilla (underground structure)

┄┄┄> Direction of the visit

0 10 20 30 40 50 m

Wall

Gardens

Nasrid architecture

Hydraulic elements

Nasrid archaeological remains

Dungeon or silo

Christian architecture

Remains of a Nasrid house in Las Placetas located in front of the southern façade of the Palacio de Carlos V

Las Placetas offer testimonials from different eras of their past such as the remains of walls located in front of the southern façade of the Palacio de Carlos V. These remains are part of the main structure of a Nasrid house built round a courtyard with a central *alberca* or water tank and surrounded by rooms; here, one can see the thresholds of some doorways with certain masonry elements that suggest that this was the entrance to the house from the Calle Real. This is an important architectural structure in the urban design of the medieval Alhambra as it marks the edge of the main road to the Nasrid Medina. All the rooms — which still conserve remains from the

Detail of the southern façade of the Palacio de Carlos V, with vertically positioned cannons. Photograph by J. Laurent (1871)

Cannons atop undercarriage supports (left photograph) that were in front of the Palacio de Carlos V. They are currently located on the parapet of the southern wall

original flooring — are found at the same level, except in the western bay, where they are at a lower level. A door is located here that may have belonged to this house or the one next door; there is a gravel pavement in front of its façade, perhaps originating from a square or a street running at a right angle to the Calle Real.

Rubble was removed from these structures in 1922 and work on them was completed over the following decade.

Cannons had been sunk into the ground in a vertical position in front the structures. The reliefs on the portal of the Renaissance palace referring to the artillery probably led to their installation on this site, which in the 19th century came to be known as the Placeta de los Cañones. Today, they are set atop undercarriage supports recreated in the late 19th century and look out over the parapet of the Alhambra's southern wall.

From these *plazas*, a surprising contrast is seen between the stony grandeur of the Renaissance palace and the modest structure of the church of Santa María de la Alhambra, a contrast that was also noted in 1576 when the mosque of the Alhambra (also located here) was torn down due to its ruinous state.

On the corner of the opposite end of the façade of the Palacio de Carlos V is the beginning of an unfinished arch. It was planned as an alternative to the Puerta del Vino, one of the fundamental constructions of the Nasrid Alhambra, whose silhouette is notable for its marked horseshoe arches.

Puerta del Vino

Today, this is a symbolic architectural element, but originally it was the main entrance to the Medina of the Alhambra, the gate inside the walled compound that protected the residential and cottage industry sector serving the court. In a way, its function today is similar to that in Nasrid times. An interior gate, it offers direct access — in a straight line — unlike the exterior gates whose purpose was to protect the interior and had bent entrances. However, its interior offers sufficient space and benches for the guards who controlled access through it. The building has an upper floor where — as

Watercolour by David Roberts (1833) with the Puerta del Vino and the Palacio de Carlos V. The Alhambra Archives

is traditional in Hispano-Muslim life, trade associations played an important role — the corps of guards assigned to duty lived.

Structurally it is one of the oldest buildings in the Nasrid Alhambra. Its construction is attributed to the era of Sultan Muhammad III (1302–1309), although the decoration of its two façades corresponds to different eras.

The decoration of the western portal — the one closest to the Alcazaba — was probably completed in the late 13th or early 14th century, although the stone tablet appearing above the lintel of the arch refers to Sultan Muhammad V who ruled in the second half of the 14th century. As this was the exterior façade, it has the traditional symbolic key appearing over the keystone of the arch.

Although the interior portal on the eastern side follows a similar design, it was decorated during the second reign of Sultan Muhammad V after 1367, the date of the military campaigns in Jaén, Baeza and Úbeda. Some of its outstanding features include lovely spandrels in its arch made of tiles decorated with the dry string technique, the windows on the upper floor framed with carved plaster work, and the remains of polychromatic paint preserved to the right of the arch. A recent restoration has revealed that the materials used to decorate the portal accentuated its naturally red-coloured appearance.

The Calle Mayor — or Calle Real — of the Alhambra begins at the Puerta del Vino and heads

east in gentle ascent. This was the main road to the medieval Medina and is still used today. One of the most important aspects of this gate is its role in the urban fabric. This can be appreciated even today by observing its surroundings: it has remained a reference point, a landmark, for the different streets inside the city.

Plaza de los Aljibes

One of the main structural modifications and first works completed in the Alhambra after the Christian conquest was the construction of a large cistern in the gully separating the Alcazaba from the rest of the Alhambra. This work was initiated by Íñigo López de Mendoza, first Marquis of Mondéjar, second Count of Tendilla and Captain General of the Alhambra.

Above the domes of this cistern — about which there are references dating back to 1494 — there was an almost spontaneous growth of a wide esplanade area that to this day has been known as the Plaza de los Aljibes.

From here, one can access the different areas inside the Alhambra's walled compound; curiously enough, it is located almost on the same site from which these areas were accessed in Nasrid times.

The *plaza* extended to the northern wall until the mid-20th century, but the archaeological excavation activity begun at the beginning of this century led to it being modified and the rubble removed so that this important part of the Alhambra — heretofore unknown — could be recovered.

Before its current layout, the *plaza* was the scene of important cultural events such as the First Festival of Cante Jondo (a flamenco music festival) in 1922 — which had an extraordinary influence in the panorama of contemporary Spanish music — or for the representation of *autos sacramentales* (religious theatrical presentations).

In the centre, site of the ancient pavilion that has been replaced by a new one, visitors and social clubs of Granada took a moment to enjoy the traditional combination of *azucarillos* (an old-fashioned sweet made mostly of sugar) and spirits.

The Aljibe de Tendilla

"In the Alhambra of Granada Your Majesty has the best cistern in the world in terms of both its construction as well as its capacity to produce very clean and clear water, and keep it so cold that it could be snow; it was commissioned by Our Majesties the Catholic Monarchs [...]" (The Alhambra Archives, Leg. L-238-4. *Aljibes de la Alhambra. Petición para que no se venda el agua de los aljibes a aguadores*). This *aljibe* was built in the streambed between the Alcazaba and the Medina inside the Alhambra in order to ensure the supply of water not only to the palace compound, but also to the city of Granada. It has a rectangular structure, with two large, nave-like spaces connected by six gates with semi-circular arches. Openings were made through the barrel vaults covering the two large spaces, creating wells through which water could be extracted. Today, the Plaza de los Aljibes is located over the roof of the *aljibe*. From the outside, only the mouth of the entrance is visible, as this area was subjected to so many modifications between the 16th and the 20th centuries that its original appearance has been lost.

Eastern façade of the Puerta del Vino. This was the main interior gate to the Alhambra's Medina

5 Palacio de Carlos V

When Emperor Charles V and his wife Isabella of Portugal visited the Alhambra in the spring of 1526, they were so astonished at the site that they decided to build a residence within its walls. This decision had the symbolic value of strengthening the Emperor's image as one of the most powerful monarchs in the world: this site — the last bastion of the Muslims — had been conquered by his grandparents, the Catholic Monarchs.

Charles I of Spain and V of Germany, king and elected emperor — a monarch who travelled throughout Europe — visited Granada in the spring of 1526 after his marriage to Isabella of Portugal in Seville. It is difficult to believe that he planned to make Granada the centre of his kingdom, but what he did want to do was build a royal residence that would be important because of its symbolic value and its location: the Muslim citadel conquered by his grandparents, the Catholic Monarchs. To carry out his plan, he decided to build an impressive

stone building integrating the three geometric shapes that represented power at that time: the exterior square (symbol of the earthly world), the interior circular courtyard (symbol of the world in its entirety), both connected by an octagonal chapel (a copy of the chapel built in Aachen by his ancestor Charlemagne) which, in turn, connects the new structure with the Muslim Palacio de Comares through the crypt located on its lower level, but in the same direction and on the same level as this building.

Aerial view of the location of the Palacio de Carlos V together with the Nasrid Palaces

Southern portal of the Palacio de Carlos V

Palacio de Carlos V

This Renaissance-style palace was commissioned by Emperor Charles V over the first third of the 16th century to serve as his imperial residence, but it was not finished, its construction being abandoned in 1637 with the roof still unbuilt. It was finally completed in the 20th century. Its enormous massive square-shaped exterior floor plan superimposed over a circular inner court changed the image of the Alhambra. Attached to the southern portico of the Patio de Comares, its architect Pedro Machuca intended that it should serve as the noble portico of the Nasrid Palaces.

❶ Façades

The palace has two floors and four façades of identical size; the northernmost is partially hidden as it is attached to the Palacio de Comares. The bench-shaped skirting board, the cornice that divides the two floors and the upper entablature that finishes the upper section create a strongly horizontal aspect for these façades on which the accentuated rustication on the lower floor stands out.

❹ Alhambra Museum

Since construction began in 1928 to recover the building, it has been used for different purposes, usually cultural. Currently, the ground floor houses the Alhambra Museum which contains objects linked to the Alhambra and the civilisation that created it, such as the Vase of the Gazelles.

❷ Portals

Located in the middle of the southern and western façades are two large decorative marble portals with a strong Roman influence; their reliefs reflect an iconographic message whose purpose is to present Emperor Charles V as a champion of world peace.

❺ Fine Arts Museum

This museum is located on the upper floor of the palace. It houses a collection of paintings and sculptures, primarily from the style typical of 16th- to 20th-century Granada. Its rooms are also used to house temporary exhibitions.

❸ Courtyard

The inside of the palace is filled with a large circular courtyard of harmonious proportions. It has a two-storey façade, and each of these floors is formed by thirty-two columns and separated by an entablature with Renaissance-style decoration of metopes and triglyphs. It has been the scene of important theatrical and musical performances.

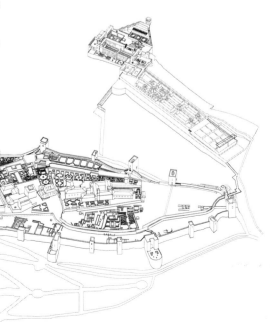

🔍 Zoom

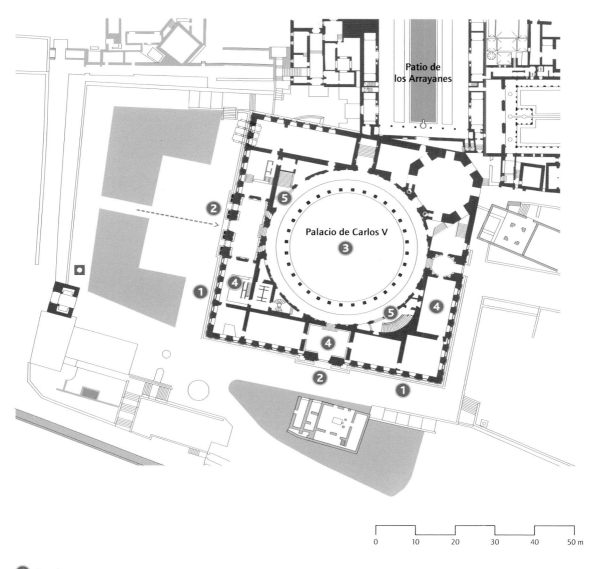

Patio de
los Arrayanes

Palacio de Carlos V
3

1. **Façades**
2. **Portals**
3. **Courtyard**
4. **Alhambra Museum**
5. **Fine Arts Museum (upper floor)**

┄┄┄┄> Direction of the visit

Wall

Gardens

Nasrid architecture

Hydraulic elements

Nasrid archaeological remains

Dungeon or silo

Christian architecture

The choice of the Alhambra as the site for this palace was an attempt to express the triumph of Christianity over Islam. To do this, it was necessary to preserve the ancient Islamic structures so that they could serve as counterpoints to the size and powerful Romanity of the new palace. The Renaissance architects were fascinated by the Roman models of Classical Antiquity. Charles V himself, as Emperor of the Holy Roman Empire (Aachen, 1520), considered himself to be part of the line of succession of the emperors of Rome. His efforts were directed in part at containing the Ottoman Empire, both in Europe (Hungary and the Balkans) where in 1529 Vienna was placed under siege, as well as in the Mediterranean (the expedition to Tunisia in 1535).

In deciding to build the palace in the "Roman" style, he was probably also influenced by the governor of the Alhambra himself, Captain General Luis Hurtado de Mendoza, whose family played an important role in the spread of Italian culture in Castile. It is also possible that the building design was suggested by Baldassare Castiglione, a friend of Rafael Sanzio, Giulio Romano and the governor.

The project, of which two original plans are preserved in the Royal Palace of Madrid, was designed by Pedro Machuca, painter, sculptor and architect, who studied in Italy under Michelangelo and was educated in art circles of the Rome of Leo X, where he received training in the Renaissance style, in which he became a pioneer in Spain. The building — financed by forced contributions from the Moors — began in 1527, on what had mainly been the land of an improvised Christian settlement that was necessary only during the first years after the conquest. Machuca directed the work until his death in 1550, leaving the façades unfinished except for the large portals located on their west and south sides. His son Luis succeeded him, creating the circular courtyard, but for fifteen years the work was halted due to the Morisco Revolt in Granada in 1568. When Phillip IV visited the city in 1628, he could not stay in the palace because,

Western façade of the Palacio de Carlos V

after ninety years of work, it was still uninhabitable. In 1637, it was abandoned definitively without the roof being installed.

Despite its scrupulous design, building the palace in the Alhambra changed the compound's image, altering both its internal structure and its connection to the city. The original project included a large *plaza* situated to the west and another smaller one to the south, which meant that significant changes would have had to be made to the entrances. In fact, Machuca intended the new building, with its *plazas* and façades, to serve as the noble portico to the Nasrid Palaces.

The Façades

The façades of the palace are characterised by their unity of colour and their horizontal design. As they are attached to the Muslim building, the southern and western façades (the latter is the palace's main façade) are more extensively decorated. Their horizontal nature is strongly accentuated by the bench — which serves as a plinth — running along the façade's entire length, as well as the cornice dividing the upper section of the building from the lower, and by the Corinthian entablature above.

Exemplifying the new taste for the Italian style is the rustication (*bugnato rustico*) across the bottom section; its unusual appearance is due to the integration of the pilasters into the rusticated area, whose ashlars have large bronze rings held by lions' heads, except in the corners where these are replaced by eagles.

Upstairs, the decorative elements appear in an alternating sequence, both on the emblems of the plinths on which the pilasters rest, as well as on the lintels over the openings for the windows. Under the cornice crowning these openings are some unusual straight garlands in the shape of a pediment, reinforcing the horizontal structure of the façade and considered by some authors to be a mannerist element.

The Portals

This horizontal design is interrupted only by the marble portals, which jut out from the façade resembling triumphal arches, contrasting in their verticality yet maintaining the differentiation of the

The western façade of the Palacio de Carlos V, with its main portal

Bronze rings, of Hispanic tradition, attached to the lower section of the façade; their function is merely symbolic (lions' heads, except at the corners, where there are eagles)

Detail of the rustication between the pilasters, characteristic of the façade of the lower floor. The distinct stone finishes made by the carvers is evident

two sections. As independent elements, the portals express the weight of Spanish tradition as opposed to the Italian. The southern portal is flanked with pairs of columns whose bases are decorated with reliefs. The ground floor has a large door with an Ionic pilaster on each side just like the columns; it is crowned with a triangular pediment displaying reclining figures symbolising the Victories. The pedestals, with reliefs of ancient and contemporary weapons, extend outward from their sides to include the lions couchant. On the upper level, the columns are of the Corinthian order atop pedestals with mythological reliefs that

— unlike on the ground floor — extend inward so as to highlight the large window in Serlian fashion. This Renaissance architectural device, consisting of combining a round arch with a lintelled opening on either side, was often used in portals, façades, etc., and widely employed by Palladio.

It was so named because it first appeared drawn in Serlio's *l'Architettura* (1537), although it was possibly created by Bramante.

The main portal is located on the western façade; both sides extend laterally, which permitted the creation of two more, smaller, accesses. The

Relief on the western façade
The façade includes the representation of historical-allegorical episodes symbolising the Emperor's desire for universal peace. In the centre of the composition are the Victories, each hoisting laurel branches and holding the Spanish imperial emblem: the Columns of Hercules and the crowned world. At the bottom points, two angels use their torches to set fire to the military armament scattered on the floor, senseless once the Emperor has imposed universal peace.

half columns — grouped in pairs — reappear up to eight times per floor, accentuating the break in the façade's horizontal design. Notable is the symmetrical relief decoration on the pedestals of the lower section, with its iconography referring to the disarmament that results from the ending of war, in an attempt to compare the palace to a new universal Ara Pacis (Altar of Peace) under the Emperor's patronage. In significant contrast, the half columns of the upper section rest on pedestals with geometric decoration — typical of the Herrerian style of the era — and on the window pediments there are three large medallions with reliefs representing the feats of Hercules.

The Courtyard

The circular courtyard — elevated in comparison to the exterior level — has two galleries, one on top of another. The lower gallery is covered with a ring shaped barrel vault made of stone — unprecedented in the Renaissance age, but used in ancient times — which probably was intended to display painted frescos. Thirty-two *pudinga* de Loja (a kind of sedimentary conglomerate containing pebbles mined in Loja) stone columns from the Doric-Tuscan order serve as the support for a lovely entablature with a frieze featuring triglyphs and metopes, creating the unique circular façade of the courtyard. A high parapet unfolds on the colonnade of the upper gallery, which was built in 1619 in Ionic style and with a design layout similar to that of the ground floor, although its roof was not completed until 1967. Of the two large staircases, the steeper — designed by architect Fernández Lechuga — was completed in 1635.

The general floor design is highlighted by the octagonal chapel in the corner nearest to the Palacio de Comares, a geometric-shaped building that became the second central structure of the palace and enjoyed great prestige during the Renaissance.

The staircase located at the northern entrance to the Palacio de Carlos V descends from the courtyard level to the western bay of the Comares

Interior courtyard of the Palacio de Carlos V, with its circular design enclosed inside the square-shaped palace floor plan

Palace, ending where there was once an *alhami* (tile-covered stone bench) that belonged to the lower hall in the residential area of the palace. This necessitated the removal of the wall shared by the two buildings. The staircase is a structure highly representative of the plan to integrate the Palacio de Carlos V into the adjacent Nasrid palaces. Built in 1580, this unique semi-direct link was part of the palace's initial plan. When the Alhambra Museum was installed upstairs in the palace's western bay, the stairwell was closed and hidden by a lobby that provides direct access to the museum. It was also necessary to modify the front elevation of the original entrance where the entrance portal to the museum was created. The recent recovery of the open space and the elevated area allows one to see how the building of the Palacio de Carlos V was built in the Muslim Alhambra was intended to respect the Nasrid Palaces and serve as a continuation of their historical legacy.

Cultural Uses

Different uses have been proposed for this distinguished building since the 16th century: everything from royal residence to more unusual suggestions, such as the military academy project from the late 18th century for the training of American nobility or the residence for the head of state during the Franco era, which never came to fruition. Indeed, the compound has always been a centre of cultural attention for the city, with bullfights being held in the courtyard, but most especially theatrical performances, large concerts and seasonal recitals. Its fate was addressed by Parliament in 1902 but the palace remained incomplete until 1923, when architect Leopoldo Torres Balbás began a programme of restoration.

In 1928 a small Arab Museum was installed, the predecessor of the Archaeological Museum of the Alhambra, created in 1942. Since then, spaces, ceilings and floors have been completed, and it has served to house administrative offices, the Archives and Library of the Council of the Alhambra, among other cultural and ceremonial uses. In 1958 the Provincial Museum of Fine Arts

Stairway constructed in 1954 by Francisco Prieto Moreno to connect the two floors of the palace

was inaugurated upstairs. Recently, its cultural use as a museum space has been enhanced with the definitive installation of the Alhambra Museum on the ground floor, the complete remodelling of the upstairs facilities for the Museum of Fine Arts, the restoration of the chapel and the crypt for temporary exhibitions and a variety of uses, and the use of rooms for institutional meetings and conferences, as well as a specialised bookstore.

The historical building that is the Palacio de Carlos V — filled with symbolism — is thus fulfilling its cultural destiny as an important space dedicated to the Alhambra's museums.

Alhambra Museum

The Alhambra Museum housed in the southern wing of the Palacio de Carlos V offers visitors the unique opportunity to contemplate artistic and archaeological objects from the monumental

Stairway directly connecting the courtyard of the Palacio de Carlos V and the Nasrid Palacio de Comares

Archaeological Museum of the Alhambra
The Palacio de Carlos V was unfinished when the Emperor died and remained so until the 20th century, when architect Torres Balbás began to restore the building. Since then, it has been used for several purposes, but always within the cultural sphere. In 1995 the century-long desire to use the inside of the palace as a place dedicated to museums became a reality with the definitive installation of the Alhambra Museum. In the image, the original exhibition hall of the Archaeological Museum of the Alhambra — created in 1942 and the predecessor of the current Alhambra Museum — in its first use of the palace as an exhibition area. Alhambra Archives

compound linked to the Hispano-Muslim culture that created it.

Created in 1870, its name was changed to the National Museum of Hispano-Muslim Art in 1962; since 1994 it has been affiliated with the Council of the Alhambra and Generalife. At that time, the museum moved to its current location and was organised using the most advanced techniques of contemporary museology. It includes seven exhibition halls that are chronologically ordered so that one can appreciate the evolution of both Hispano-Muslim art and of the complex itself; these exhibition halls house the best collection of Nasrid art in existence, most of which proceeds from excavations and interventions carried out in the Alhambra.

Perhaps the most remarkable object in the museum is the Vase of the Gazelles from the 14th century and made of gold-coloured ceramic, along with a vase from the Simonetti collection

and large fragments of other vases, including the neck of a piece from the Hirsch collection. In the pottery collection, there is a remarkable Caliphate-era plate from Madinat al-Zahra' (Medina Azahara), as well as numerous pieces of household objects from the Nasrid period, some of considerable size. Also noteworthy are the fragments of Fatimid pottery acquired in Cairo; the ceramic collection is one of the largest in the museum and includes a curious group of small toys. Tile panelling, such as that from the Sala de las Aleyas in the Palacio de Comares — which was in the Mexuar — and ceramic tiles, such as those from the Peinador de la Reina, are among the most important examples of floor tiles.

Of the numerous pieces of carved plaster — besides those from excavations and restorations throughout the Alhambra — are those originating from the mirador of the Patio de la Acequia in the Generalife, from the Palacio de los Alijares,

Copy of the project (1793) to convert the Palacio de Carlos V into the campus of a military academy, which never came to fruition. Alhambra Archives

Courtyard of the palace during the "coronation" of romantic poet José Zorrilla as National Poet Laureate in 1889. Photograph by Ayola

Hall in the Alhambra Museum with the Vase of the Gazelles in the centre; behind, the door from the Sala de Dos Hermanas and other objects found within the Alhambra

and from the Palacio de Dar al-Arusa on the Cerro del Sol.

The collection of wooden items includes the door and latticework screen from the Sala de Dos Hermanas in the Palacio de los Leones; pieces displaying inlay work, such as the small Nasrid chest with marble fragments on one of its sides, a cupboard having two large doors from the house belonging to the Princes of Granada, a *jamuga (*scissors chair) whose back is made of embossed leather, and a peculiar chess board, all from the 14th or 15th centuries. Mention should also be made of various pieces of Nasrid and Mudejar armour, parts of Toledo Mudejar eaves from the 11th century, and some Almohad and proto-Nasrid planks from the Casa de los Tiros.

Included in the marble collection are the Caliphate-era fountain from the Alamiriya de Almanzor Palace, and various Nasrid fountains and basins including that of the Lindaraja. Remarkable too are a Caliphate-era capital and base from the 10th century as well as other capitals, bases and peduncles from Nasrid columns of various eras, the Nasrid sultans' *maqabriyyas* (tombstones), a pair of lions and the stone marking the foundation of the *Maristán* hospital in the Albaicín (14th century); there are also (although incomplete) a curious sun dial and a varied collection of stone braziers from various eras.

In addition, the museum exhibits a small but important selection of coins, glassware, fabrics and documents including a Nasrid Qur'an. Lastly, the collection of metallic objects features outstanding pieces such as an 11th-century copper mosque spire or *Yamur* from the Cadí Mosque in Granada and several Caliphate-era oil lamps from different sources.

Exhibition hall in the Fine Arts Museum of Granada, where masterpieces of painting and sculpture are conserved

The museum is divided into the following exhibition halls:

Hall I: Faith, science and the economy
Hall II: Emirate and Caliphate-era art
Hall III: Art from the Caliphate to the Nasrids
Hall IV: Nasrid art. Public buildings
Hall V: Nasrid art. The Alhambra and architecture
Hall VI: Nasrid art. The Alhambra, material culture
Hall VII: Nasrid art. The Alhambra, material culture

Fine Arts Museum of Granada

Located on the top floor of the Palacio de Carlos V, this museum contains a select collection of paintings and hosts temporary exhibitions. It was created as a result of Church property reforms that took place in the 19th century, and so the majority of its collection consists of religious-themed paintings from Granada dating back to the 16th through the 18th centuries. The pieces originated from monasteries such as the Cartuja Monastery, or groups of paintings that decorated the inside of the convents of San Francisco, the Merced, the Trinitarians or the Discalced Augustinians. After its location at various sites in Granada, it finally moved to the Palacio de Carlos V in 1958 on the occasion of the four hundredth anniversary of the death of the Emperor, and has been located here ever since.

Some of the most outstanding works from among its significant pieces are an enamel piece by Limoges, the *Burial of Christ* by Jacopo Torni, the *Thistle Still-Life* by Juan Sánchez Cotán, and other baroque, neoclassical and romantic masterpieces. There are also paintings from Granada from the 19th and 20th centuries, among which the works of Manuel Ángeles Ortiz stand out, with the museum conserving an important selection of works from his "Albayzín" and the "Paseo de los Cipreses" series.

The Vase of the Gazelles, one of the ceramic masterpieces from medieval Muslim times. The Alhambra Museum

The Alcazaba: the Kasbah

On the western side of Sabika Hill — the side closest to the city — rises the Alcazaba with the Torre de la Vela dominating the Vega and protecting the palace-city of the Alhambra. When Al-Ahmar — the first Nasrid sultan of the kingdom of Granada — chose Sabika Hill as the location for his palace, it was already the site of an old red castle that, once renovated, was converted into the defensive fortress of the entire compound. It comprised several towers and up to three segments of superimposed walls. Members of the military lived inside, in what is known as the *barrio castrense*, or military district.

Once the decision to build a new city was taken, the Nasrid dynasty sought to protect the delicate beauty of their residence and the magic of its surroundings by placing them in the naturally solid defensive site that is Sabika Hill. An old red castle stood on its peak — the oldest building in the Alhambra — which, once renovated, would serve as a defensive fortress for the entire compound. Despite having been built in the Early Middle Ages — perhaps a partial reconstruction of a late Roman building — it was given the name Alcazaba Yadida; the earliest documentary reference to this site dates back to around 860. The first Nasrid sultan, Al-Ahmar, rejected the Alcazaba of the Albaicín, the old Qadima, a fortified ancient Roman forum built on a sturdy Iberian wall. Around 1238 he decided to take up residence on the adjacent mountain — more strategically situated — in order to found the new *qasbah* (Kasbah), the services district for the new administration and the seat of his kingdom for the next two and a half centuries.

He rebuilt on the foundations of the ruins of some towers and reconstructed almost all the walls, which dated back to before the 11th century, when the castle had protected Granada under the rule of the Zirids, when it was the capital of one of their *Taifa* kingdoms.

Structure of the Alcazaba

The Alcazaba is shaped like a triangle. Its western corner is closest to Granada, its privileged domain. It is in this corner that the great Torre de la Vela was built, and it has been a symbol of the city

Aerial view of the Alcazaba

The Alcazaba is shaped like a triangle. The eastern section is separated from the rest of the Alhambra by a large reinforcement wall that runs from north to south between three strong towers: Homenaje, Quebrada and Adarguero or Hueca. Three other towers finish the wall on its western side: Hidalgos, Vela and Pólvora. Though completely integrated into the Alhambra, it is completely independent from it and as a military site, it is heavily fortified. In the upper part of this picture taken from the north, the 11th century compound can be seen. Beginning with the Nasrids, different types of towers and reinforcements for the walls were added.

The Torre del Homenaje, the Torre Quebrada and the Torre Hueca close off the Alcazaba compound toward the east

Alcazaba

The Alcazaba occupies the western part of the hill, in the area that advances on the city like the bow of a ship. Its function is clearly defensive, not only because of the strength of its walls and towers, but also because it houses the military district, the living quarters of the troops whose duty it was to provide immediate defence to the sultan and the palace-city. In the corner nearest Granada is the Torre de la Vela, from which the entire surrounding area can be seen.

① Torre del Homenaje

Located on the northern section of the wall, adjacent to the Plaza de los Aljibes, this is the highest tower in the Alhambra and its terrace offers the best panoramic view of the Alhambra. At its base is the Torre del Cubo, built during Christian times as a circular bastion to provide greater defence.

④ Torre de la Vela

This Torre de la Vela — or Torre Mayor as it was called when it was built in the 13th-century Nasrid era — has been a reference point in the life of the residents of Granada. According to tradition, it was on its terrace that the standards of the Catholic Monarchs were raised on the very day that Boabdil turned over the keys to the city. Its ringing bell has announced many events to the residents of Granada.

② Military District

Inside the Alcazaba, the foundations of the walls of a number of buildings that formed a homogenous and complete neighbourhood have been recovered. This is where the living quarters for the sultan's guard and some of the troops that defended the Alhambra were located. Among the buildings are living quarters offering all kinds of services, the *tahona* (bakery) with its oven, latrines, baths, a cistern, etc.

⑤ Torre de la Pólvora

Located to the south of the Torre de la Vela and jutting out from the wall, this tower has been an important defensive element in the history of the Alhambra. This small tower is the starting point for the wall that joins the Alhambra to the Torres Bermejas.

③ Puerta de las Armas

Located in the tower of the same name, it was the only of the Alhambra's four large exterior gates that during the early Nasrid era connected directly to the city of Granada; it was used by the residents of the city who came to conduct business at the court.

⑥ Jardín de los Adarves

During medieval times, the Jardín de los Ardaves was the site of a defensive trench between the wall and a smaller wall built around 1550 in the southern part of the Alcazaba. The transformation of the trench or rampart into a garden occurred in the 17th century when the Moorish threat no longer existed after the Moors were expelled in 1609.

① Torre del Homenaje

② Military District

③ Puerta de las Armas

④ Torre de la Vela

⑤ Torre de la Pólvora

⑥ Jardín de los Adarves

Bastion or Ravelin

┄┄┄> Direction of the visit

▇ Wall ▇ Nasrid architecture ▇ Nasrid archaeological remains ▇ Christian architecture

▇ Gardens ▇ Hydraulic elements ▇ Dungeon or silo

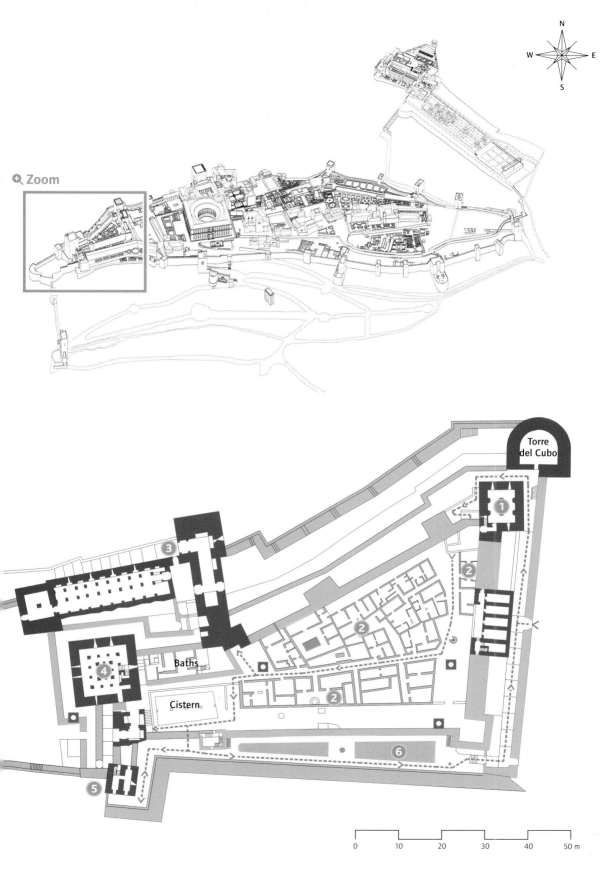

N
W · E
S

Zoom

Torre del Cubo

1

2

2

3

2

Baths

4

2

Cistern

6

5

0   10   20   30   40   50 m

Entrance to the Alcazaba via the gate located at the base of the Torre Quebrada, in the Plaza de los Aljibes

ever since. At the other end, to the east, extends the rest of the Alhambra, and so it required a strong reinforcement wall, which was built running from north to south between three strong towers: Homenaje, Quebrada and Adarguero or Hueca (as they were called by the Christians).

After the Nasrid era, the occupation of the Alhambra fortress by the Catholic Monarchs led to an important plan to renovate and adapt the fortress to the new techniques of attack and defence of this type of compound in response to the massive use of the newly emerging artillery based on the use of gunpowder. These changes began in 1492 with the building of the artillery bastions that protect the large gates of the Alhambra, and were completed around 1589 with the construction of the artillery turret or Torre del Cubo, on the site that had previously been occupied by the disappeared Puerta de la Tahona, in the southeast corner, under the Torre del Homenaje.

Adding to this apparently complex defensive system was the natural gorge separating the bluff of the Alcazaba from the rest of the Alhambra, a ravine that drains into the northern valley of the Darro River. Renovations continued in 1494 with the construction of the large two-part cistern commissioned by Tendilla, the roof of which served as the platform for a wide esplanade. The construction project for the Palacio de Carlos V contributed to this design. Although the planned Plaza de Armas was never built, the terrace created became what today is known as the Plaza de los Aljibes.

Visiting the Alcazaba

Visitors enter the Alcazaba — whose original Arabic name *(Alhizán)* describes very well its castle-like image — through the Alhambra's eastern inner wall. Once inside, its military nature becomes immediately obvious. There are reinforcement towers dating back to Nasrid times built on top of the superimposed walls, whose northeastern section is very important to the Alhambra's strategic defence.

Torre del Homenaje and Torre del Cubo

The Torre del Homenaje dominates the entire perimeter of the Alhambra like a sentinel watching over all that occurs within the Medina. The highest point in the fortress is located on its terrace; it allows visual contact with the watchtowers distributed across the surrounding mountains — possibly via mirrors or smoke signals — in order to obtain up-to-date information regarding the movement of enemy troops.

Later, the Christians would reinforce the base of this tower with the Torre del Cubo, whose cylindrical shape offered more protection from artillery than the square-shaped Nasrid towers like the one around which it was built, the Torre de la Tahona. The strategic value of the Alcazaba can be clearly appreciated from both the terrace of the

The Torre del Homenaje is one of the largest defensive towers in the Alcazaba. The Torre del Cubo at its foot was built during the Christian era

Plan and elevation views of the Torre del Homenaje

The Torre del Homenaje — which had six floors in its interior, as can be seen on the elevation view — was, from a strategic point of view, the most important tower of the Alcazaba. The highest point in the fortress is located on its terrace. It was the watchtower from which the surrounding area was observed in order to monitor for potential attacks. During the Christian era, around 1586, its lower section was reinforced with the Torre del Cubo, whose circular shape provided a better defence against artillery.
Alhambra Archives

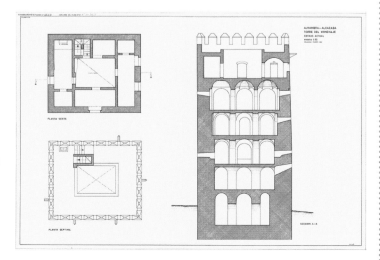

The Alcazaba is reinforced by three walls: the interior and the highest has small protruding solid stone towers; the middle one corresponds to the closure of the compound; and the last, which protects the access road from Granada, corresponds to the general perimeter of the Alhambra

Torre del Cubo and the rampart that encircles the base of the Torre del Homenaje.

This northern area displays an architectural layout unique within the Alhambra, of great physical beauty, which consists of three closely-built walls: the highest belongs to the compound of the 11th-century Zirid *taifa*, and has three small solid towers that project outward from the wall; the middle wall is the site of the *adarve* (rampart or walkwalk) built when the Nasrids enlarged the compound; and the lowest is an outer wall protecting the wide street used by the residents of Granada to enter the Alhambra during the Nasrid era.

Various unique elements used for protecting the compound can be seen here. *Alambores* or scarps — sloped wall reinforcements making potential assaults more difficult — were built at the base of the three walls. A curious perpendicular parapet was installed at the foot of the Torre del Homenaje that — in addition to forcing a winding, circular ascent — hides the

entrance to the fortress so that no one could monitor the changing of the guard that patrolled the area. Lastly, we come to the gate to the upper compound, which has a bent passageway and a section without a roof so that potential attackers could be harassed from above.

Military District

Today, the interior of the Alcazaba is an open-air space that is, nevertheless, occupied almost entirely by a labyrinth of walls and roads. This is a case of anastylosis, that is, the architectural recovery of the archaeological remains of a Nasrid-era military district found at the level of the wall's base. In the early 20th century, almost the entire area was covered with soil or rubble. When it was removed, the layout of an outlying neighbourhood that complemented the palace city came to light. This neighbourhood was separated from the rest of the city, and was where the military contingent — probably selected for their absolute loyalty to

The military district, discovered at the beginning of the 20th century, was a neighbourhood in which the troops assigned to defending the sultan and his court lived. It included all the services available in any other residential district: a bakery with oven, steam baths, cistern, etc.

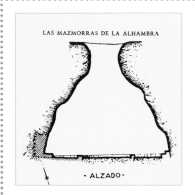

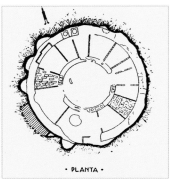

The dungeons of the Alhambra

A dungeon was discovered In the Plaza de Armas in the Alcazaba around 1930. In elevation view, it seems to be shaped like a narrow-necked *tinaja* (a pottery vessel for holding liquids), the top of which is at ground level. Its base is wider and has brick walls radiating out from the middle that mark off cells for the inmates. There was no better place than the Alcazaba to hold important prisoners that could be used in prisoner swaps with the enemy.
Drawings of the ground plan and elevation by Torres Balbás. Alhambra Archives

The terrace of the Torre de las Armas is a spectacular vantage point from which the extensive surrounding area can be seen, including the layout of the Alhambra with respect to Granada

the sultan — whose duty it was to protect the Alhambra lived.

It is the kasbah of the Alhambra, filled with homes, military quarters and services typical of a military community.

The area closest to the northern wall was occupied by houses grouped together and laid out just like any neighbourhood, with bent entrances to avoid indiscreet looks from the side streets or passageways used to reach them. The houses, though of varied design and size, were all designed around a small interior patio that opened onto the main room, a latrine, an *alacena* (pantry cupboard) and a stairway to the upper floor, just as in any Hispano-Muslim home. A main street runs longitudinally, separating this area from the area immediately to the south, where the dividing walls and layout of the areas are more regular; these are probably barracks or shelters for the young guards who did not yet have their own

families to live with as did their comrades in the adjacent neighbourhood.

The neighbourhood includes some elements related to military life, such as dungeons, silos for storing provisions, and storage areas for weapons and ammunition and — as in any other neighbourhood — it contained the necessities for ordinary life: a *tahona* for cooking prepared foods for each family or for preparing the daily rations, and a spacious steam bath house for both regular and ritual hygiene, with all of the necessary requirements such as the adjacent cistern, which was rebuilt in the 16th century.

Currently, two spectacular vantage points can be accessed from inside the Alcazaba, from which one of the most admired aspects of the Alhambra can be observed: its relationship with the extensive territory around it. The Torre and the Puerta de las Armas and the Torre de la Vela are very different from one another and yet, from their rooftops, they

The Torre de la Vela with the midday sun reflecting off of its western face

both offer spectacular views of Granada, the Vega, the valley of the Darro River, the lower city, the Albaicín, Sacromonte, etc. Most importantly, they offer an overall view of the entire compound of the Alhambra and the Generalife.

Puerta de las Armas
The Puerta de las Armas — one of the first constructions undertaken in the Alhambra in the 13th century — is the only one of the four large exterior gates that connected directly with the city of Granada until well into the 14th century. The progress of the Christian conquest led many Andalusians to seek protection in the new neighbourhoods on the outskirts of Granada. This caused the city to expand, transforming the urban fabric and customs of the local population, such as the need to go up to the palace to tend to official matters. From its terrace, one can see — to the west — the connection to the city below

across the left bank of the Darro River and — to the east — the entrance to the palace city via the street running along the outer wall. The northern wall of Granada — which connects it to the Alhambra — can also be made out, as well as the upper Albaicín, the neighbourhood of the Sacromonte and San Miguel Hill.

Torre de la Vela
The entire Alhambra fortress seems to gravitate round the impregnable structure of the Torre de la Vela — called the Torre Mayor in the Nasrid era — which has marked the daily life of the people of Granada since the early 13th century.

In the 16th century it was also referred to as the Torre del Sol, as the midday sun reflects on its façade, which serves as a sun dial for the city. Inside, the different floors feature handsome examples of building techniques such as brick pillars, a central vault, side galleries that are also

GRANADA.—ESTADO DE LA HISTÓRICA TORRE DE LA VELA,
después de la tormenta del 22 de Mayo.—(De croquis remitido por D. Valentín Barracheguren.)

The Torre de la Vela
The elevation view clearly shows that the upper floors widen gradually widened in order to lighten the weight of the building.
After the Christian conquest of the Alhambra, a bell — replaced on several occasions — was installed on the terrace of the Torre de la Vela. The current bell dates from 1773, and it was installed in its current location in 1840. This bell has been present in the life of Granada residents, informing them of many important events. Cross-section and engraving, Alhambra Archives

domed, a basement with a dungeon, and a terrace at the top. As is characteristic of the large Nasrid towers, the interior spaces become successively larger on the upper floors in order to lighten the load of the building and to ensure its stability. With all certainty, the stairway — at least in the middle section — was not located in the same place as the current one. As in the majority of the Alhambra's towers, there were large battlements on the roof terrace that — over time and due to regular earthquakes in the area — collapsed, with some still lying at the foot of the tower. Tradition has it that this is where the well-known ceremony in which the standards of the Catholic Monarchs were raised after they conquered the city on 2 January 1492 took place. It was also known as the Torre de la Campana, because — just as in other Christian fortresses won back from the Muslims — it housed a bell used to sound the alarm for the local population. From historical documents, we know that — due to the frequency it was rung, as well as poor weather conditions — the bell was replaced in 1569, 1598, 1624, 1640, 1655 and, lastly, 1773, when the current bell was installed. In images dating from the 16th century, the bell is shown in the tower's northeastern corner; it was moved to its current site in 1840. A lightning bolt destroyed the belfry, which was reconstructed in 1882. With its different day- and nighttime military bell strike

patterns, the Torre de la Vela has marked daily life in Granada and its surrounding areas. Thanks to its regularity, until very recently it was used by the farmers of the Vega to determine the shifts for irrigating crops. It was also rung at particular times to sound the alarm about fires and popular uprisings, and to mourn the deaths of royalty. As a result, in 1843 Queen Isabella II granted the city the privilege of including the Torre de la Vela on the city's official coat of arms. Throughout the year, it tolls in celebration of various events, such as 2 January, the day the city was conquered by the Catholic Monarchs; 7 October, celebrating the Virgin of the Rosary and the anniversary of the Battle of Lepanto; 12 October; the day celebrating Columbus's arrival in America; and in Holy Week, during the citywide procession of the Brotherhood of Santa María de la Alhambra. One of Granada's most deeply rooted traditions consists of climbing the Torre de la Vela every year on 2 January to ring the bell, which supposedly ensures that marriageable young women will become engaged during the coming year. Currently, the regular nightly strikes are done mechanically.

In front of the Torre de la Vela extends what is called the Revellín (Ravelin), an artillery bastion that has been compared to the bow of a ship anchored to the hill. Documents from the late 15th century referred to it as the "Baluarte de la Mezquita de Sobre Darro" (Bastion of the

Mosque Overlooking the Darro). In front of it — in addition to traces of an early connection of the compound with the city — can be found other significant elements, including the gate to the upper compound of the Alcazaba, which has a circular brick vault and on whose façade is a stone horseshoe arch, partially hidden by where the wall has been enlarged.

Along the base of the Torre de la Vela runs a rampart or barbican which was the natural path to the interior of the Alcazaba, which is separate from the rest of the walled compound. It leads to the large exterior Puerta de las Armas and the building that housed the easily recognisable stables.

The Ravelin — which is the final component of the Alhambra's apparently complicated system of walls and towers — is, in turn, connected to the walls that protect Granada to the south and that cross the current Cuesta de Gomérez until they reach Mauror Hill, where the Torres Bermejas are located.

Torre de la Pólvora

The Torre de la Pólvora — which survived the medieval era, becoming even more important during the Christian period — must have played an important protective and monitoring role in the complex's defensive programme. Significantly, it has maintained its name throughout the years, despite the fact that in documents from the 16th century it was referred to as the Torre de Cristóbal del Salto. This tower is somewhat smaller in size in comparison to the other, larger towers of the Alhambra, but it had an important strategic value. The Torre de la Pólvora protected the southern side of the emblematic Torre de la Vela and acted as a sally port for the rear entry to the gate and the western rampart, today buried under the Jardín de los Adarves, an area whose strategic importance increased during the 15th century due to the advances in artillery and the art of siege warfare.

The Torre de la Pólvora stands on a recently recovered artillery platform from the 16th century

Two centuries later, taking advantage of the terracing of the area between the segments of the Alcazaba's wall, it would be turned into the current recreation-oriented landscape from which the Torres Bermejas and the Carmen de Peñapartida can be seen.

It is perhaps for this reason that it was this place in the Alhambra that was chosen in 1957 to immortalize in stone the well-known words of Mexican poet Francisco de Icaza: *"dale limosna, mujer, que no hay en la vida nada como la pena de ser ciego en Granada"* (Give him alms, woman, for there's nothing worse than being a blind man in Granada).

Jardín de los Adarves

The space currently occupied by this garden was part of the programme for adapting the Alcazaba to the new artillery techniques. To do this, in the 17th century the moat between the fortress's two southern walls was filled to its present level. Around 1540, the retaining wall was built with a slightly sloping elevation against the existing outside wall — which it used as its base — employing a very refined 16th-century technique consisting of vertical brick pilasters combined with horizontal brick rows surrounding masonry boxes. It is topped by a continuous semi-circular

parapet with pieces of stonework of the same design that were highly effective against a direct impact from artillery. This space was originally a wide platform designed to support the light artillery of the era, which recoiled when fired over the parapet. This wall between the bastions first appears on the 1528 map of the Alhambra known as La Planta Grande, attributed to Pedro Machuca. The construction of this wall has been dated between 1550 and 1555, based on documents relating to massive purchases of brick and cornices (pieces carved in quarter round shape from limestone from Alfacar with which the parapet was finished). The technical team that carried out the project consisted of Luis Machuca as Master Builder, Gonzalo de Lorca as Head Builder, and Juan de Marquina serving as Head Surveyor (upon his death in 1552, he was replaced by Bartolomé Ruiz).

The wall runs parallel to the inner defensive wall, forming an angle at its northern end to include the Torre de la Pólvora, thus incorporating it into the defensive system as the final bastion in the wall. The wall of the southern side of this tower has two well-built openings for the artillery, curved so they could be used to aim sideways and below, sunken so that small cannons could fire downward to strike at the foot of the wall.

Fountain in the Jardín de los Adarves
In 1624, the kettle drum-shaped central fountain in the Jardín de los Adarves was installed on top of the fountain in the Patio de los Leones where it remained until 1954, at which time the Fuente de los Leones was restored to its original design. The original site for which this fountain was carved is not known with certainty, though it must have been installed somewhere in the palace. Photograph by J. Laurent (ca. 1872)

The Jardín de los Adarves — named for its location between the segments of the walls on the southern side of the Alcazaba

This space was not long used for military purposes, due mainly to the disappearance of the threat posed by the Moorish community whose uprising — neutralized between 1568 and 1571 — led to them being definitively expelled in 1609.

The exact date that the ramparts were converted to a garden is unknown, although there is a document stating that the first of the two pillars — still visible today decorated with a representation of water genies on dolphins — was constructed in 1628, so it is possible that the remodelling took place around this date. In 1624, the central kettle drum-shaped fountain was attached to the top of the fountain in the Patio de los Leones, where it remained until 1954, when this fountain was restored to its original design.

These changes in the ramparts are due to Íñigo López de Mendoza y Mendoza, Fifth Marquis of Mondéjar, who inherited the title after recovering the position of Governor of the Alhambra in 1624. They are part of a lovely legend — one of many that are part of the Alhambra's magical heritage — according to which some gold-filled jars of fine porcelain were found in the ramparts, hidden perhaps in the times of the conquest. The Earl is supposed to have spent part of this gold to design the garden and decorate it with fountains. Some of these jars must form part of a series of large golden earthenware cups, about twenty examples of which are preserved in various museums and collections worldwide, two in the Alhambra Museum.

7

The Nasrid Palaces

The *Dar al-Mamlaka,* with its different royal palaces commissioned by the sultans of the Nasrid era, makes up what we know today as the Nasrid Palaces. Although they are located in a single compartmentalised space, each palace can be identified with the sultan who had it built. Currently, they comprise three independent areas: the Palacio del Mexuar, the Palacio de Comares and the Palacio de los Leones. To these three, we can add another: the palace modified for use by the Christian royalty, an area of the Nasrid Palaces adapted to serve as the residence of Emperor Charles V while his palace was being built.

The Alhambra, viewed from the outside — particularly from the Albaicín — is a walled compound fortified by strong towers built on the edges of steep precipices that make it difficult to access.

However, the palaces that lay behind these naked walls — and many of the interior rooms of the towers — are fragile works of delicate architecture and subtle decoration. The contrast is so intense that it produces an unsurpassable aesthetic emotion.

The Nasrid Palaces are the residences that the different Muslim sultans inhabiting the Alhambra built and enlarged during their reigns for their own use and that of the court.

The Alhambra Palace o *Dar al-Sultán*
As in all Muslim palace-cities, in the Alhambra, the site of power, the *Dar al-Sultán,* residence of the sultans where their family and occasionally, ceremonial lives transpired, was the focal point around which the city was structured and based. The so-called Nasrid Palaces constitute a single space that was compartmentalised in a manner similar to the traditional nomadic settlements that developed into the first Muslim cities.

Over the course of more than two and a half centuries in the Nasrid Alhambra, numerous constructions, enlargements and renovations — at times, of a radical and traumatic nature — were carried out. Each of the palaces is identified with the sultan who commissioned its construction; there are, therefore, at least half a dozen palaces when, in reality, the royal space — the centre of

power — should be but one single space. Although we call them the Palacio de Comares, the Palacio de los Leones, and the Palacio del Partal, or we call them Serrallo, winter or summer palace, we are actually referring to a single place: the Alhambra Palace or, in any event, the palantine area of the Alhambra.

The Royal Palace
Beginning in the second half of the 19th century — from the perspective of a modern interpretation of this group of palaces — the manuals used at the time identified these palaces as *cuartos* (rooms); so they are listed as the Comares Room, the Room of the Lions, etc. In fact, the Arabic expression that designates a habitable space is *al-Dar,* one of whose meanings is precisely "room." And Arabic texts tend to refer to it as such: *Dar al-Sultán.* Based on this interpretation, it is understandable that the Muslim palaces in the Alhambra are referred to as the Old Royal Palace, to differentiate it from the New Royal Palace, that is, the Renaissance Palace of Emperor Charles V.

Thus, today this group of Nasrid Palaces comprises three independent yet connected areas: the Mexuar area, and the areas called the Comares Room and the Room of the Lions. Of the palace areas identified, two of them — the Palacio de Comares and the Palacio de los Leones — still have most of their annexes, thanks to, among other factors, the fact that, historically, those in charge agreed to keep their spirit alive and, above all, to continue using their rooms.

Detail in perspective of how of the palaces forming the Royal Palace of the Alhambra rise one above the other

The Nasrid Palaces

As the seat of the sultanate's court, perhaps the most remarkable sights of the Alhambra are the palaces commissioned by the Nasrid sultans. Behind the bare walls, devoid of any decoration, that mark the outside of the compound, we find a series of buildings of subtle architecture and fragile, delicate ornamentation that produce an intense aesthetic emotion. These were the residences used by the different Nasrid sultans for themselves and their courts. These palaces are currently divided into three main areas independent of — yet connected with — each other.

❶ The Mexuar

This is the oldest of the preserved palaces. In Nasrid times it served as a hall for audiences and important meetings. The main hall is accessed via two courtyards, and has an elevated seating area where the sultan sat. In the rear is a small room that served as an oratory from which the Albaicín can be seen, and is oriented differently in order to meet religious requirements. Its decoration is the result of various interventions undertaken between the 16th and 20th centuries.

❸ Palacio de los Leones

The most remarkable of the Nasrid Palaces, it dates from the second half of the 14th century, under Muhammad V. Its rooms are distributed around the Patio de los Leones, the best-known of all of the spaces in the Alhambra. The palace receives its name from the central fountain in this courtyard, consisting of twelve lions from which water pours forth. It was constructed expressly to serve as a residence, and its rooms — the most outstanding of which is the Sala de Dos Hermanas — are exquisitely decorated.

❷ Palacio de Comares

Built during the era of Yusuf I, the Nasrid sultans established the Salón del Trono in this palace, which also served as the residence of the sultan and his family. The entire palace — situated around the Patio de los Arrayanes or Patio de Comares — is an architectural and decorative marvel, attaining a perfect harmony between the constructed elements and nature that creates a microclimate and a level of humidity, air flow and fragrance that all contribute to the wellbeing of its inhabitants.

⊕ **Zoom**

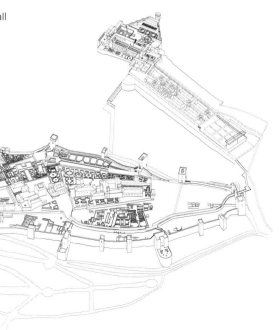

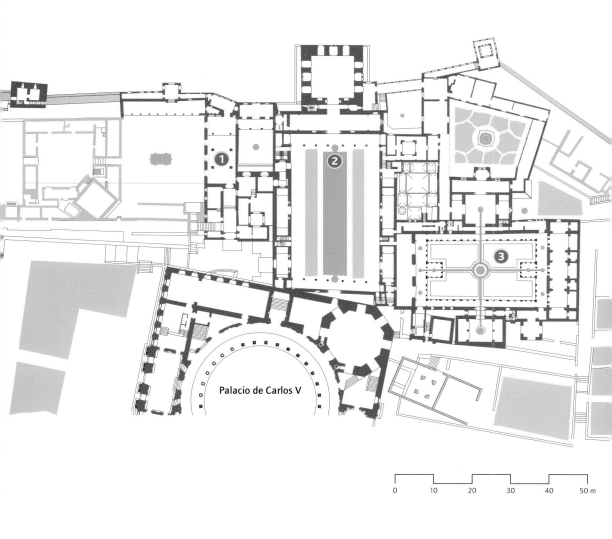

Palacio de Carlos V

| 0 | 10 | 20 | 30 | 40 | 50 m |

1 The Mexuar

2 Palacio de Comares

3 Palacio de los Leones

| | Wall | | Nasrid architecture | | Nasrid archaeological remains | | Christian architecture |

| | Gardens | | Hydraulic elements |

7.1 The Mexuar

The area called the Mexuar is considerably different from its original layout although — based on descriptions from the era and the architectural structures that still exist — we know that it was distributed among three areas surrounding courtyards at different levels and halls used for a variety of purposes. It was the heart of the first Nasrid palace built in the area, and throughout the 14th century it was used fundamentally for bureaucratic activities and the administration of justice.

The first two courtyards of the Mexuar were used for bureaucratic activities and the administration of justice. They have been recovered archaeologically, and can be currently identified largely from the bases of the walls that jut up between the garden spaces. This area forms what we refer to generically as the Mexuar, or Council.

With the help of texts describing its original layout and the architectural structures that have been preserved — transformed over the Christian era to a greater or lesser extent — we can categorise the Mexuar's distribution into three contiguous areas: the new (or second) Mexuar, the private (or first) Mexuar and the Sala del Trono.

Patio de la Mezquita

The first of the courtyards — the Court of the Mosque — has various elongated halls that open onto a central courtyard, and were most certainly used as court administration offices. It is likely that the office located at the south is the office referred to in texts as *Qubbat al-'Ard*, where secretaries attended to official correspondence and judicial appeals; it had a private area in which the sultan could occasionally receive greetings from his subjects. Adjacent to it, and above a fountain used for ritual washing, is the so-called Mezquita Vieja or Mezquita del Sultán, a small oratory with its adjacent minaret. Some Arabic texts have referred to it as being "badly decorated" because it is not correctly oriented towards Mecca. Built under Sultan Isma'il I (1314–1325), it was respected and

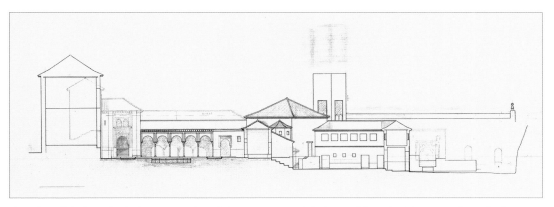

Elevation of the hypothetical reconstruction of the two courtyards in front of the Sala del Mexuar, drawn in the Technical Office of the Alhambra during the 1950s. Alhambra Archives

The Sala del Mexuar with the oratory in the background

The Mexuar

Its architectural and decorative design has been considerably modified over the centuries, since following the Christian conquest one of its areas was designated as the governors' residence. It comprises two extensive courtyards that must have had buildings attached to its wall, and a large hall — that of the Mexuar — which was also repeatedly adapted to the different uses assigned to it over time.

1 Patio de la Mezquita

The first courtyard was called the Madraza de los Príncipes during the middle of the 20th century due to its apparent similarity to the Madraza in Granada. It contains the remains of various elongated halls — probably government administration offices — opening onto a central courtyard.

2 Patio de Machuca

The second courtyard, the Patio de Machuca, is accessed via a wide staircase. In its centre is a pool with fluted edges, referred to in Arabic texts as a *zafariche de peregrina forma* (peculiarly shaped pool). It underwent significant modifications during the Christian era, when it was converted into a residence for governors and for architect Pedro Machuca.

3 Sala del Mexuar

This was the main hall of the palace built under Isma'il I (1314–1325). It was modified by Muhammad V and converted into a Christian chapel in the 16th century. During some eras, it was the site of the sultan's throne.

4 Oratory

This is a small mosque, oriented as required toward Mecca. In the 19th century, it was opened up on to the Sala del Mexuar by breaking through the wall and lowering the floor level. A spectacular view of the Albaicín can be seen from its windows.

5 Courtyard and portico of the Cuarto Dorado

During the 14th century, the sultans received their subjects in the Cuarto Dorado. It was accessed via a narrow door so that the guards could control who entered. The portico is held up by slender columns with reused capitals carved out of stone. In front of it is the portal through which the Palacio de Comares is accessed.

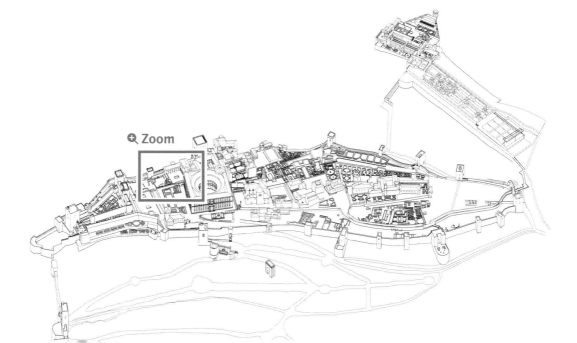

Zoom

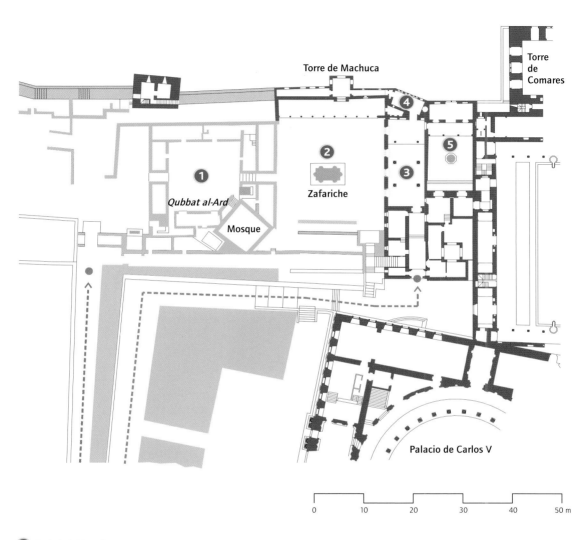

Torre de Machuca

Torre de Comares

Qubbat al-Ard

Mosque

Zafariche

Palacio de Carlos V

N
W E
S

0 10 20 30 40 50 m

1 Patio de la Mezquita

2 Patio de Machuca

3 Sala del Mexuar

4 Oratory

5 Courtyard and portico of the Cuarto Dorado

● Entrance. Visit schedule checkpoint

┈┈> Group entrance

┈┈> Individual entrance

■ Wall

■ Nasrid architecture

■ Nasrid archaeological remains

■ Christian architecture

■ Gardens

■ Hydraulic elements

Detail of an engraving of *Les delices de L'Espagne et du Portugal* (Lisbon, 1715), with the Mexuar buildings existing at the time. Alhambra Library

Aerial view of the Mexuar courtyards. In the centre of the second courtyard, the pond or "peculiarly shaped pool" stands out

integrated into the remodelling carried out in the second half of the 14th century. In modern times, the courtyard has been referred to as the Madraza de los Príncipes due to its apparent similarity to the city's Madraza and because — as it was located inside the palace — it must have been designed for use by its residents.

Patio de Machuca

Access to the second courtyard is via a staircase. The centre of the courtyard holds an astonishing pool with fluted edges referred to in Arab texts as a *zafariche de peregrina forma* (peculiarly shaped pool).

Originally, smaller circular fountains appeared on both sides, as well as water spouts shaped like small lions that poured water into the interior, but these elements have since disappeared. The northern side of the court has a porticoed gallery with nine arches — recovered thanks to early 20th century restorations — that leads to a small balcony jutting out of the wall. Built under Sultan Yusuf I (1333–1354), it was known by the word for "victory" (*al-nasr*) in Nasrid times and, more recently, as the Torre de los Puñales because a dagger was found within its walls during restoration work. Both the tower as well as the entire courtyard are called Machuca, as it was this architect's residence.

A line of cypresses shaped like arches fills the now disappeared southern gallery that served as the entrance to what is known as the Sala del Trono. Currently, this area has been considerably modified by adaptations made during the Christian era, particularly when it was used as the residence of the Alhambra's governors. In the so-called "Planta grande" design plan from 1528 — attributed to Pedro Machuca (and today preserved in the Royal Palace of Madrid) — this area appears referred to as the "Mexuar court where the German queen sat." In any event, we can imagine it as it was during Nasrid times thanks to an original text that has recently come to light. Written by Ibn al-Khatib — vizier to Sultan Muhammad V, the great reformer of the Alhambra who lived in the second half of the 14th century — it recounts a story about the *Mawlid* celebration commemorating the birth of the Prophet Mohammed celebrated here during the winter of 1362.

Sala del Mexuar

Three main stages can be identified in the evolution of the Sala del Mexuar: the first corresponds to the era in which the central palace structure was built under Sultan Isma'il I (1314–1325); the second, in which his grandson Muhammad V adapted this space to his palace programme; and the third, its conversion into a Christian chapel during the 16th century.

Access to this hall was via a narrow courtyard leading to a delicate lintelled portal, representative of Hispano-Muslim architecture with its wide wooden eave above the pilastered corbel. The tiling of the lower section has been lost, but the exquisite ceiling of the threshold remains. This has been referred to in Nasrid texts as the Vestíbulo del Alcázar, and it was the result of closing off the original stuccoed entranceway — some of whose remains, integrated into the wall, are visible from the inside — from the era of Muhammad V.

The hall — in which the sultan's throne was located during some eras — consists of a square-shaped central space bordered by four slender marble columns whose capitals maintain their polychromatic decoration; originally, they supported a "very high dome [...] encircled by a sea of flawless glass," as described in the previously mentioned Arab text describing the *Mawlid* celebration of 1362. This was dismantled around 1540 in order to add an upper floor with rooms. This square-shaped space fits inside another, rectangular area with tiled baseboards on the four walls, over which an epigraphic panel originally displayed a poem that declared "[...] covered with pure gold leaf [...] between ground lapis lazuli." Today, the following inscription can be read: "the Kingdom [...], the Grandeur [...] and the Glory is of God," words intentionally selected by Moors

Entrance courtyard to the Sala del Mexuar, with a delicate lintelled portal and a characteristic wide wooden eave

converted to Christianity due to its similarity to the Latin litany *Christus regnat, Christus vincit, Christus imperat*. This hall was transformed into a chapel after the conquest, but the wooden ceilings of the perimeter areas have retained their original design. For the conversion of the Mexuar into a Christian chapel, it was necessary to lower the level of the floor and to add on the rectangular space in the back, a court that Arabic texts referred to as "the small room of the treasure of the perfume." Currently, it is separated by a high wooden railing which, in the space's new function as chapel, was used for the choir.

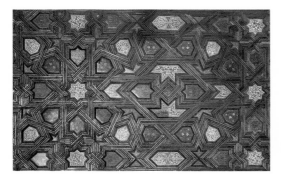

Coffered ceiling at the threshold of the entrance door to the Sala de Mexuar

Detail of the epigraphy in the Sala del Mexuar: *(al-mulk li-l-lah, al qudra li-l-lah, al-'iza li-l-lah* (The kingdom [...], the Grandeur [...] and the Glory is of God)

View of the Sala del Mexuar with the choir created during the **Christian era.** Photograph from the late 19th century. Alhambra Library

Interior of the Sala del Mexuar converted to a chapel, ca. 1925. Alhambra Archives

The tiles for this space were brought in from outside. In its decoration, based on star shapes or *sinos,* the Arabic Nasrid motto appears alternately in a symbolic manner with the Imperial Spanish coat of arms displaying the two-headed eagle and with the coat of arms of the Christian governors of the Alhambra. The original glass dome described in the 1362 text — similar to a *lantern,* a small windowed tower installed in the ceiling and lighting the entire area — has not been preserved. The current window shutters were installed during the first third of the 16th century in order to adjust the level of light in the chapel.

Court and Portico of the Cuarto Dorado
Passing through a narrow doorway, we reach the court where the sultan received his subjects in the Alhambra during the second half of the 14th century. This is why the small door with the horseshoe arch allows only one person at a time to pass through it, making it easier for the guards to control the visitors who were guided across the first gallery of columns to the interior of the waiting room. In the era of the Catholic Monarchs the Muslim coffered ceiling of this space was repainted with gold-coloured ornamental motifs and decorations and the monarchs' emblems

Oratory
In the restorations of the Alhambra undertaken between 1868 and 1889, a small, adjoining Muslim oratory was incorporated into the Sala del Mexuar, for which it was necessary to knock down the wall and lower the level of the original floor, evidence of which is the small ledge that runs under the windows. This building — oriented as required in the direction of prayer — still conserves the polygonal-shaped *mihrab* (niche indicating the direction of prayer) with a horseshoe arch in its front wall or *qibla.* The entire northern side is open toward the Albaicín, with a view that invites Believers to meditate on the grandeur of Creation through the landscape and nature. This is reinforced by the inscription on the *mihrab* asking them to: "come pray and be not one of the negligent" (Qur'an, second part, sura VII, ayah 205).

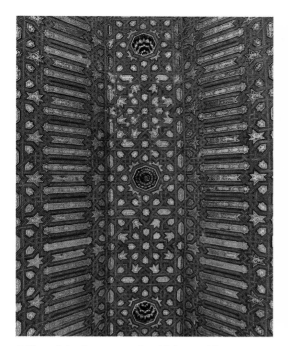

Ceiling of the Cuarto Dorado with its Nasrid coffered ceiling repainted with the heraldic and decorative motifs of the new Christian residents

The central window of the Cuarto Dorado transformed in the Christian era into a balcony with Mudéjar seating in front of it

were added, since which time it has been known as the Cuarto Dorado. Christian renovations of the room also altered the rest of the decoration, particularly with the closing of the side windows and the transformation of the central window into a balcony with two benches facing each other in front of it and curious capitals, imbuing it with a bi-cultural ambience typical of Mudéjar art.

The portico, formed by three slender arches, still has some of its original decoration, with the middle Almohad-style capitals — carved out of stone — being particularly noteworthy. At the end of the 15th century, it was hidden by a large Moorish arch, immortalised in 1871 by painter Mariano Fortuny in one of the most repeated images in the Orientalist pictorial tradition of the Alhambra. It was torn down in 1965.

The upper level of the building that today we know as the Mexuar was used in modern times as the residence of the governors of the Alhambra. However, it was converted into

a Christian palace much earlier, practically right after it was conquered at the end of the 15th century. In the design plans of the 1528 *Planta grande*, appearing above the portico in the Cuarto Dorado is the note "chamber where the empress sat"; clearly the transformation of the area had already taken place. It was still used as a residence in the 19th century, as mentioned by North American writer Washington Irving when he asked the governor for lodging so he could to write his *Tales of the Alhambra* in 1828. Additional adaptations were required in order to make the upper floors more habitable, such as building the corridor overhanging the courtyard of the Cuarto Dorado — drawn by John F. Lewis around 1835 — to directly connect to the upper floors of the Mexuar and the adjacent Palacio de Comares. This curious projection of a cantilever over a corbel — dismantled at the beginning of the 20th century — is known in contemporary historiography of the Alhambra as the Corredor

Drawing by J. F. Lewis displaying the portico of the Cuarto Dorado in 1835, with the Moorish arch added in the 15th century and dismantled in the mid–20th century, as well as the wooden corridor, removed earlier. Alhambra Library

de Harriet, as it had been sketched by Richard Ford's wife during their stay in the Alhambra between 1830 and 1832.

The marble central basin is a replica of the Lindaraja fountain, one of the most beautiful pieces in the Nasrid hydraulic system, preserved today in the Alhambra Museum; with the changes made by the Christians, it ended up appearing out of context. The grille located next to the portico allows light to enter the dark underground hallway used for security purposes by the palace guards. In early Nasrid times, the courtyard was probably not entirely enclosed, but instead open at its northern end to the city's scenery over the wall. In fact, underneath the Cuarto Dorado there is a passageway used by guards for making their rounds that was originally uncovered above the rampart or upper part of the wall, just as there is in the rest of the Alhambra.

The growth of these palace-related structures during the 14th century made this courtyard a middle ground of great symbolic nature between the semi-public and private areas. This was clearly recognised by the Christian kings, who added their own identifying icons here. This is why it is one of the sites that best represent the Alhambra's treasured values of cultural integration.

The side walls of the courtyard are still in their original condition, with large undecorated surfaces of smooth lime stucco that reflect the light and highlight the façade that rises solemnly in front of the Cuarto Dorado.

Court and portico of the Cuarto Dorado

7.2 Palacio de Comares

In addition to having been the residence of the sultan and his family during certain periods of time, the Palacio de Comares contained the Salón del Trono — a spectacular area inside the tower — following the Islamic concept of the multifunctionality of spaces. The palace is structured around a large rectangular courtyard onto which rooms open and in which the open-air environment, architecture, vegetation and water all combine to offer its residents a foretaste of the oasis awaiting them in Paradise.

The Façade of the Palacio de Comares

The portal of the Palacio de Comares — one of the supreme works of Islamic art — was commissioned by Sultan Muhammad V in 1370 in commemoration of the conquest of the city of Algeciras, of importance to the Nasrid sultanate from both a military and a commercial point of view for its strategic control of the Strait of Gibraltar. Before it, seated on his throne — most certainly a luxurious *jamuga* (folding chair with curved legs) — in the centre of the three-level tier, the sultan would preside over ceremonial events elaborately dressed as though an inseparable part of the throne, protected by a superb wooden eave, a masterpiece of Islamic woodwork. The allegorical nature of this impressive façade is accentuated by the quote of the "Throne Verse" from the Qur'an over the middle window of the upper floor. Other texts, such as the four-verse poem engraved between the medallion shapes at the base of the eave, insist on its royal nature: "my position is that of a crown," and describe its function: "my gate is a fork in the road [...]; the Western world believes that in me lies the East." Of the two gates, the right-hand gate accesses the interior of the palace, where the private life of the sultan and his family took place. The gate on the left leads to a chamber that was possibly filled with the "treasure of the military payroll," mentioned in the 1362 text recounting the *Mawlid* celebration. This royal

Detail of the ceiling in the entranceway to the Palacio de Comares

The wooden ceilings used in Nasrid palace architecture are elements of great symbolic and decorative importance. In this case, the wooden latticework has a great ornamental value and offers a cultural combination of motifs and emblems from the Catholic Kings — gilded between 1496 and 1497 — above characteristic Muslim geometric pieces. From a circle, a star or *sino* is created, in this case of sixteen points, and prolonged, developing the decorative scheme on the ceiling. These ceilings utilise the design method known as *ataujerado*, integrating latticework, strips and geometric pieces nailed into a panel attached below the ceiling. This representative sample is located at the entrance to the Palacio de Comares, behind the door.

Façade of the Palacio de Comares in the Patio de los Arrayanes, in front of the portico of the Cuarto Dorado

Palacio de Comares

Commissioned by Yusuf I, its splendid decoration was finished by his son Muhammad V. It is accessed via the façade with two gates located in the courtyard of the Cuarto Dorado, built by Muhammad V. The different service areas are through the right-hand gate, while the gate on the left leads to the main chambers. The magnificent Patio de los Arrayanes — with its central water tank flanked by rows of myrtles and a portico on each of its shorter sides — is located in the centre of the palace. Inside the tower is the largest hall in the Nasrid Alhambra: the Salón de Comares. The only completely preserved steam baths from Muslim times are also found in this palace.

❶ Façade of the Palacio de Comares

It marks the separation between the public and private areas. Exceptional due to its architectural and decorative concepts (overall decoration, its epigraphy, the wooden eave with medallions), its construction probably marks the peak of Nasrid art.

❷ Patio de los Arrayanes

As in other Hispano-Muslim homes, the court is the heart of the residence, with rooms distributed around it and a water tank integrated into its architecture, breaking up the horizontal structure of the space, harmonising with the subtle plant life and softening the light with its mirrored surface.

❸ Sala de la Barca

The Sala de la Barca — a multi-purpose palace space located on the way from the court to the Salón del Trono (rather like travelling from the desert to the inside of a Bedouin tent), is where the new sultan would pray for divine assistance before taking possession of the throne.

❹ Salón de Comares

This hall is the largest chamber in the compound and the site of the sultan's earthly power; its magnificent ceiling has references to the end of times. Its construction design and decoration represent both a synthesis and a prototype of Islamic art in the West.

❺ The Southern Pavilion

Similar to the Sala de la Barca, it was torn down in order to build the Palacio de Carlos V, leaving behind only the interior bay of the courtyard. However its three-storey façade was maintained as a kind of backdrop to preserve the original appearance of the courtyard.

❻ *Hammam* or the Baths of Comares

An essential element of Islam, the Baths of Comares are located between the Palacio de Comares and the Palacio de los Leones. It can be accessed directly from the Patio de los Arrayanes next to the sultan's rooms, for whom it was reserved.

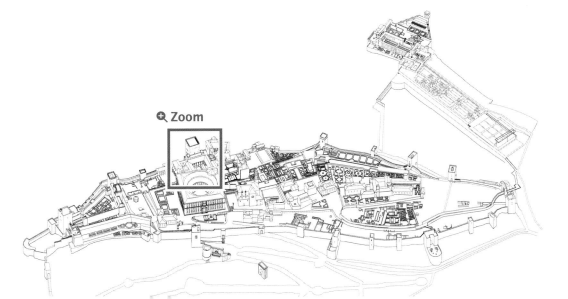

🔍 Zoom

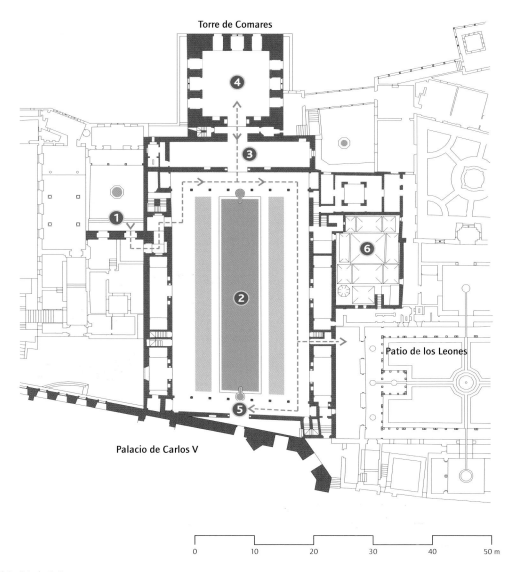

Torre de Comares

④

③

①

②

⑥

⑤

Patio de los Leones

Palacio de Carlos V

```
0        10        20        30        40       50 m
```

① Façade of the Palacio de Comares

② Patio de los Arrayanes

③ Sala de la Barca

④ Salón de Comares

⑤ Southern Pavilion

⑥ *Hammam* or the Baths of Comares

------> Direction of the visit

█ Nasrid architecture   █ Christian architecture   ▨ Hydraulic elements   ▨ Gardens

image is reinforced by the rich and varied colour palette used on the tiles of the baseboard and on the the frames of both doors that are today restored with other stucco-based materials that resemble these tiles.

The palace is accessed via an indirectly lit ascending passageway with a double bend; there are doors opening in opposite directions at the ends of the passageway, protecting the guards inside and allowing them to control access by preventing anyone from entering the rooms or escaping from them. The wooden ceiling — one of the most remarkable decorative elements in this passageway — is also evidence of the bi-cultural mix that integrated gold-coloured motifs and the emblems of the Christian kings on the Muslim planking made of geometric pieces. In contrast to the dark passageway, a burst of light greets visitors when they emerge into the Patio de los Arrayanes.

Patio de los Arrayanes or Patio de Comares
Every corner of this palace is representative of the Hispano-Muslim architectural design used in houses: the bent entrance to the open-air courtyard, the centre of the residence, equipped with a source of water of some type and with a variety of plants, the heart of family life around which the rooms were distributed. The houses that have been preserved in different parts of the Alhambra all have a similar layout, although their proportions and decoration differ. Here, in the centre of the courtyard is a spectacular pool that for years has given the courtyard its name, the Patio de la Alberca, also known as the Patio de los Arrayanes for the carefully trimmed beds of shrubs that run along the length of its longer sides. Water, vegetation and open sky bring nature into the palace in a way that is both symbolic and physical, helping to create a system with a microclimate, humidity, ventilation and fragrance that resembles an oasis in an earthly foretaste of what awaits in Paradise. The water tank forms a part of the building and aesthetic designs of the palace. Its

Central area of the palace: the water tank in the Patio de los Arrayanes with the northern façade and the Torre de Comares in the background

Fountain in the water tank of the Patio de Comares
On the ground of the Patio de los Arrayanes, in front of the largest arch of the porticos on the shorter sides, are some "schematic fountains" that supply water to the pool in a surprisingly unique way: the water gushes from the spout in the circular part of the fountain, flowing quickly toward the exit channel where it pauses before spilling smoothly and soundlessly on to the surface of the pool. These are not the original spouts installed, but replacements. The marks from the water spattered from the original spouts can still be seen on the surrounding flooring.

still surface reflects the surrounding architecture like a mirror, breaking the horizontal design of the courtyard through the creation of depth and verticality. At the same time, it brings direct sunlight into the space, filling it with nuances that may be more spectacular around midday, when the sun is high above and illuminates the northern portico, reflecting its carved plasterwork in the pool's water. Located on the shorter sides, in front of the central arch of the respective porticos, one can appreciate the symbiosis between architecture and nature, often sought but rarely achieved as

The state of the portico in the northern pavilion of the Palacio de Comares after the devastating fire of 15 September 1890. As a result of the fire, the entire wooden ceiling covering the Sala de la Barca collapsed. The pieces salvaged from the fire allowed a complete reconstruction of the ceiling after painstaking work that was finished in 1965. Alhambra Archives

it has been in the Nasrid Alhambra. Under these arches, the two uniquely designed "schematic fountains" supply the pool in a surprising manner: the water, gushing from the circular part of the fountain, flows rapidly toward the exit channel, where it pauses before spilling into the pool, thus preventing ripples from forming on the surface of the water.

The doors on the sides of the court lead to four rooms serving as living spaces that are separate from but integrated into the palace. They all have the same layout: a lower main room with a direct entrance from the court via the large framed arches with carved plasterwork decorations that stand out against the monotonous façade. Of the other, smaller, arches, four connect to the respective stairways ascending to the upstairs chambers. They open on to the courtyard via double-arched mullioned windows with wooden latticework shutters. The arch nearest to the northern portico provides access to the palace baths.

Sala de la Barca

The Sala de la Barca is the antechamber to the Salón del Trono, the centre of power in the Alhambra's palatial architecture. An old epigraphic text refers to the space as a large tent for the sultan with a canopy unfolded — the gallery of the portico — in front of it.

The tower and hall are laid out in the traditional inverted T design: a hall running lengthwise with a tower-balcony projecting from it at a right angle toward the north over the main wall. This tower-balcony has an interior square-shaped alcove suitably sized and decorated for use as the dynasty's throne room. One of the Alhambra's most characteristic decorative and functional elements — the *taqa* — can be found in the walls forming the thresholds of the entranceways to the main rooms of the houses and, since this a palace, they are particularly remarkable.

The Sala de la Barca receives its name not — as popularly believed — from the ship-like shape

Mihrab in the small private oratory of the sultan located between the Sala de la Barca and the Salón de Comares

Taqa in the threshold of the entrance to the Salón de Comares framed by a poem which metaphorically explains that its function is to hold vessels

of its ceiling, but from the Arabic word *al-Baraka* (the Blessing), as within it, the new sultan prayed for divine assistance before taking possession of the throne in the adjacent Salón de Comares or Throne Room. Its creator, Sultan Yusuf I, never saw it completed, as he was assassinated in 1354. His son Muhammad V was responsible for most of its decoration and his name appears on the plasterwork.

Its lovely semicircular framework has circular caps at its ends, with geometric ornamentation based on wheels formed of stars. It has been known as the Cuarto Dorado or "Golden Room" since the end of the 16th century, as its ceiling had been completely painted over. A devastating fire in 1890 caused its entire ceiling to collapse. Some pieces were salvaged, allowing for its reconstruction, completed in 1965.

A baseboard made of tiles with different designs covers the lower section of the walls in the entire chamber, including the wide alcoves designed to hold beds that prolong the room at both ends beyond the large semicircular arches. To the left, a small door leads to a double bend and the palace's main latrine, where remains of the baseboard's original paint can still be seen; the door of the alcove opposite was created in the 16th century to connect it to the bathrooms of the royal Christian palace.

Rich fabrics or tapestries were likely hung on the wide undecorated surfaces of the walls, and the floor was covered with large rugs. A wide doorway leads to the Salón del Trono, crossed by a hall that to the left leads to the upstairs stairway and, to the right, to a small oratory – a private place of prayer for the sultan.

Salón del Trono

The Salón del Trono, also known as the Salón de Comares or the Sala de los Embajadores, located inside the Torre de Comares, is without doubt the most remarkable room in the palace and in the entire Alhambra. Inside is a synthesis of the architectural, aesthetic and symbolic

Salón del Trono of the Palacio de Comares, inside the largest tower in the Alhambra

Detail of the area where the wall meets the ceiling in the Salón de Comares
The *arrocarabe* or wooden support frieze with epigraphic ornamentation found at the top of the walls in the Salón del Trono is evidence of the importance of this hall as a maximum expression of earthly power of divine origin. Sura 67 of the Qur'an, written here in white letters, manifests the undisputed supremacy of God. The first ayah (verse) begins on the northern side and runs across the four walls. Both the ceiling and the Qur'anic inscription serve to legitimise the sultan, who ruled under them.

concepts of Hispano-Muslim culture, of which it could be considered the undisputed universal manual. The interior space is an example of proportional perfection: a cube within the largest tower in the Alhambra, decorated on all sides.

In this *qubba* (square-shaped room with dome), earthly and supernatural power can be felt and the epigraphic decoration on its walls confirms this: a poem written on them states that this is the throne of the dynasty; under the ceiling, at the highest point on the wall, sura 67 of the Qur'an — known as "The Kingdom" or "The Dominion" — reveals the unquestionable supremacy of God. The sura is proportionately distributed, written in white letters on the wooden wall under the ceiling across the four sides of the tower, with the first verse or ayah appearing on the northern wall and the thirty-first ending on the eastern. The Torre de Comares is oriented to the four cardinal points, further symbolising the power of God in the heavens and on Earth.

The name "Comares" originates, in part, from the Arabic word *arsh*, which — as with many Arabic words — has two meanings: pavilion — or tent — and throne. It was undoubtedly chosen with the intention of pointing out that the hall was equivalent to an extraordinary Bedouin tent in which lived an exalted individual.

The three thick exterior walls of the tower are perforated at ground level with three openings in each, which were made to hold nine small rooms.

There are four pairs of similar rooms, with the ninth — located in front of the entrance — being more beautifully decorated, as it was used by the sultan. Thus, with their three-way distribution, the rooms break the horizontal appearance of the cartouches located above their arches. The walls of the large hall are completely covered with decorations. The lower section is covered with tiled baseboards featuring different geometric combinations, while above there are different plasterwork panels placed both vertically as if they were tapestries and horizontally, decorated with epigraphy and with star-shaped designs on plant-

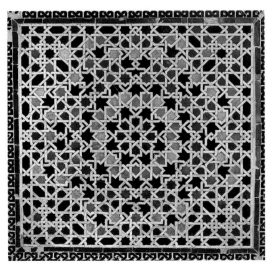

Detail of one of the tiles on the baseboard in the Salón de Comares

The interlacing or "complex linking" ornamentation of the ceiling of the Salón de Comares, together with its symbolic function, combine to form a masterpiece of Islamic carpentry. Left, the reconstruction of the original colours of the ceiling done by painter and restorer Manuel Maldonado, based on research by Brother Darío Cabanelas, OFM, in the 1960s

filled backgrounds. Currently, only the colouring of the ceramic baseboards can be seen in its original state, but it is possible to appreciate the remains of the polychrome on the carved plaster and imagine the actual symphony of colours that must have covered the entire area. Even the window coverings — today, recreations of the old wooden latticework — must have included brightly coloured translucent glass. A second row of windows with latticework shutters in the upper part of the walls provides ventilation and light to the room.

Although the floors in important rooms like this were commonly covered with large rugs — and abundant evidence of this has been preserved — only a few pieces of the original flooring remain in the square section in the middle of the floor; there are also other pieces dating from the 16th century and later which had been reused. There were probably marble slabs in the doorjambs of the rooms, as there are in other areas of the palace.

The totality of the room's decoration reaches its climax in the majestic ceiling, a masterpiece of Hispano-Muslim carpentry created using the interlacing or "complex linking" technique, inherited from the Mudéjar masters who passed it down to future generations, and who referred

to it as "assembly" carpentry or "white" carpentry. It consists of seven panels of wood, stacked one on top of the other and braced against the wall, on to which the 8,017 different parts that make up the design are nailed. The decoration's geometric motif — rows of wheels made of stars — is a copy of the heavens, symbol of the cosmos, of the grandeur of Creation. Thus, the ceiling is the eschatological representation of the seven

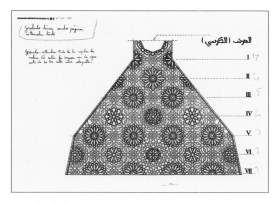

Drawing by Leopoldo Torres Balbás made when he was curator of the Alhambra (1923–1936) showing the ceiling of the Salón de Comares with its Muslim representation of the seven heavens. Alhambra Archives

Room in the Salón de Comares converted into a gate

Central room of the hall that was occupied by the sultan

Central detailing of the floor of the hall with the Nasrid Order of the Sash emblem

heavens that, after death, a Believer's soul must pass through — based on its worthiness — before reaching the eighth heaven: Paradise, the throne of God (represented here by the central Mocárabe dome). The roots of the four trees of Paradise are grafted on to it, symbolized by the peaks of the ceiling, which also may be identified with the rivers of Paradise irrigating the different levels of heaven. Thus, the ceiling served to legitimise the sultan seated below it, under the same celestial vaults "in which there exist no defects or imperfections," according to the Qur'an, so that he might carry out his eminent judiciary functions.

The Catholic Monarchs and Emperor Charles V must not have been unfamiliar with the profound symbolism of the hall. During their stays in the Alhambra, the royal flag was flown from this tower and not from the Torre de la Vela, as would have been expected.

With the arrival of the Christian kings and the creation of the New Royal Palace, various renovations were carried out in this symbolic and splendid hall that converted the first room to the right into the Emperor's Chambers.

Southern Pavilion

The southern side of the Patio de Comares has a large vertical façade without recesses that covers the entire bay which is, nevertheless, divided into three floors. The ground floor, behind a portico like the one at the front, has spatial characteristics similar to those of the Sala de la Barca, although it is smaller so that the stairwells for two stairways leading to the upper floors could be built, as shown by the small doors found at the far ends of the gallery.

Referred to in old documents as the Sala de las Aleyas or Sala de las Helias, some of its decorations can still be seen on the inside face of the wall. Some of the wall's elements, such as the tiled baseboard, were removed in 1537 so they could be reused in the Mexuar. The upper floors have a similar layout, opening on to a courtyard, with an elongated central space and *alhamíes* (tile covered benches) at the ends.

On the ground floor, a double mullioned window marks the centre of the space; upstairs, there is an elegant lintelled construction in the middle of the gallery that replaces the need to use

Southern façade of the Palacio de Comares with the Palacio de Carlos V joined to it in the background. The two long rows of myrtles are not original: after numerous changes in the vegetation used, they were planted in the 19th century and have become an integral part of the courtyard.

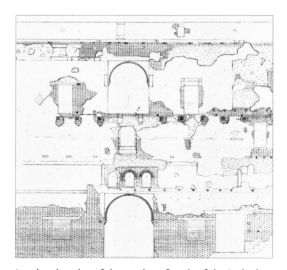

Interior elevation of the southern façade of the Patio de los Arrayanes showing the decorative remains and the original layout. Copy (1988) of unsigned original. Alhambra Archives

a larger arch that would have required raising the ceiling even higher.

Nineteenth-century historiography interpreted the presence of this unique and special space within the palace as the site of the indispensable harem: it was referred to as the Seraglio, based only upon the cultural aesthetic of Orientalism. More recently, its chambers were believed to have been the site where future sultans lived and studied.

This façade has been maintained as a kind of stage rigging or "theatrical backdrop," as the building behind it was torn down in order to build the Palacio de Carlos V to which it is attached. It would not have been difficult for the Renaissance architect to remove the Nasrid façade and to make an opening in the new façade, creating a continuous portal with its large windows opening directly

Stairway directly connecting the Palacio de Carlos V with the Palacio de Comares, located by the side wall of the room in the southwest section

onto the courtyard; however, he opted to maintain the original image or aesthetic composition and build a rather awkward stairway that would connect the two palaces in the southwestern Nasrid alcove, where the solemn Portada del Príncipe was located and which served until 1924 as the entrance for visitors to the Alhambra palaces.

At the other end of the courtyard, the Catholic Monarchs connected the Nasrid Palacio de Comares directly with the Palacio de los Leones via the door accessing the top floor of the living area located in the southeast, changing the architectural design typical of the last stage of the Hispano-Muslim era.

It is worthwhile to pause for a moment to gaze at the reflection of the Torre de Comares on the surface of the pool below that makes it seem bigger than it is, as well as at the effects of the light as it reflects off the architecture itself.

The *Hammam* or Baths of the Palacio de Comares

Among the unique Islamic architectural structures preserved in the Alhambra, one of the most noteworthy is the *hammam* or baths in the Palacio de Comares, referred to until quite recently as the "Royal Baths" because they were reserved for use by the Catholic Monarchs.

Today we know that each palace within the Alhambra had its own *hammam*, but this is the only medieval Islamic bath in the Western world that has been preserved almost in its entirety. Adopted by the Islamic culture from the old Roman *termae* or public baths, they soon became a fundamental part of the Muslim world.

Due to their state of preservation and special nature, the baths of the Alhambra usually cannot be visited, although glimpses of them can be seen from other spaces.

Located between the Palacio de Comares and the Palacio de los Leones and close to the palace rooms, they have a door opening directly onto the courtyard next to the bay housing the sultan.

Almost all of the elements in these baths have been preserved, along with the structural modifications associated with a change in their use and in their maintenance that was more token than practical. The entrance — on the same

Sala de las Camas in the *Hammam*
In the Islamic culture, bodily hygiene is an inescapable principle of socio-religious nature. For this reason, the *hammam* or baths are an essential part of the palaces of the Nasrid sultans. The baths in this palace are the only ones in the Western world from this era that have been preserved almost in their entirety, practically converting them into objects of worship during centuries. Due to their state of preservation and special uniqueness they are not on exhibit to visitors, but glimpses of them may be caught from other spaces. Coloured engraving by Alexandre Laborde (1812)

level as the Patio de los Arrayanes — leads to a vestibule for undressing with an alcove for that purpose and a separate ventilated latrine. From this *apodyterium* or entry into the baths, one descends a steep stairway to the resting room — the *bayt al-maslaj* — the most remarkable area in the baths. It is popularly known as the Sala de las Camas or the Hall of the Beds, due to the two wide, slightly elevated chambers located one on each side of the main room. This entire area is ventilated and illuminated by a small windowed tower installed in the ceiling, very common in Nasrid architecture. The room's decorative elements — fountain, flooring, columns, tiling and carved plaster — are for the most part original, although the ceilings and plasterwork were repaired and repainted in bright colours during the second half of the 19th century by the Alhambra's "restorer of ornaments decorator" Rafael Contreras. The doors on either side of the beds are part of the baths' original structure: in addition to the entrance door, the door opposite it opens onto a storage area; the doors at the front lead to a latrine located behind the alcove and in the room and to the baths' steam rooms.

The entire area in the *hammam's* steam room is covered by vaults filled with slightly conical fluted and star-shaped skylights. They had glass windows that could be moved from the outside; someone would be assigned to open or close them in order to regulate the amount of steam in the rooms.

Next is a small space used as a passageway — the *bayt al-barid* — containing a fountain with cold water, followed by the middle part of the baths, the *bayt al-wastani*. This is a wide, heated area with a central area flanked by slightly pointed triple horseshoe arches.

Opposite the entrance area, another passage leads to the baths' final heated room, the *bayt al-sajun*, which has two large fountains located under wide *iwánes* (enclosed pavilions) from which pour out cold and hot water.

Lantern in the main room of the *Hammam*. Typical of Nasrid architecture, it was used to ventilate the area and provide lighting from above

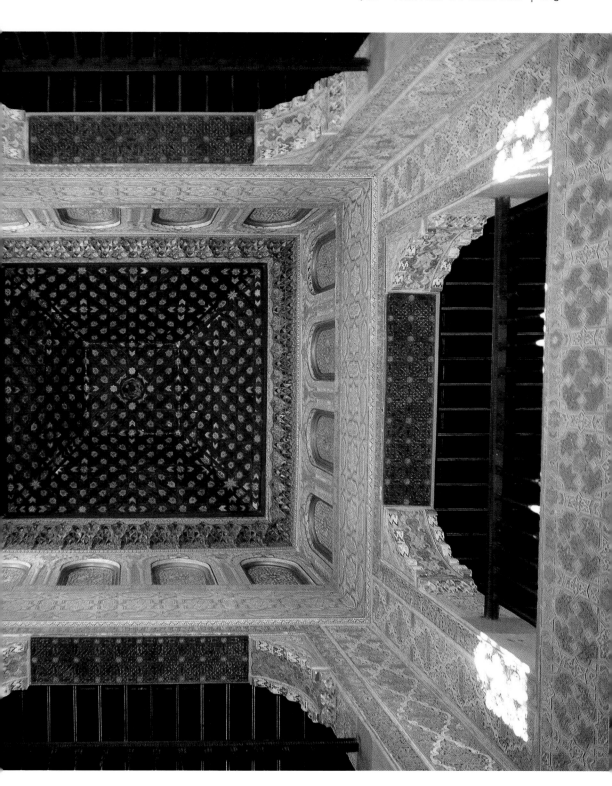

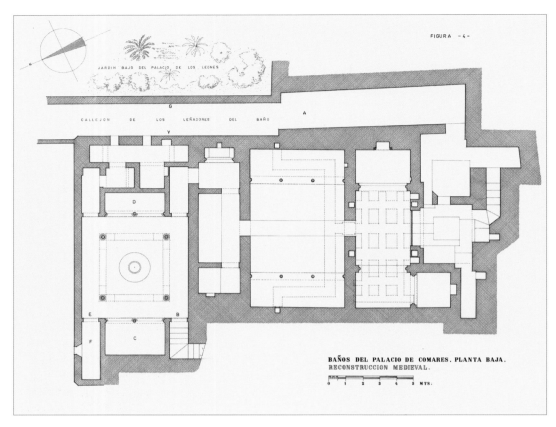

FIGURA -4-

JARDIN BAJO DEL PALACIO DE LOS LEONES

CALLEJON DE LOS LEÑADORES DEL BAÑO

BAÑOS DEL PALACIO DE COMARES. PLANTA BAJA.
RECONSTRUCCION MEDIEVAL.

0 1 2 3 4 5 MTS.

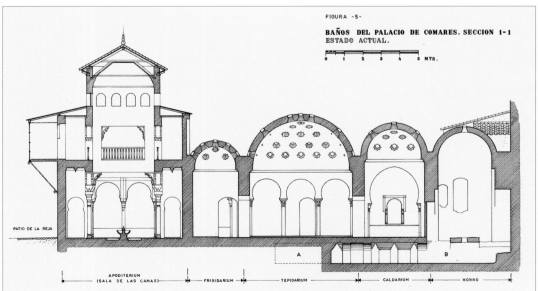

FIGURA -5-

BAÑOS DEL PALACIO DE COMARES. SECCION 1-1
ESTADO ACTUAL.

0 1 2 3 4 5 MTS.

PATIO DE LA REJA

APODITERIUM (SALA DE LAS CAMAS) — FRIGIDARIUM — TEPIDARIUM — CALDARIUM — HORNO

Reconstruction of the original ground plan and elevation of the *Hammam*, based on the research of Jesús Bermúdez Pareja, published in *Cuadernos de la Alhambra* (no. 10–11), 1974–75. Alhambra Archives

Decoration of tiles in the cold room of the baths, simulating the wave-like movement of water

Ceramic baseboard from the 16th century with the initials for "Plus Ultra" from the royal emblem of Charles V

Detail of the polygonal skylights in the main vault of the *hammam*

The hypocaust is located under the floor of this room, and next to it, behind the solid arch in the back, are the oven (*al-furn*) and the boiler with an area for storing wood and a back service door.

The steam rooms have marble floors with pipes running underneath to maintain the heat; this meant that thick-soled shoes had to be worn here. Similarly, in the walls clay pipes of different sizes and diameters were installed to carry the hot air and steam from the boiler so that the rooms could reach the appropriate temperature and humidity required for bathing.

Some of the ceramic baseboards in these rooms were renovated in the 16th century, and the initials of the imperial motto "Plus Ultra" can be seen on some of them. A new exit to the adjacent courtyard — the Patio de Lindaraja — was also built.

Numerous visitors and artists, from Hieronymus Münzer in 1494 to the avant-garde artist Henri Matisse in 1910, have been captivated by the atmosphere and mysterious light in the Baths of Comares, one of the most fascinating sites in the Alhambra. Many artists have expressed their impressions of these baths in numerous works, including the printing plates of Alexandre Laborde (1812), the notes of Richard Ford (1831) and the map created by James Cabannah Murphy (1813) including details such as the piping circuits or the boiler of the *hammam,* to mention but a few.

Partial view of the central room of the *hammam*

7.3 Palacio de los Leones

Commissioned by Muhammad V (1362–1391), the Palacio del Riyad or Palace of the Garden is organised into two terraces of different levels with rooms arranged around a rectangular-shaped courtyard that, instead of a water tank, contains the most famous fountain in all of the Alhambra — the Fuente de los Leones, with a porticoed gallery on its four sides. This was a residential palace, and in its four main halls — Mocárabes (west), Reyes (east), Abencerrajes (south) and Dos Hermanas (north) — leisure time activities, celebrations and musical events were held. Upstairs were other alcoves where day-to-day palace life transpired.

The *Qasr al-Sultán* — the Nasrid royal palace — was enlarged by Muhammad V (1354–59 and 1362–91) during his second mandate, the era considered to have been the culmination of the the sultanate.

It was named Palacio del Riyad or Palace of the Garden, perhaps because it was built on land occupied by a courtyard-garden surrounded by simple rammed earth walls belonging to the previous palace.

Distributed across two terraces on different levels, its main rooms are organised around a rectangular-shaped cross-platform courtyard. These two levels — or *paratas* — are built between the Baths of Comares, its cistern and future entranceway, and the exceptional *qubba* (square-shaped room with a dome) of the *Rauda* which opens onto Calle Real Baja and the hill to the Partal.

Its main entrance was probably located at the southwest corner, with a bent access from Calle Real.

Currently the direct connection from the Palacio de Comares follows the remodelling done after the conquest in order to install the Christian Royal Palace in the Alhambra. The first surprise upon entering the palace is the porticoed gallery that runs along the entire perimeter of the courtyard. Although the porticos seem similar to those appearing in Mudéjar patios, these serve as a side passageway that links and serves as a place around which to organise the different

---

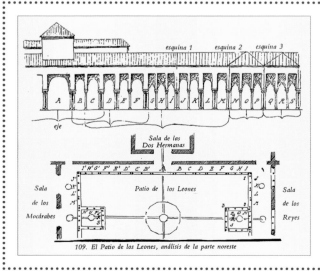

109. El Patio de los Leones, análisis de la parte noreste

Porticoed gallery of the Patio de los Leones

Arranged around the entire perimeter, this gallery consists of arches supported by columns following a proportional design system based on the diagonal of a square. On the narrower sides there are portico-like pavilions covered by roofs with semi-spherical domes. On the ground underneath are "schematic fountains," also found in the Patio de los Arrayanes, in which water flows from all four sides to the central fountain.

The illustation at the left was taken from the research work of Professor Georges Marçais, *Melanges d'histoire et d'archeologie de l'occident musulman*, 2 vols., Algiers (1957).

The Patio de los Leones occupies the central space where all the rooms of the palace converge

Palacio de los Leones

In this palace, Nasrid decoration reached an extraordinary level. The openwork on the wall sections resembling lace, its slender columns, the exquisite plasterwork of its walls, the colourful tiles, the Mocárabe ceilings and the perfection of its proportions together create an atmosphere conducive to a pleasure-filled existence.

❶ Sala de los Mocárabes

This rectangular hall was originally covered with a *mocárabe* ceiling (also knowns as a "stalactite ceiling") that was destroyed in an explosion in 1590. Its current vault is from the 17th century.

❷ Patio and Fuente de los Leones

The emblematic Fuente de los Leones — for which the palace is named — consists of a central basin surrounded by twelve outward-facing lions with spouts in their mouths.

❸ Sala de los Abencerrajes

The square-shaped Sala de los Abencerrajes is covered with a delicate eight-pointed star-shaped celing using pendentives as a transitional device. Its *mocárabe* decoration is one of the most exquisite in Islamic art.

❹ Patio del Harén

Located above the Sala de los Abencerrajes, this court contains a residential area with two porticos, one of which is supported by columns with serpentine capitals reused from another site.

❺ Sala de los Reyes

This hall is distributed in a series of rectangular- and cube-shaped spaces (the cube is a symbol of perfection) that form a harmonious architectural combination. Three of its rooms have decorated ceilings with unique paintings of court scenes.

❻ Sala de Dos Hermanas

The Sala de Dos Hermanas is the palace's main hall and is the most richly decorated. On the upper level, windows with delicate latticework open onto the interior of the *qubba*, which is covered with one of the most spectacular *mocárabe* ceilings in the Alhambra.

❼ Sala de los Ajimeces

This gallery get its name from the hanging wooden balconies and latticework that enclose the two large double-paned and arched windows facing each other on the two larger sides.

❽ Mirador de Lindaraja

The Mirador de Lindaraja is one of the Alhambra's many jewels. It originally opened onto the Albaicín over a garden-orchard that extended towards the northern wall.

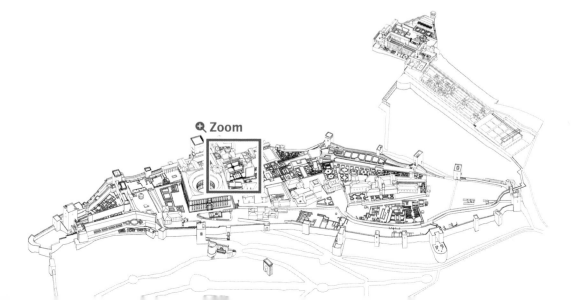

🔍 Zoom

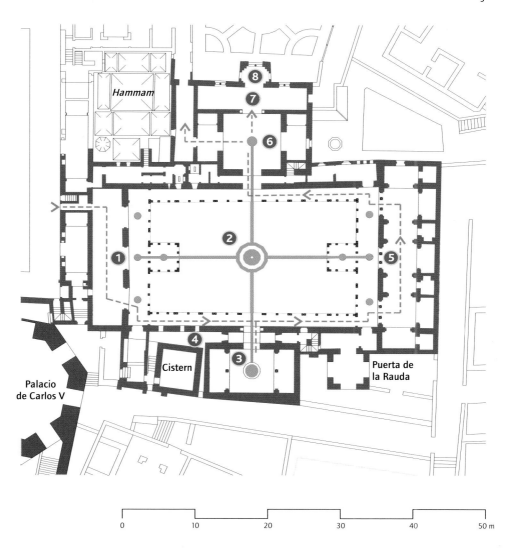

Hammam

Palacio
de Carlos V

Cistern

Puerta de
la Rauda

0	10	20	30	40	50 m

1. Sala de los Mocárabes
2. Patio and Fuente de los Leones
3. Sala de los Abencerrajes
4. Patio del Harén (upper floor)
5. Sala de los Reyes
6. Sala de Dos Hermanas
7. Sala de los Ajimeces
8. Mirador de Lindaraja

------> Direction of the visit

■ Nasrid architecture   ■ Christian architecture   ■ Hydraulic elements

View of the Palacio de los Leones from the cornice of the Palacio de Carlos V (1986). Alhambra Archives

areas of the palace, as though they were Bedouin tents grouped together and surrounding an oasis. Under the eaves there are arches supported by one hundred and twenty-four columns that follow a proportional design system based on the diagonal of a square and that here probably attains the maximum degree of perfection.

At the centre of the longest axes is a main arch serving as a portico, while cube-shaped pavilions — whose ceilings are covered with semi-spherical domes — project onto the court. On the ground are embedded "schematic fountains."

Sala de los Mocárabes

This hall serves as part of the palace's living quarters, and is an entrance or reception hall opening onto a court via three large *mocárabe* arches that helped to provide light and ventilation. Its name refers to the no-longer existing ceiling that once covered it. Completely covered in a "stalactite ceiling," it was probably one of the most beautiful rooms in the entire Alhambra. Destroyed in 1590 by the explosion of a nearby powder magazine, it was torn down and divided into two spaces by a grille; one of these was covered by the plaster vault designed in 1714 by painter Blas de Ledesma specifically for the visit of the monarchs Phillip V and Isabella of Parma, and it is their initials — "F.Y." — that are found at the far end. Just a few remnants of the original mocárabe vault can be seen where its base once met the upper part of the enclosing wall, and on which faint traces of the polychromy of the former ceiling can be made out. A similar situation has occurred with the walls of the room, which originally must have had traditional tiling on their lower section, leaving the upper part ready for hanging tapestries or plasterwork.

Patio de los Leones

The name by which this palace is universally known comes from the fountain in the centre of the palace, heir to the the eastern Islamic tradition of using animal figures as fountains, widespread throughout Al-Andalus since the 10th century. According to some researchers, the origin of this tradition may be the "Bronze Sea" from the Temple in Jerusalem described in the Bible, in this case, substituting its twelve bulls with twelve lions. Although similar, the figures are different to one another and they are all positioned with their backs to the fountain in an intentionally symbolic posture. Far from the hieratic figures they were believed to be until very recently, the lions were most meticulously sculpted. The block of marble was most certainly selected by the master sculptor, who used the natural veins in the stone to enhance the modelling of the figures. Not only do these serve to highlight their different fur coats and the folds around their slightly open jaws, there are other fine details, such as the delicate hair on their extremities or the uniqueness of each toe, in keeping with the naturalistic decoration of the palace.

As has been documented in the Alhambra's Historical Archive, the Fuente de los Leones underwent a radical change in appearance during the second half of the 16th century. The new fountain had a pyramid-shaped structure, with the cylinder-shaped centre support and the main basin raised by balusters that apparently rested on the back of the lion figures, in addition to a second basin that had the medieval spout

The Sala de los Mocárabes, whose original dome — which gave its name to the hall — was partially restored during the early 17th century. Right, detail of the remains of the original dome

The lions of the fountain

The twelve lions — seemingly identical — each have features that set them apart from the others. They all appear in alert position, with their tails folded inward, ears perked, teeth clenched, in a tense posture, waiting for the slightest gesture or order from their master the sultan. On the other hand, the association of water — purifier, fountain of life — with the image of the lion — guardian of power — is lost in the dawn of Humanity, but symbolically integrated into the traditions of the great monotheistic religions. In this recently restored sculpture, one can clearly see how the veins in the block of marble chosen by the sculptor serve to highlight the rounded shape of the lion.

hidden in its base. This basin is currently found in the Jardín de los Adarves, where it was installed in 1954.

In 1624 sculptor Alonso de Mena worked on the fountain, which he repaired and cleaned. During the first third of the 19th century, a set of spouts was added and around 1837 it was finished through the addition of a spout at the top in order to "beautify" it in accordance with the taste of the times.

After several attempts and tests that began in 1945, in July 1966 the fountain was returned to its hypothetical original state by removing the added piece, and the original fountain was moved to the Alhambra Museum.

The fountain's basin, carved into a twelve-sized shape from a single piece, had an ingenious hydraulic system that permitted it to maintain a constant water level. This system was beautifully described and extolled in the evocative metaphors of the twelve verses of the *qasida* or Arabic poem written by poet and vizier Ibn Zamrak and carved on the basin's outside edge. Below is a translated version of the poem.

> Blessed be the One who granted Imam Mohammed
>   the beautiful ideas for decorating his mansions.
> For are there not in this garden wonders that God has
>   made incomparable in their beauty,
> and a sculpture of pearls with a transparent light,
>   whose edges are trimmed with seed pearls?
> Molten silver flows through the pearls, which it
>   resembles in its pure white beauty.
> Water and marble seem to be one in appearance, and
>   we know not which of the two is flowing.
> Do you not see how the water spills into the basin,
>   but the hidden spouts hide it immediately?
> It is a lover whose eyes brim over with tears, tears that
>   it hides for fear someone will reveal them
> Is it not, in fact, like a white cloud that pours its
>   flowing water onto the lions
> and looks like the hand of the Caliph, who, in the
>   morning, lavishes his favours on the war lions?

Detail from a photograph from 1857 highlighting the craftsmanship of the fountain. Photograph by J. Pedrosa

The fountain basin

Called in Arabic *manhuta min lú'lú* (pearl sculpture), the Fuente de los Leones was created from a single piece of white marble. On the exterior border of the basin appears a poem by vizier Ibn Zamrak in beautiful Arabic calligraphy in praise of the sultan who commissioned the fountain. It was most likely carved on site from a block especially selected by the artisans, like the twelve lions, sculpted from pieces with veins whose geometric or rounded shapes could be brought out. A subtle polychromy — unfortunately lost due to centuries of aggressive mechanical cleaning — was applied to the entire fountain in order to highlight its decorative elements.

Those who gaze upon the lions standing in a
 threatening posture [know that] only respect
 [for the Emir] contains their anger.
Oh! descendant of the Ansares — and not through an
 indirect line — heritage of nobility, who despises
 the fatuous:
May the peace of God be upon you and may you live
 long and unharmed, multiplying your feasts and
 afflicting your enemies!

         Ibn Zamrak

The entire open space of the palace is shaped like a cross-platform courtyard, highlighted by the four platforms or branches beginning from the cardinal centres. These platforms have small water channels carrying water from several fountains embedded in the pavement — known as "schematic fountains" — that converge at the central fountain.

The cross-platform shape of the courtyard signalled a break with earlier patios in the Alhambra, leading historians to closely analyse it. Some have found influences from the cloistered courtyards typical of the architecture used in monasteries on the Iberian Peninsula, or from the architecture of palaces such as that of the Norman Siza in Palermo, while others believe that it came from a North African tradition rooted in the Zirid Palace of Asir in Algeria. Some more recent precedents are found in the courtyard of the Castillejo in Murcia, dating from the second half of the 12th century, or in the Qarawiyin Mosque in the Moroccan city of Fez, among others. Recently, in the Patio de las Doncellas in the Alcázar of Seville, an original cross-platform court with low-lying gardens between the platforms has been discovered, built during the reign of Pedro I

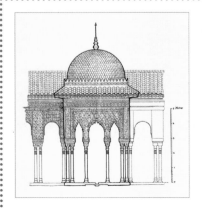

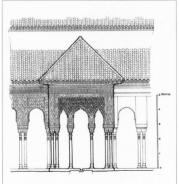

Oriental pavilion

This pavilion has been the site of one of the most important pages in European architectural restoration: in 1859 its roof was "restored" with a spherical dome of glazed ceramic to fit with what was understood to be the "Arab style." In 1934 Leopoldo Torres Balbás disassembled it and rebuilt the current roof — as seen in the elevated views — which was strongly opposed by the more conservative sectors of the country.
Alhambra Archives

The Patio de los Leones surrounded by the porticoed gallery and with the fountain in the middle, where the branches or channels meet accentuating its cross-platform structure

(1334–1369), with a roof added in 1584 due to its poor state of conservation. Although the court may have had a similar fate, current research suggests that it was paved with slabs of marble and, perhaps, planters for small trees. In any case, the palace had a garden to the north on the lower terrace opposite the main *qubba*, the area currently occupied by the Patio de Lindaraja.

As for its symbolic significance, it is considered to be an early representation of Paradise, common to the Christian and Muslim religions, whose branching into four rivers is represented here by the channels of the cross-platform.

Sala de los Abencerrajes

This hall is designed as an independent home within the palace. The entire structure revolves round the large *qubba* graced inside by a magnificent three-dimensional *mocárabe* dome. Through it, the architect hoped to balance the size of the larger *qubba* located opposite in the tradition of double domes seen in other palaces. Similarly, the pavilions jutting from the upper floors were intended to balance the effect of the cube-shaped pavilions of the courtyard, thus highlighting the cross-platform design and its four-part division.

The central area of the hall is at the same time a copy of a courtyard, with a twelve-sided polygonal central fountain, translating the immaterial ("the best vault is the celestial vault") into the material (the beautiful *mocárabe* dome in the shape of an eight-pointed star) in a wonderful three-dimensional transition from the square-shaped floor by the use of pendentives, also done in *mocárabe*.

Today, 16th-century tiles from Seville decorate the hall's baseboard, which unfolds behind a double arch in the two side rooms, both raised with small steps. The dwelling has no openings to the outside except for the tall windows that beautifully illuminate the dome

Star-shaped *mocárabe* ceiling in the Sala de los Abencerrajes

Schematic fountain

In the middle of both the floors of the pavilions in the Palacio de los Leones, as well as in its interior halls, there are small canals that carry water to the middle of the courtyard, like streams flowing "between the feet of the Believers", according to the Qur'anic reference. The fountains are referred to as "schematic" due to the fact that they are found — in this case, in a palace — embedded into the pavement from which the water bubbles forth with a soft whisper and without splashing, combining nature with architecture. Subtle details such as this make the Palacio de los Leones a unique place.

and the door, originally closed with a large wooden door with a wicket. A small passageway behind the gate leads to a latrine and a stairway to the upper floor where there are several rooms, one of which has a small window above the door to control all those who entered.

Complementary Spaces: Patio del Harén and Puerta de la Rauda

As domestic spaces, the halls inside the palaces of the Alhambra include other complementary areas and secondary rooms, corridors, latrines, upper chambers, etc.

Next to the original entrance to the Palacio de los Leones, a stairway leads up to the Patio del Harén, a room that was separate from the other halls in the palace and located above the Sala de los Abencerrajes

Mocárabe

The Palacio de los Leones is filled with the best examples of *muqarnas* — mocárabe design on the ceilings, roofs and arches — in the Alhambra and, perhaps, in all western Islamic art of the second half of the 14th century. They are created by superimposing prism shapes combined geometrically. The surface is then decorated with varied motifs and colours that accentuate the play of light. The mocárabe ceilings are very light, "almost ethereal". Today we know that these ceilings are not only decorative but also have a structural function.

Owing to their unique characteristics, the complex nature of their preservation, the difficulty of accessing them, or the path the tour follows, some of these are not included in the general visit. However, the majority may be visited under special conditions during

Detail of the Puerta de la Rauda from outside with the access to the Patio de los Leones in the background

special visiting hours. Included among these is the courtyard known as the Patio del Harén, located on an upper floor above the Sala de los Abencerrajes. Its name comes from the collective romantic imaginary of the 19th century. It is actually another independent dwelling, accessed from the palace entrance, and taking advantage of the cistern that controlled and distributed the water supply throughout the palace and its surroundings.

Inside are the original *al fresco* baseboards as well as two small, reused green serpentine capitals, unique in the Alhambra.

Also forming a part of the palace is the so-called Puerta de la Rauda, which probably belonged to a previous palace. Square-shaped and made of brick, it contains a horseshoe arch in front and a set of windows above supporting a splendid umbrella dome on squinches that imitate the traditional look of red brick. This slender building probably served as the majestic portal to the Palacio de los Leones, into which it would be integrated after later remodelling during the second half of the 14th century. It may be accessed through the gardens known as the Jardines del Partal.

Sala de los Reyes

This space was integrated into the palace but had its own purpose, most likely both royal and recreational, as seen in the painted scenes appearing on the three eastern side ceilings. Returning to the image of the oasis surrounded by a camp of Bedouin tents, the Sala de los Reyes

Vaults of the Sala de los Reyes
Three wooden vaults were made on the ground individually like the frames of a ship, using a technique known as false vault. It includes several phases: first, the perimeter of the structure is set up like a false ring of large white poplar rails, to which were attached semi-cylindrical-shaped beams or ribs whose ends form quarter spheres; next, in the middle, thick pine boards — on the semi-spherical ends, they were cut into triangular shapes — were nailed onto the inside of the beams; lastly, the outside was coated with vegetable tar — a biological barrier against humidity — as well as a layer of plaster to protect the other side. The gaps in the curved pieces were plugged with wooden wedges and vegetable fibres.

presents the grouping of various alcoves round one long area, opening on to a courtyard to the west via a gallery of columns, similar to the Sala de los Mocárabes. Here, however, instead of a single, one-piece ceiling, there is the alternative formula of three square-shaped *mocárabe* ceilings that divide the room into sections, separated perpendicularly by high double *mocárabe* arches, offering depth and a harmonious interchange of lights and shadows. Once again, the palace offers a perfect distribution of cubic spaces — symbolic of perfection — that are grouped like tiny cells in a harmonious architectural group filled with light and colour.

Five rectangular rooms open onto the main hall, all raised via steps and separated from each other by small dressing rooms or storage areas. The three eastern rooms are roofed with vaults made of planks covered with paintings of court scenes; the painting in the middle shows well-known individuals meeting in an animated social debate, sitting on cushions on a platform, dressed in typical Nasrid attire, all carrying the unique jineta sword, suggesting that they were sultans — kings —, hence the name of the hall. It was also referred to as the Sala de la Justicia because of the group being interpreted as a tribunal deliberating.

The other two vaults represent different court scenes, such as challenges between gentlemen — a Christian and a Muslim — for the hand of a

maiden, in which the Muslim wins, following a joust of several successive competitions.

These representations — whose decorative origin may lie in Gothic minium paintings — are one-of-a-kind examples, authentic jewels. The may have been influenced by the *quattrocento* art of northern Italy, or even by the circle of Avignon; let us not forget that Nasrid Granada had a large colony of merchants from Genoa and Venice who greatly influenced the court. The technique is equally impressive: executed with tempera paint and egg and then varnished, they were first drawn by dotting their outlines on the surface of sheepskins prepared with various layers of plaster and assembled with bamboo splinters to completely cover the concave arch of the plank vaults, called "ships" by the artisans on account of their shape.

This remarkable space within the palace was surely the scene of celebrations and parties during the Nasrid era. The Catholic Monarchs built a chapel here that continued to function as such until the 17th century, used as the headquarters for the parish of Santa María de la Alhambra while the construction of the new church was being finalised.

The roof of the Sala de los Reyes underwent significant modifications in 1855: an individual roof was created for each of the three painted ceilings, replacing the original common roof, leading to a lack of ventilation in the voissoirs of the ceilings that caused it to deteriorate.

The three painted vaults in the Sala de los Reyes: a) southern vault; b) middle vault; c) northern vault

a)

b)

c)

At the end of 2006, a restoration project was undertaken on the roofs to prevent further damage.

All of the roofs of the Palacio de los Leones were altered — especially after the second half of the 19th century. One of the most noteworthy was the remodelling undertaken in the eastern pavilion, whose restoration was a milestone in Spain. In 1859, "restorers of ornaments" Juan Pugnaire and Rafael Contreras reconstructed the pavilion with a roof of coloured glazed tiles. In 1934, the architectural curator of the Alhambra at the time, Leopoldo Torres Balbás, dismantled the roof, setting off a huge debate in the world of restoration and receiving international attention in the press. This debate was rooted in the intellectual dispute over "stylistic restoration" versus "scientific restoration" taking place at the time.

Sala de Dos Hermanas

The palace's main room — around which the rest of the palace turns — is the main *qubba* inside of which is the Sala de Dos Hermanas. This Christian name refers to the two marble slabs on the floors of the room. It had upstairs rooms and a lower floor opening up to the garden-orchard. The layout of this hall is similar to that of the Abencerrajes, located opposite, only larger and with a more ornate decoration. Unlike the other hall, it is open to the outside, and on the upper floor there are windows covered in delicate wooden latticework that open up on the interior of the *qubba*. Without a doubt it must have boasted one of the best views of the Alhambra of its time.

Entrance to the hall was via the gallery in the courtyard, up three steps, passing through a magnificent wooden doorway with two large panels and a wicket, one of the masterpieces of Nasrid carpentry, today preserved in the Alhambra Museum. Behind it, the corridor crossing it connects to latrines on the left and a stairway leading upstairs on the right. A small

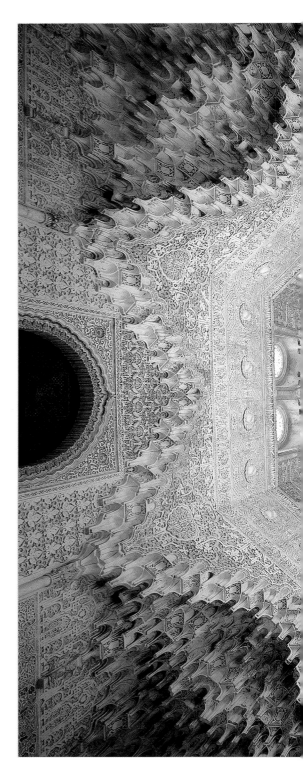

Interior *mocárabe* ceiling in the Sala de Dos Hermanas, the pinnacle of architectural decoration in the Alhambra

canal channels water from the usual schematic fountain located in the middle of the room to the Fuente de los Leones.

The Sala de Dos Hermanas is covered with one of the most exquisite *mocárabe* domes in all of Islamic art. Starting from one of the eight points of the central star, there is a three-dimensional design that unfolds into sixteen small domes situated over the same number of windows covered in latticework that softens the light as it changes throughout the day. It is the maximum evolution of the lantern (a windowed tower that allows light to enter from above), a technique so characteristic of Nasrid architecture. Exquisite double windows rest on the octagonal drum of the dome that uses *mocárabe* squinches in the corners to transition into the square shape of the room.

A sober but lovely tile baseboard whose design is based on strips of colour embellishes the lower part of the *qubba*. Above it, written on alternating rectangular and circular cartouches, is the twenty-four line poem composed by Vizier Ibn Zamrak for the circumcision ceremony of the prince, son of Muhammad V, which probably took place here (from the original translation into Spanish by: José M. Puerta, "La Alhambra de Granada o la caligrafía elevada al rango de arquitectura," in *7 Paseos por la Alhambra*, 2007, ch. 8, p. 374):

I am the garden *(ana al-rawd)* adorned by beauty:
gaze upon my loveliness and my stature will be
   explained to you.

For my lord the Imam Muhammad I equals
the noblest thing that will exist or has ever existed.

By God! His lovely building, in happiness, surpasses
any others that have been built.

How many delights for the eyes!
The soul of he who is benevolent renews his desires
   here.

The five Pleiades find refuge at night here
and the languid breeze becomes sublime.

A splendid vault — peerless — exists here
whose beauty is both hidden and manifest.

Two alcoves flank the hall, slightly raised by a step, inside which the typical *alhamí* or rest area is located at the far end. Both have elegant ornamentation of plasterwork and lovely panelling on their upper sections as well as windows facing outwards; the left alcove was converted into a door to connect to the rooms that were added during the Christian era.

Perhaps in no other site within the Alhambra do art and nature combine in such a perfect manner as in this palatial residence, with its plant-inspired ornamentation of figurative *atauriques* in the interior and the gardens surrounding the hall on the outside.

Sala de los Ajimeces

The main *qubba* extends north via the hall crossing it, whose name refers to the two wide mullioned windows *(ajimeces)* that are found in the centre of the longer sides and that

Sala de los Ajimeces

Detail of the play of light reflected on the face of the western wall in the Sala de Dos Hermanas

had hanging wooden balconies covered with latticework. The walls which today are empty and whitewashed were once covered with rich silk fabrics, the remains of which are found in museums. An elongated *mocárabe* vault with small consecutive domes covers the entire hall.

Mirador de Lindaraja

At the far end, opposite the entrance area and protruding from the inferior garden of the palace is the exquisite Lindaraja balcony, one of the most beautiful corners of the entire Alhambra. As its name implies, this *mirador* was originally open-air, facing the Albaicín, above a garden-orchard that extended below to the northern wall of the palace-city. Its interior holds the most exquisite decoration in the palace, with varied geometric compositions and epigraphs, and delicate carved plasters that frame the front window under a *mocárabe* arch. The baseboards, made up of small tiles displaying a simple but colourful succession of stars, are completed with inscriptions having characters cut out of black ceramic pieces on a white background, laid out like a puzzle. In the lantern tradition, the balcony is covered with a roof of coloured crystals assembled in

Detail of the baseboard of the entrance threshold of the Mirador de Lindaraja. The arabic inscription is created using cut and assembled ceramic pieces

a wooden vaulted structure, exemplifying the majority of the *ajimeces* or mullioned windows of the palatial Alhambra.

In 1528, a residence for Emperor Charles V was built around the lower garden, enclosing it like a cloister and radically changing its original appearance. Currently, this area is known as the Patio de Lindaraja.

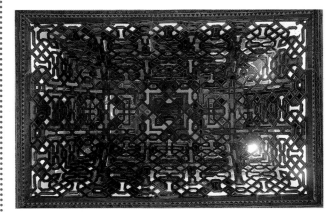

The Mirador de Lindaraja ceiling

This ceiling, with a lantern structure, was made from pieces of coloured glass assembled in the wooden vault structure. It is the only example of its type preserved in the Alhambra. Its formal finish recalls the appearance of the closures — the latticework shutters — of the majority of the windows in the palatial areas of the Alhambra. The Arabic text of the *Mawlid* from 1362 describes a spectacular glass ceiling in the Mexuar that must have been similar to this one. Muhammad V must have liked this type of roofing which probably also existed in his no-longer existing Palacio de los Alijares.

The back of the Sala de Dos Hermanas with the Mirador de Lindaraja jutting out from it

7.4 The Palace Converted into the Christian Royal Palace

After Boabdil handed the Alhambra over to the Catholic Monarchs, following a long period of siege, the new rulers installed themselves in most of the space within the palace and allocated funds for its preservation. Their grandson Emperor Charles V visited the Alhambra in 1526 with his wife Isabella, and commissioned the construction of some rooms around the Muslim palaces, today known as the Emperor's Chambers.

Immediately after the 1492 conquest of Granada, the Catholic Monarchs initiated an extensive programme of renovations and construction works in the Alhambra in an attempt to stop the advanced state of deterioration that had occurred following the long siege and to ensure its future preservation. To this end, the monarchs arranged for a regular allocation of funds, which we know about thanks to the Granada-born Moor, Francisco Núñez Muley: "this intent and desire was that of Their Highnesses [...] for this purpose the rich *alcázares* (fortified palaces) of the Alhambra and other smaller ones are maintained as they were during the times of the Moorish kings." A similar request was made by their grandson and heir, the future Emperor Charles V, from Flanders in 1517 to the marshall of the kingdom on the eve of his journey to take possession of the throne: "in order to determine the best manner of accommodations for home and court [...] and so that these accommodations provide comfortable and worry-free lodging." In June of 1526 the emperor and his wife Isabella of Portugal reached Granada and took up residence in the Alhambra. The monumental complex created such a positive impression on the illustrious guests that they decided to establish an important imperial seat and centre for their dynasty here. In 1528 the construction of six "new rooms" in the area around the Muslim palaces was approved. These would form a kind of royal suite, known today as the Emperor's Chambers.

Coat of arms above the chimney in the Despacho del Emperador
When the Christian kings took control of the Alhambra, they respected the palaces, the decoration and the symbols of their Nasrid predecessors, but at the same time tried to instil their own style and symbols in the areas where they lived. During the construction of the Palacio de Carlos V, a garden area between the Muslim palaces was remodelled for the emperor to live in. Inside these residences we find many decorative elements that refer to the Christian culture, such as the marble coat of arms found above a large fireplace, an architectural element that was not a part of the Nasrid Alhambra. The coat of arms displays all the symbols of the Emperor: The Pillars of Hercules — of mythological origin — that marked the end of the world known during Antiquity, on which the motto "PLUS ULTRA", the two-headed Habsburg eagle, — symbol of the Holy Roman Empire — and the royal crown appear.

Patio de Lindaraja the appearance of which resembles a Christian monastic cloister

The Palace Converted into the Christian Royal Palace

After Emperor Charles V visited Granada in 1526, he decided to make his residence in the Alhambra. To this end, the gardens located between the Palacio de Comares and the Palacio de los Leones, bordering on the northern wall, were remodelled and impressively decorated to serve as chambers for the Emperor. Access to these rooms was via a door made from what had previously been a window in the left-hand room off the Sala de Dos Hermanas.

❶ Emperor's Chambers

There is a large Renaissance fireplace included in the chambers. The wooden panel design of the ceiling is the work of Pedro Machuca — the same architect who designed the Palacio de Carlos V — carried out in 1532.

❷ Salas de las Frutas

One of the most inconographic programmes of the Spanish Renaissance was carried out in these halls. The creators of these paintings were Julio Aquiles and Alejandro Mayner.

❸ Peinador de la Reina

Occupying the top floor of the Torre de Abu-l-Hayyay is this imperial studiolo or study known as the Queen's Dressing Room consisting of one private chamber entirely decorated with Renaissance paintings.

❹ Patio de la Reja

This courtyard was included in the construction of the rooms for the Emperor's use. Its name comes from the overhanging latticework-filled corridor that connects the rooms.

❺ Patio de Lindaraja

The Lindaraja court has a garden, a central Baroque fountain and porticoed galleries on three of its sides. On the fourth side is the Mirador del Lindaraja.

❻ Sala de los Secretos

Located under the Sala de Dos Hermanas, the Sala de los Secretos is accessed via the Patio de Lindaraja. Its empty, square-shaped interior covered with a spherical vault causes sounds to reverberate creating sounds similar to murmurs, hence its name.

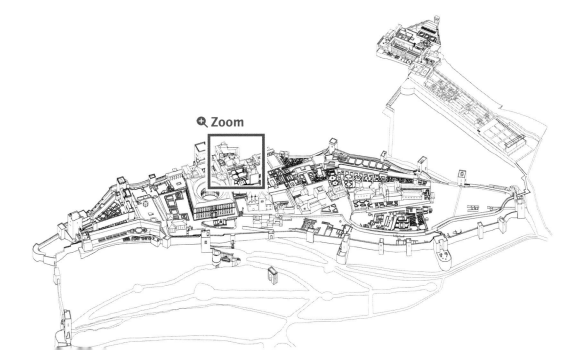

🔍 Zoom

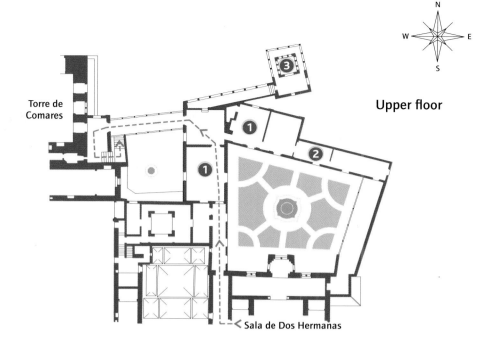

Torre de Comares

Upper floor

① Emperor's Chambers

② Salas de las Frutas

③ Peinador de la Reina

< Sala de Dos Hermanas

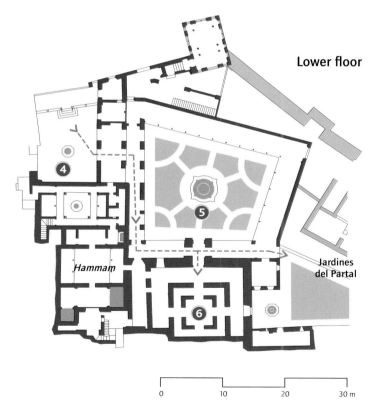

Lower floor

Hammam

Jardines del Partal

① Emperor's Chambers

② Salas de las Frutas

③ Peinador de la Reina

④ Patio de la Reja

⑤ Patio de Lindaraja

⑥ Sala de los Secretos

------> Direction of the visit

▨ Wall

▨ Christian architecture

■ Nasrid architecture

▨ Gardens

▨ Nasrid archaeological remains

▨ Hydraulic elements

0   10   20   30 m

Despacho del Emperador

Since 1870, this area can be accessed directly through the window of one of the rooms in the Palacio de los Leones that was converted into a door. The corridor connecting the Muslim and Christian palaces runs along the top floor of the 16th century cloiseter-like patio next to the *Hammam* in the Palacio de Comares. Along this itinerary, the vaults of the baths can be viewed with their skylights, as well as the main room of the upper floor, later converted into an entrance to the baths.

Down this hallway is the Despacho del Emperador with its large fireplace and decorated panels designed around 1532 by architect Pedro Machuca, author of the Palacio de Carlos V project plan. Next to the Emperor's Office, an antechamber precedes the royal bedchambers, which occupy the entire northern part of the area. In the 16th century, a legend was spread that "in this room Emperor Charles impregnated the empress Isabella, his wife, with the prudent king to be, Phillip II," which is entirely untrue.

Habitaciones Imperiales

Today the rooms of the Imperial Suite are also known as the "Rooms of Washington Irving," the North American writer and author of the famous *Tales of the Alhambra*, who lived here in 1829.

Detail of the ceiling in the Sala de las Frutas representing a still life

The first Council of the Alhambra placed a tablet over the door in his memory in 1914.

Salas de las Frutas

One of the most impressive iconographic programmes of the Spanish Renaissance was carried out in these rooms and their annexes. From among these, the Salas de las Frutas are particularly noteworthy, with ceilings painted around 1537 by Julio Aquiles and Alejandro Mayner, disciples

The Habitación del Emperador with the large Renaissance fireplace and above it, the royal coat of arms

Vaults from the *Hammam* of seen from the entrance to the Office

Salas de las Frutas

of Rafael Sanzio and of Giovanni de Udine. This pictoral representation of the products from the gardens surrounding the Alhambra recalls the tradition of the still-life paintings in the large Italian residences of the time. From here we enter the chamber referred to in 16th-century documents as the Habitación de la Estufa, which was modified when the lantern of a Nasrid tower was turned into an Italian-style gallery that opened on to the outside. This integration of the Muslim and the Christian with the surrounding scenery — so typical in the Alhambra — may be appreciated from one of the most beautiful balconies looking out over the Albaicín and Sacromonte, located in the open-air gallery beyond the antechamber to the Habitaciones del Emperador.

Peinador de la Reina

This tower probably built under Nasr Ibn al-Yuyyus (1309–1314) and later remodelled by Abu-l-Hayyay — Yusuf I — (1333–1354), from whom it also received its name, is the only one that diverges from the regular design style of the Alhambra towers. Inside, it contains a private pavilion that juts out from the main wall, to the upper part of which was added the aforementioned Renaissance-style gallery that surrounds the medieval lantern which would later be popularly known as the Peinador de la Reina.

Remodelled around 1537, it was decorated between 1539 and 1546 by the previously mentioned Julio Aquiles and Alejandro Mayner with frescoes of mythological scenes such as the Fall of Phaeton or scenes from the *Metamorphoses* by Ovid that remind one of rooms in the Vatican. Among other themes found here are the pictoral representations of the Imperial Armada's invasion of Tunisia in 1535 — based on sketches by Dutch painter Jan Cornelisz Vermeyen, who accompanied Charles V — as well as the ports of Cagliari, Sicily and Trapani, or the ruins of Carthage. On the pilasters, one can see the ornamental motifs of formal Italian classicism together with some others that are more curious, including

The belvedere gallery, added to the Nasrid tower in order to create the so-called Peinador de la Reina

one of the first pictoral representations of corn cobs together with the two-headed eagle of the Emperor's emblem.

Because of their unique characteristics, these rooms are not included in the official itinerary, and may be visited only by prior registration during some of the special programmes offered by the monumental complex.

Paintings from the Peinador de la Reina

Inside the Peinador is a synthesis of the most impressive pictoral repertory of the Spanish Renaissance. Its artists were Julio Aquiles and Alejandro Mayner, disciples of Rafael Sanzio. In addition to mythological iconographies with some very curious details, such as corn cobs or a crab holding a shell, there are landscapes and scenes from the Imperial Armada, such as the battle scene on the right representing the 1536 invasion of Tunisia. This detail shows the fleet that sailed to Africa. It is significant that, in the Alhambra — the last Muslim stronghold in Spain — there is an artistic representation of the conquest of Tunisia by the imperial troops of Charles V.

The Peinador de la Reina is representative of the integration of Nasrid decorative elements on the ground floor with Renaissance paintings of historical and mythological scenes upstairs

The Torre del Peinador was connected to the royal rooms via a gallery above the wall that serves as a balcony from which to view the scenic landscape below.

The Christian remodelling of the palace created a direct connection with the large Torre de Comares in 1530 via an open two-story gallery. This took on its current structure in 1618, when columns and capitals from other renovated sites of the Alhambra were included, some of which were considered masterpieces and have since been removed and preserved in the Alhambra Museum.

Patio de la Reja

From the gallery, we travel down to this picturesque courtyard named after the grilled overhanging balcony that runs across the upper part of the southern wall. It was built between 1654 and 1655 to protect the nearby rooms and to serve as an open corridor between them. In the middle of the courtyard, a small fountain with a white marble cup-shaped basin completes the look — both unique and traditional — of this curious corner. From the western wall of the courtyard, it is possible to see the room in the basement of the Palacio de Comares, underneath the Sala de la Barca, which in the 17th century was known as Sala de las Ninfas because of the statues of women stored here.

Patio de Lindaraja

Next to the Patio de la Reja we find the Patio de Lindaraja, greatly contrasting with the Nasrid courtyards in its cloiser-like style. Receiving its name from the Nasrid balcony found on its southern side, it was an open-air garden until the 16th century, and was later enclosed by the three bays of the Habitaciones del Emperador. On the lower floor, there are porticoed galleries for which columns from other sites of the Alhambra were used. The cloister-like sensation is accentuated by the design of the garden, which has a central Baroque fountain made of stone from Sierra Elvira, made around 1626. At that time, a cup-shaped Nasrid marble basin

The Patio de la Reja with its grillework balcony serving as a corridor between the rooms

The Patio de Lindaraja is one of the corners in the Alhambra that has most attracted painters across the ages, as demonstrated by this painting by Joaquín Sorolla from 1910. Madrid, Museo Sorolla

The Patio de Lindaraja with its central fountain, the Mirador de Lindaraja above to the right and, underneath, the entrance to the Sala de los Secretos

The baths of Comares from the western gallery of the Patio de Lindaraja

From the western gallery of the Patio de Lindaraja one can access the interior of a corridor located under the Habitaciones del Emperador. Both gallery and corridor were built during the Christian era over the Callejón de los Leñadores, through which firewood for the ovens of the Comares *Hammam* was supplied. From here one can see the middle room, the only space created to enter the *Hammam*. It is also possible to see the door throughh which fuel was fed into the baths' furnace — the leñera (woodshed), there are next to where the boiler was located. At the back of the hall there are some open areas through which some of the water conduits to the Alhambra's palaces can be seen. This area displays a surprising cultural symbiosis that is also a feature of other sites in the Alhambra.

decorated with wedge shapes and an epigraphic inscription — probably intended for the Palacio de los Leones — was placed on top of it. In March 1995 it was replaced by the current replica, so that it could be restored and preserved in the Alhambra Museum, where it is exhibited today with the name of this courtyard. References from throughout the 19th century have established this courtyard as one of the most romantic corners in the Alhambra.

The western gallery of the courtyard provides access to a covered corridor belonging to the final section of the medieval lane named Callejón de los Leñadores used to provide firewood for use in the Baths of Comares. Here, the service area for the baths and the site of various underground drainage channals from the 14th-century palaces can be seen.

Sala de los Secretos
This hall belongs to the Palacio de los Leones, although today it is an independent structure that forms the northern façade of the Patio de Lindaraja. The lower floor of the Mirador de Lindaraja — whose structure juts out over the courtyard — make the portico seem like an entrance, complete with pointed horseshoe arches. The Sala de los Secretos consists of an interior square-shaped room covered with a spherical vault that produces a reverberating or refracting sound in the room's corners, accentuated by the lack of furniture, producing in one the sensation of overhearing someone murmuring supposed confidences or secrets, thus earning it its name. The central space is surrounded by covered hallways with open half-barrel vaults and openings along its axis; at the main entrance threshold there is a small but elegant square-shaped ribbed vault.

The gallery used to exit the Patio de Lindaraja was named in recent times Chateaubriand's Gallery, as the signature of the famous French writer and politician is found here. The columns used to build it come from one of the Mexuar courtyards that was torn down.

The Sala de los Secretos located under the Mirador de Lindaraja

7.5 The Partal

Until relatively recently, the wide terraced area generally known as the Jardines del Partal — including the palace after which it was named — was in the hands of private owners. Subsequently it was acquired by the government for inclusion within the monumental compound. The Partal was one of the areas that underwent the most modifications over the 20th century as a result of a landscaping and architectural plan that has integrated many of its recovered archaeological structures into a large area of great scenic interest.

Following a narrow landscaped path that looks out directly onto the Sacromonte, we leave the northern wall of the Alhambra — next to which the remains of walls and pavements that make up what is called the Patio de la Higuera can be seen — to our left. A small pergola leads to an esplanade in the lower section of the Partal, presided over by the architectural structure which lent its name to the entire area: the portico of the Palacio del Partal. This large area in the Alhambra's monumental complex, as we se it today, is the result of the landscaping and architectural planning initiated in the 1930s which now accommodates large crowds of tourists in a large space designed for relaxation.

The houses in this area of the Alhambra, including the palace, were in the hands of

Aerial view of the terraced section of the Partal

The Palacio del Partal or Palacio del Pórtico, one of the oldest palaces in the Alhambra, with its impressive large water tank and tower known as the "Observatory"

The Partal

The large area known as the Partal is presided over by the Palacio del Pórtico and the Torre de las Damas. This extensive space covers terraced and landscaped areas in which the integration of buildings, architectural remains and plant life offers visitors a moment of relaxation during the visit to the Alhambra. The Torre de las Damas is a large balcony offering a panoramic view of the Albaicín, Generalife and the spacious Jardines del Partal that border the water tank in which the lovely image of its porticoed gallery is reflected.

❶ Moorish Houses

Attached to the wall to the left of the Palacio del Partal are some two-story Nasrid houses without courtyards that underwent remodelling in the 16th century. They conserve some important decorative remains.

❷ Palacio del Pórtico

Located near the Torre de las Damas, this architectural structure forms part of the oldest of the palaces conserved. It consists of a portico of five arches opening onto a garden with a large central water tank.

❸ Oratorio

To the right of the palace is a small building from the era of Yusuf I, facing in the direction of Mecca, in alignment with the wall. Both the inside and the outside of the Oratorio are decorated with plasterwork.

❹ The *paratas*

The terrain of this sloped area is organised into landscaped terraces or *paratas* containing architectural elements and building remains that came to light during a series of archaeological excavations.

❺ The Rauda, cemetery of the sultans

This was a partially covered cemetery designed like a garden in which the gravestones of some of the sultans who reigned over the Alhambra have been discovered.

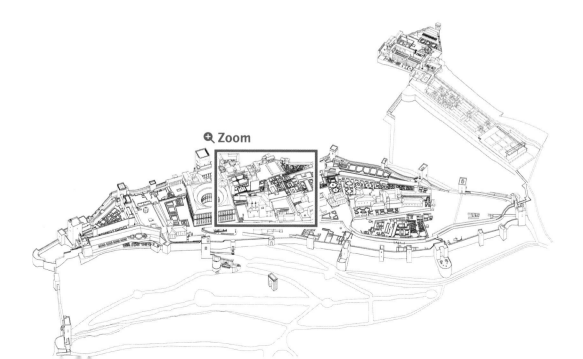

🔍 Zoom

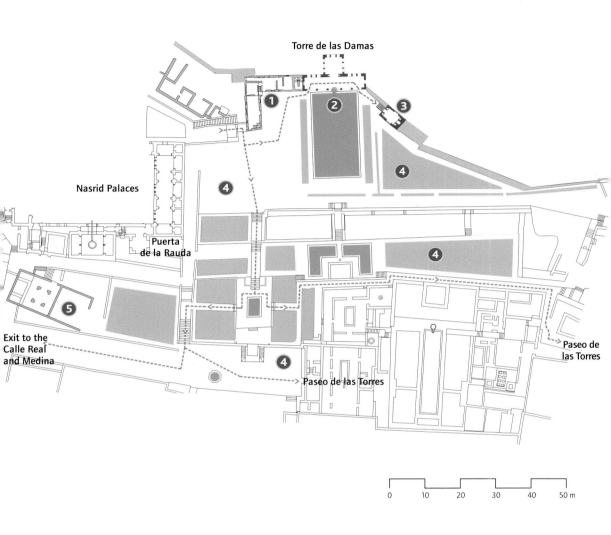

Torre de las Damas

Nasrid Palaces

Puerta
de la Rauda

Exit to the
Calle Real
and Medina

Paseo de las Torres

Paseo de
las Torres

0   10   20   30   40   50 m

1. Moorish houses

2. Palacio del Pórtico

3. Oratorio

4. The *paratas*

5. The Rauda, cemetery of the sultans

- - - - - > Direction of the visit

▨ Wall   ▨ Nasrid architecture   ▨ Nasrid archaeological remains

▨ Gardens   ▨ Hydraulic elements

private owners. Since the mid-19th century, there have been acquisitions and expropriations permitted the area to be recovered and a series of archaeological explorations to be carried out. Walls, pavements and architectural elements were repaired — especially over the first third of the 20th century — and plants were added to the area, until the archaeological remains, architectural repairs, vegetation and landscape were integrated into a lovely paradigm that has had a great influence on the Alhambra, and that offers visitors a large area of open natural space with benches that invite them to take a break during their visit.

The Jardines del Partal extend from the Torre de las Damas to the Rauda. This is the same place in which the gardens surrounding the royal palaces — also terraced — were located.

Moorish Houses

To the left of the Torre de las Damas — which dominates the Partal area — there are some small, two-story Moorish houses featuring various elements from the Nasrid era (known since the 17th century as the Casa de González Pareja, the Casa de Villoslada, the Casa de los Balcones and the Casa de las Pinturas, one of which is attached to the Torre de las Damas. Originally independent from one another, they probably shared a common courtyard similar to a small *plaza* between their walls.

Inside the Casa de las Pinturas are the remains of an important wall decoration done in the first half of the 14th century. It is the only example conserved in situ of a figurative Nasrid painting. It was discovered in 1908 by architect Modesto Cendoya when he removed a layer of

The Casa de las Pinturas, attached to the Palacio del Pórtico in the Partal

Casa de las Pinturas
This house shellers the only remains of Nasrid wall paintings preserved on site. Created over the first half of the 14th century, they show court and ceremonial scenes. The details — sometimes done in the style of miniatures — of the naturalistic scenes are astonishing. These paintings were covered when the house was attached to the previously free-standing pavilion. As a result, under the paintings, the paint on the outside of the pavilion — based on a red brick design with white joints and an epigraphic strip — has been conserved.

finishing plaster from the wall. These paintings — of tempera on stucco — are organised in three horizontal spaces and feature very interesting festive court and ceremonial scenes that provide information about life during that time period. Its delicate state of preservation requires that it be restricted from public exhibition.

Palacio del Pórtico
Located atop the wall, with an architectural structure that develops around the Torre de las Damas, this palace is one of the oldest of the palaces preserved in the Alhambra. Its layout recalls that of the Palacio de Comares: a large central water tank presided over by a portico of five arches, behind which the main room is located inside the tower. The decoration — damaged from the effects of time and weather — has the typical tiled baseboard, wide plasterwork panels — originally polychromed up to the wooden support frieze — that reach the frame and a wood-framed ceiling. Its decorative style makes it possible to attribute its construction to the era of Sultan Muhammad III (1302–1309).

The upper room — a pavilion typical of Nasrid architecture called the "Observatory" — juts out above the portico of the palace

A small *mocárabe* dome — the oldest in the Alhambra — in the so-called "Observatory" of the Partal

Ceiling of the turret in the Palacio del Partal, currently in the Museum fur Islamische Kunst, Berlin

Jutting out above the portico of the Torre de la Damas is a turret inside which is a balcony with windows facing the four cardinal points, characteristic of Nasrid architecture and similar to those of the other palaces, such as Comares or Generalife. Due to its extraordinary views and the sultan's well-known love of astronomy, in modern times it has been called the "Observatory"; the small *mocárabe* dome inside is the oldest in the Alhambra.

Unlike the neighbouring Palacio de Comares and Palacio de los Leones — whose general structures have been kept more or less intact since the Nasrid era — the Palacio del Partal has had different private owners, and thus was remodelled into a residence, as can be seen in the photograph from the early 20th century. It was incorporated into the Alhambra complex about a century ago, on 12 March 1891, the date on which its last owner, Arthur von Gwinner, ceded the title to the Spanish government. The building was then converted into a simple two-story house, with the finishing plaster on its walls covering the majority of the original structure and decoration.

Unfortunately, the wooden ceiling in the interior of the balcony was dismantled by von Gwinner, turning up in Berlin in the early 20th century. Currently, it is one of the most impressive pieces in the Islamic Art collection of the Pergamon Museum in the German capital.

One of the most altered sites of the Alhambra, numerous restoration techniques have been carried out here.

The Palacio del Pórtico del Partal with the Torre de las Damas on the left

Between 1923 and 1924, Leopoldo Torres Balbás, then architectural curator of the Alhambra, freed the portico's façade of the added elements and reconstructed the entire arch from the preserved remains; the central arch appeared almost in its entirety and the side arches were rebuilt, imitating the rhomboid-shaped ornamentation with the typical *sebka* style decoration of "pieces of perforated plaster that from a distance give the impression of being very old," according to the illustrious architect. This solution — which has had a great subsequent influence — is the architectural equivalent of the *rigattino* applied to paintings.

Another later intervention — this time by architect Francisco Prieto Moreno — consisted of substituting the brick pillars of the portico with slender marble columns and capitals. During excavation work carried out in the gallery during the 1920s, some of the foundations of the central columns that had been lost appeared, while a number of pilasters were found at the far ends. Due to the rapid nature of the work and the lack of resources, the brick pillars were initially left standing throughout the gallery, but some columns were carved and stored away for a time until — after consultations with Torres Balbás — they were finally installed in 1959.

During the last decade of the 19th century, two large 14th-century marble lion statues (originally from the Maristán in the Albaicín) stood in front of the Partal gallery.

The Oratorio del Partal, next to the house of the squire Astasio de Bracamonte

In 1955 they were moved so that they could be restored; today, they are conserved in the Alhambra Museum, because nothing related to their conservation, chronology, purpose or context justifies them being in front of the gallery.

The Oratory

The Oratory is attached to the main wall of the compound, to the right of the Palacio del Pórtico. Its decorative elements tie it to Sultan Yusuf I (1333–1354). The building's mandatory orientation coincides precisely with the alignment of the wall. It has a rectangular shape and — because it is located above the gardens — access to it is via a small staircase. The left wall facing the water tank is decorated with plasterwork as though it

were a façade, just like most of the interior and exterior walls. The Oratory has a double window with a column in the middle. The structure is made of brick, with a tile-covered frame made of crosspieces inside, under a tiled roof. The wall facing shows traces of the battlements that were there before the Oratory was built.

At the entrance is the *mihrab* (the niche indicating the direction of prayer), whose *qibla* (wall holding the *mihrab*) is attached to the Casa de Astasio de Bracamonte, the house belonging to the squire to the Count of Tendilla, governor of the Alhambra beginning in 1492. This building — which may also possibly date from the Nasrid era — was remodelled in the 16th century. The structure of the house is older than that of the Oratory, as it conserves

Interior of the Partal Oratory, with the *mihrab*

remains of imitation brick painting like that
on the exterior of the Torre de las Damas,
which was subsequently attached to the Casa de
las Pinturas.

The *Paratas*

The land in this area has a series of terraces or
paratas carved into its slopes beginning at the
wall of the fortress on the left bank of the Darro
River and rising toward the upper Alhambra. This
area was probably the site of the first planned
settlement of the Nasrid dynasty.

The layout of a garden in ascending terraces
is reminiscent of the design created by the
Caliphate of Córdoba in the 10th century for
the Madinat al-Zahra' Palace, which had a great
influence on the Hispano-Muslim world. In
fact, on the nearest *parata* — perfectly parallel
to the Partal's portico — is preserved the floor
of a small pavilion belonging to this palace,
which served to enclose it at its southern bay.
Beginning at the esplanade located on the lower

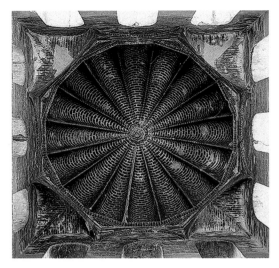

Dome of the Puerta de la Rauda

terrace, visitors may continue their visit to the
Alhambra by climbing the stairs that begin at a
leaf-covered portal.

Puerta de la Rauda

From here we can visit the building known as the
Puerta de la Rauda because of its proximity to the
cemetery of the sultans. Rectangular in shape,
inside it has a magnificent umbrella dome, with
the typical trompe l'oeil paint that imitates red
bricks with white joints. It is a *qubba* or pavilion,
open on three of its sides with large horseshoe
arches; the fourth side connects to the interior of
the Palacio de los Leones, into which its structure
would be integrated, although the *qubba* of the
Rauda dates from an earlier era, thus highlighting
its role as a link between the palaces that were
located in this area.

Jardines del Partal

Walking through the Jardines del Partal,
visitors pass through a new stepped and
plant-covered arcade that shelters a small
fountain and a large courtyard surrounded
by gardens flanking a water tank. All of the
remains of the buildings correspond to original
structures discovered during the archaeological
excavations of the first third of the 20th century,

The Puerta de la Rauda of the Partal (1986).
Alhambra Archives

running perpendicular to it, there is another, secondary but wider street that probably led through the upper *parata* to the Alhambra's upper area where the Medina or court city was located, organised round Calle Real Alta.

At the right angle created by the junction of the two streets and hidden among gardens is the structure of a house built around a traditional courtyard with a small central water tank. Behind it, at a more elevated level, is another structure with a similar layout.

In front of the balcony in the street through which the itinerary continues one can see the beautiful portico of the Palacio del Partal silhouetted against the scenery of the Albaicín and the Sacromonte. The parapet serving as a barrier is actually a wall marking the boundary of the Palacio del Partal, in front of which are the remains of what must have been a beautiful pavilion that lay parallel to the portico. Part of its original ceramic pavement has been preserved. Surrounded by two curious pools forming a U-shape and dominating the steps down from the gardens, this lovely space is reminiscent of the Madinat al-Zahra' to which Hispano-Muslim architecture is so indebted.

The Partal from the small pavilion situated opposite the Palacio del Pórtico

including a pillar embedded into the wall enclosing the upper *parata*, flanked by two stairways accessing the terrace. A small balcony that dominates the area.

Currently, this courtyard is a central point from which to continue the visit of the Alhambra. From here, visitors may head in the direction of the Generalife, following the wall on which are built various towers. They may also choose to visit the upper area where the remains of the Nasrid's dynasty cemetery — known as the Rauda — are, as well as the exit towards the Palacio de Carlos V and Calle Real. This latter option allows visitors to continue towards the Alcazaba or to leave the monumental complex.

The central *parata* of the Jardines del Partal gives visitors an approximate idea of the area's original urban fabric: following along a section of narrow street paved in the original pebblestone, which might have been Calle Real Baja, the main street connecting the palaces in the Alhambra, the remains of the Palacio de Yusuf III can be seen in the upper area, while the general structure of the Palacio del Partal can be seen on the lower *parata*.

This section of road is thus a privileged observation point from which to see the Jardines del Partal. Near the beginning of this street, but

Two Options: the Torres and the Medina

The Jardines del Partal complete the route of one of the three sections into which the visit to the Alhambra monument is divided: the Nasrid Palaces. The other two areas — the Alcazaba and the Generalife — may be visited next, if they have not already been seen. Likewise, visitors may see the Palacio de Carlos V, or choose to leave the monumental compound.

From the Partal, there are two options for continuing the visit: either following the Paseo de las Torres or entering the Medina.

The Generalife may be reached from the Partal without leaving the compound following the inside of the Alhambra's wall, along which there are several towers that are representative of those in the compound.

This route passes through gardens and architectural remains (recovered in part thanks to the excavations and restorations carried out in the 20th century) and boasts lovely views of the landscape surrounding the Alhambra.

After completing this route, visitors may leave the Alhambra's walled compound to visit the Generalife and the surrounding area. Both the car park as well as the area of complementary services offered by the monumental complex can be reached from this point, as can the woods and the accesses to Granada, if the visit is over.

The Alhambra's upper Medina — the urban area which has undergone many changes over time — may be accessed from the Partal as well; along this route there are many interesting sites. This is the option for visitors who have not yet visited the Alcazaba, the interior of the Palacio de Carlos V or its exhibition areas (Alhambra Museum, Fine Arts Museum, Exhibition Hall, Bookstore/Shop, etc.).

The Rauda, Cemetery of the Sultans

Rauda means garden, leading us to believe that this area was intended to be used as such, in a space that is typical of the Alhambra, next to the main mosque and palace from which it is separated only by Calle Real Baja. The term in classical Arabic is used to name — within the multipurpose spaces that are so characteristic of Muslim culture — a funeral garden. Islam confers a special significance upon the relationship between burial and the environment, as the antechamber to Paradise. Some tombs, despite being located inside a building, were left unroofed, or closed with a lattice gate that ensured contact with nature. The Rauda was most likely a partially covered cemetery treated like a garden. In the centre it had a building that is reminiscent of the mausoleums of the Saadi princes of Marrakech, although these were built later. According to information from the Moorish interpreter of Arabic Alonso del Castillo, in 1574 — as a result of the construction being carried out on the Palacio de Carlos V — the tombstones of Muhammad II, Isma'il I, Yusuf I and Yusuf III were discovered. It is possible that the Rauda occupied in part some remains of a previous burial site, as indicated by the walls of tombs

Interior of the cemetery of the Rauda with the remains of the central *qubba* and the main door in the background

Tombstones

These are two of the tombstones that — along with a few other remains — were recovered from the Rauda of the Nasrid sultans of the Alhambra. Today, they are in the Alhambra Museum, in the hall of the Palacio de Carlos V nearest the Rauda or cemetery of the sultans. These large marble stones were placed at the heads of the tombs of the most distinguished individuals — such as the sultans — whom they praised with metaphors. Large slabs of stone were also placed over the sultans' tombs and, on top of these, other pyramid-shaped stones called *maqabriyyas*. The tombstones were probably polychromed. The texts written on them have great historical and epigraphic value.

found near the Palacio de Carlos V, some of which were discovered near the building.

Access to the Rauda was via Calle Real Baja, through a small entrance hall and a gate with a horseshoe arch that still conserves traces of a rhombus-shaped decoration on its spandrels. The remains are rectangular and have the same orientation as the mosque. In the middle, the tilted pillars attest to the fact that there was a lantern (square windowed tower set into the roof), whose upper window with its wooden latticework is preserved in the Alhambra Museum. During the removal of rubble, many decorative remains were also discovered, including tile-covered baseboards and fragments of plasterwork.

The presence of a cemetery at such an early date may have helped to increase activity in this area of the compound, which during that era was empty of buildings; beginning in the first third of the 14th century, it would be the centre of the large Nasrid Palaces. The Rauda was not an isolated building in the urban fabric of the Alhambra; it occupied a section in the middle of the road from the palaces to the mosque and the Medina. Its original boundaries are unknown, although it probably extended beyond the current garden area.

The Rauda is the Alhambra's mausoleum, although it is known that there was another cemetery outside its wall. According to writer and vizier Ibn al-Khatib, the first emir buried here was Muhammad II, who died in 1302. After Isma'il I was assassinated, he was buried next to his grandfather on 9 July 1325. There is also information mentioning the burial of Yusuf I, who died tragically in 1354: "The sultan, upon whom God has taken pity, was buried on the same day, in the cemetery of his palace, next to his father." Similarly, there is the tombstone of Yusuf III, who died in 1417, as well as that of Prince Yusuf, brother of Muley Hacén.

After the Christian conquest and as part of the agreements reached, their descendents were allowed to disinter the remains of their relatives from the Rauda, and these were moved on muleback to an unknown site in the Alpujarras.

Both the vertical and horizontal tombstones, carved in white marble, are true epigraphic jewels. It is almost certain that they were polychromed, possibly with golden letters on a blue background. In the 19th century, they were displayed in the Sala de los Reyes of the Palacio de los Leones next to pieces from other sites, in what was the Alhambra Museum's first exhibition space. The stones and decorative remains of the Rauda are preserved in the Alhambra Museum, where they have a hall dedicated to them.

Other Alhambra Palaces

The Nasrid dynasty's first settlements were built in the central area of the highest point of the hill but, over time, they fell into disuse or were used for other purposes. This is where the Palacio de los Abencerrajes — which would later become the Convento de San Francisco — and the Palacio de Yusuf III were built. Of the first and last, only ground level archaeological remains are left. The second — for the most part also torn down and subjected to alterations since the 15th century — is now the site of a national parador.

Modern research regarding the Alhambra has revealed that, together with the Nasrid Palaces conserved — such as the Palacio de los Leones or the Palacio de Comares — there were others that apparently functioned as the Alhambra's first settlements but which, as the dynasty grew and became stronger, fell into disuse or were destined for other purposes, perhaps complementary to the new buildings. There are three such complexes, and all three are found adjacent to one another, in an upper, central area, on a slight slope. It was an excellent place to get water from the water channel, with good visibility in all of the cardinal directions, and the site of what would become the urban framework of the city where the two royal streets — Calle Real Alta and Calle Real Baja — converged.

The original names of these palaces are unknown and we can scarcely imagine their evolution during the Nasrid era although, after the 16th-century Christian conquest, the three had secondary purposes, as they were not chosen by the new monarchs. They did, however, serve to house economic, religious and military powers: the Accounting Office, the Franciscan convent and the governors' headquarters.

Palacio de los Abencerrajes

In the upper area of the Alhambra — more or less in the centre of the Medina, where some of the more important streets are located — are the archaeological remains of the palace known as the Palacio de los Abencerrajes. In 1501 the Catholic

Baths of the Palacio de los Abencerrajes
Partial view of the *hammam*, partially recovered in 1982, with the remains of the Palacio de los Abencerrajes. The excavations have resulted in the discovery of elements that are typical of the baths, such as the *bayt al-maslai*. Although they are known as the Baños del Palacio de los Abencerrajes, it is possible that they were an independent public bath house built next to the palace's baths that fell into disuse or became part of the new baths. They had a separate access — most likely directly from Calle Real — as can be assumed from the stairway that has been recovered. Archaeological excavations being carried out will reveal still-hidden elements that will provide more information about its architectural layout and decorative scheme.

Central pavilion of the Nasrid palace converted into the Convent of San Francisco at the end of the 15th century

Other Alhambra Palaces

On the highest part of Sabika Hill, where Calle Real Alta and Calle Real Baja meet — that is, an important point in its urban fabric — the oldest buildings of the Nasrid dynasty were built. We know of the existence of three important palaces in the area: the Palacio de los Abencerrajes, the Palacio de los Infantes — later to become the Convento de San Francisco — and the Palacio de Yusuf III. Of the three, the partial remains of only one have been preserved: the palace that was converted into a Franciscan convent during the Christian era and that today is a national parador. Archaeological studies of the other two are ongoing in order to determine how they were laid out.

❶ Palacio de los Abencerrajes

Excavation was begun the 1930s; its remains indicate that it had a large room in a tower over the southern wall, a large water tank flanked by gardens and a *hammam*.

❷ Palacio de los Infantes (Convento de San Francisco, Parador Nacional)

Originally a Nasrid palace built in the 13th century, in 1494 the Catholic Monarchs converted it into a Franciscan convent. It was heavily damaged during the Napoleonic occupation and suffered various other misfortunes, until 1954 when it was included as a unique building within the network of national *paradores*.

❸ Palacio de Yusuf III

Also called the Palace of Mondéjar or Palace of Tendilla, as it was the residence of the governors of the Alhambra, it was demolished in the 18th century when Phillip V stripped the family of its titles.

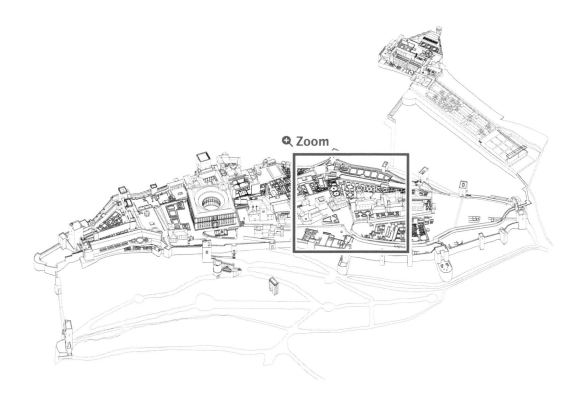

⊕ Zoom

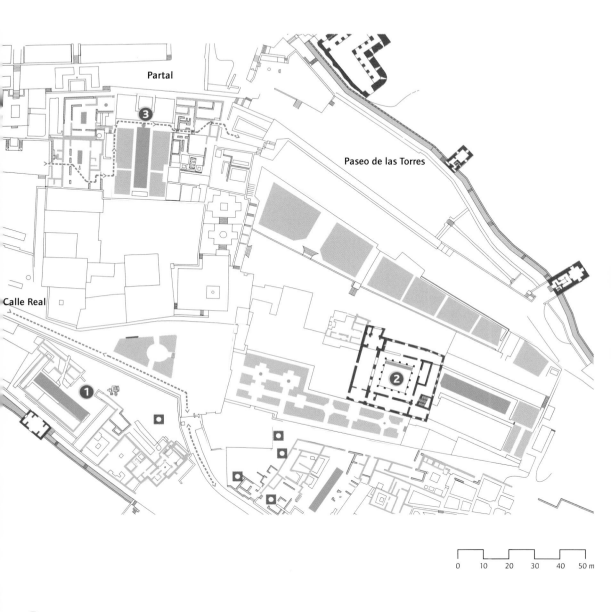

Partal

Paseo de las Torres

Calle Real

0   10   20   30   40   50 m

1 Palacio de los Abencerrajes

2 Palacio de los Infantes (Convento de San Francisco, Parador Nacional)

3 Palacio de Yusuf III

┈┈┈> Direction of the visit

	Wall		Nasrid architecture		Nasrid archaeological remains		Christian architecture

	Gardens		Hydraulic elements		Vault or silo

General view of the remains of the Palacio de los Abencerrajes. The central part of the palace can be seen in the image's background, with the *hammam* at the front

Monarchs ceded it to the head accountant of the Royal Council, Juan Chacón, and ever since, it has been called the Casa de la Contaduría or the Palacio de la Contaduría, a name that has survived in the *plaza* located where its entrance is assumed to have been. The entire parcel of land upon which it was built was found to be in a sad state of abandonment during the second half of the 19th century as a result of Napoleonic troops blowing up parts of the upper area of the Alhambra; since that time, the area has been called − significantly − the Secano. In the late 19th century, the rubble was removed and many architectural and urban remains were discovered. Other curious objects were also found, such as a single coin with the mint mark of the Alhambra, leading us to believe that there was a Nasrid mint in the area.

A number of excavations carried out after the 1930s have demonstrated the importance and the size of this palace. Based on the structures preserved, its most important area was located round a tower-hall built over the wall to the south of the fortress, where the Torre de los Carros and

the Torre de las Cabezas now stand. In 1958 a reconstruction project was carried out to rebuild the tower's main floor, which contained three alcoves. The square middle room opens to the outside via a wide opening, onto which, in turn, open two smaller elongated side rooms. Under this room, via a vaulted tunnel, passes Calle de Ronda or del Foso, which runs along the inside of the Alhambra's wall.

A curious small tunnel begins under one of the rooms that leads to a gap in the street. This is possibly a drain or an emergency exit. The main chamber of the tower opens on to an elongated room of which only the foundations remain. It possibly served as an open gallery or traditional portico.

In front of the façade of the reconstructed tower, the central open-air area of the palace extends lengthwise. This must have been a rectangular courtyard, with an elongated central water tank with slightly sunken gardens along its longer sides. This would have been the traditional three-part courtyard composition, with the central water element (water tank or pool) surrounded by

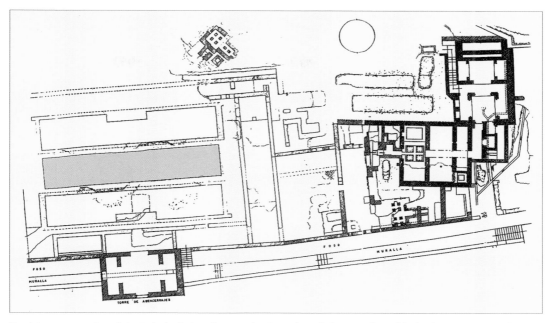

Partial reconstruction of the Palacio de los Abencerrajes from the existing remains, with the *hammam* to the right.
Alhambra Archives

gardens or vegetation. The overhanging gallery in front of the tower may have extended like a pavilion into the interior of the garden space, a typical design in Hispano-Muslim architecture.

The wall of the eastern border apparently acted as the façade of the bay's courtyard, extending north behind a second parallel wall to the first; between these walls there must have been various rooms or alcoves that would have closed off the patio in this part of the palace. The northern wall, parallel to the longer sides of the courtyard, probably was the boundary of the building's rectangular space.

Toward the east it is difficult to determine the palace's boundaries, as it still has not been completely excavated, although they are assumed to have extended some metres into a bay that closed off the building.

Remains of foundations and walls belonging to two baths have been found at the eastern end of the courtyard. In 1982 work aimed at cleaning and repairing part of the structures was begun, although it has not been definitively determined whether or not they belonged to the palace or

were a separate building. Since the 1990s, a series of archaeological campaigns has been undertaken, and these have gradually uncovered some of the original structures and the boundaries of the buildings have been determined: the eastern bay of the palace — partially remodelled into living quarters and reused during the Christian era; a modestly-sized *hammam*, with direct access from Calle de Ronda, part of whose annexes were shared with or enlarged into a second larger bath house, accessed via Calle Real.

Front and back of a Nasrid coin minted in the Alhambra's mint, discovered during the excavations of the Palacio de los Abencerrajes. Alhambra Museum

Plasterwork preserved in the Alhambra Museum, originally from the Palacio de los Abencerrajes

These baths were accessed via a stairway from the upper floor that leads to a room with a lantern and a rest area with two side alcoves. Completing the baths were corridors, latrines, etc. Some of the more remarkable areas include a small room with a marble floor and a large basin, the typical hypocaust, and the conduits for exhausting the smoke and hot steam outside. To the west would have been the boilers and other necessary bath elements. Remains of different types of flooring have been preserved, including clay bricks covered with mortar and glazed and unglazed stone of various sizes in white, green and black. The remains of baseboards with glazed green strips were also found.

Towards the south there is also evidence of buildings facing Calle de Ronda. All of this confirms how large the Palacio de los Abencerrajes was, extending toward the north to the edge of Calle Real Alta, where the main entrance was most likely located. Archaeological data confirm the importance of the repair work carried out on the floor which — free of other uses — has become a reference for the recovery of the Alhambra's heritage. The Alhambra Museum conserves many pieces from the explorations and excavations carried out. Among these pieces are the spandrels of an arch, panels decorated with *sebkas* (diamond-shaped patterns) carved in limestone and showing the original marks of the compass and square, epigraphic and geometrically decorated panels, and ceramic pieces with green, red and blue colours, originally part of the tiled baseboards in the rooms of the Palacio de los Abencerrajes. The latest explorations have led to the recovery of some remains that were believed to have been lost, such as part of the fountain for the water tank and various pavements.

Palacio de los Infantes (Convento de San Francisco, Parador Nacional)

Part of the national network of Spanish paradores, in 1954 this state hotel was installed in the building occupied by the royally-sponsored Franciscan convent in 1494, which was built on top of a late 12th-century Nasrid palace remodelled in the mid-14th century.

It is located in the upper Medina of the Alhambra, in what was most likely an important urban area in the Nasrid fortress, where several streets converge with the areas occupied by their first palace settlement; this Nasrid palace is located in a zone between the Palacio de los Abencerrajes and the Palacio de Yusuf III and, of the three, it is the one located at the highest point, hence its strategic importance and possible influence over later constructions.

The convent was accessed from the end of the current route of Calle Real. Almost all of the preserved convent belongs to the building remodelled in the 18th century, although some interesting remnants from the Nasrid era and the 16th century have survived. It was also badly damaged during the Napoleonic occupation and, in 1840, it was put up for auction, although it finally became property of the Crown. At the beginning of the 20th century, the convent was

Convento de San Francisco, in whose interior are the remains of a Nasrid palace. The compound is currently a national *parador*

found to be in a lamentable state of ruin; it was restored between 1927 and 1928 by Leopoldo Torres Balbás, who converted it into a residence for artists and distinguished personalities.

The remains preserved from the Nasrid palace – which had been remodelled so many times – are laid out around a central space with an elongated and narrow courtyard, quite similar to the Patio de la Acequia in the Generalife, although it is much smaller. It has the typical three-part design with the central water element and the side gardens and – just as in the Generalife – there is a central water channel called the Acequia Real or the Acequia del Sultán from which water is provided, although possibly the section in the palace was a branch of the main channel that flowed a few metres more to the south at a higher elevation. The palace's water channel probably originated at the large water tank located to the east and crossed the courtyard

from east to west, supplying the building and the gardens and orchards that extended below.

The boundaries of the parcel of land on which the Nasrid palace stands are difficult to determine, although they surely continued across the lower *paratas* through the orchards and gardens, reaching the northern wall. To the south, the boundary may have been Calle Real. To the west, it probably reached the entrance gate to the Franciscan convent, called the Compás due to the shape of its entrance atrium; in front of the gate facing Calle Real there was probably a small *plaza*.

The palace's central axis was most likely defined by a pavilion with a balcony that was remodelled when the convent was converted to a chancel, where the tombs prepared for the Catholic Monarchs were located until 1521, when the Royal Chapel was finished in the city. This area underwent many changes when it was converted into a church, with the room in front of the observation point

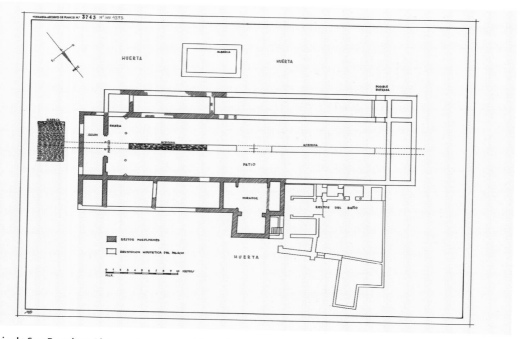

Palacio de San Francisco. The remains preserved from the Nasrid palace indicate that it had a long, narrow central courtyard similar to that of the Generalife, with gardens on both sides. Copy (1957) of the original map. Alhambra Archives

becoming a transept that conserved fragments of the marble flooring that most certainly had belonged to the palace. Apparently, a tiled baseboard similar to that in the Sala de los Reyes in the Palacio de los Leones disappeared shortly before the restoration, although the *mocárabe* vault and the entrance vault were both conserved, as were the arches corresponding to the three remaining sides with their inscriptions of the Nasrid motto and praise of Muhammad V. The plasterwork resembles that in the Sala de Dos Hermanas and the Sala de los Abencerrajes, so it probably dates back to the last third of the 14th century.

A rectangular-shaped room (known today as the Sala Arabe or Arabic Hall) located on the ground floor and belonging to the original palace was also

The baths in the Palacio de San Francisco

Toward the middle of the last century, work was begun to remove rubble from the parcel of land occupied by the *hammam* of the Nasrid palace. Recently, scientific excavation work in the building has come to an end, after having brought to light many important elements from its original structure, despite the fact that a large part of it was demolished in modern times. Today, it is included in the gardens of the Franciscan convent, where it awaits final repair.

preserved. It was probably preceded by a portico that extended into the courtyard. Inside, there are alhamíes (low benches of tile-covered stone) at the far ends – slightly raised – as well as part of the original baseboard and remains of the decorative inscriptions with the dynasty's motto. In the back are spaces for small water channels and the remains of an eave, suggesting that there was no upper floor and that it did not extend out further toward the exterior, where the large water tank mentioned earlier is located. During the convent's restoration, remains from two of the courtyard entrance arches were found. The foundation of a wall running parallel to the central water canal and enclosing the courtyard to the south was also discovered, as were remains from other rooms or alcoves at the front. Behind the wall bordering the property appeared the remains of another water tank.

To the north of the courtyard – between the easternmost room and the balcony – there were at least two other rooms. Under one of these, the remains of the canals belonging to the *hammam* of the palace were discovered. These rooms were torn down in modern times owing to their extreme state of deterioration, which affected the crypt of Queen Isabella I, who had been buried briefly next to the baths. The baths were gradually covered over by soil and remained unnoticed until the middle of the 20th century, when work was carried out to recover and repair this facility, although shortly afterward it was forgotten once again and ended up being covered in vegetation until the early years of this century, when its historical role in the Alhambra was recovered as the result of archaeological and conservation projects.

It was accessed via one of the most important halls in the palace – the *mirador* or balcony. There was a wide opening – currently closed – through which one descended a stairway to the baths located below the level of the Acequia Real that supplied it with water. The entrance has been conserved, along with a vestibule with two alcoves or beds and a central fountain. From here, through a bent corridor, the cold/warm room containing a bathing pool is reached. The path of the water can be seen here, originating in a lead pipe, reaching the pool and escaping via a clay drain to a conduit that runs through the baths and collects water to

Detail of the Arab hall, belonging to the Nasrid Palace, integrated within the Franciscan convent that today is a national *parador*

carry outside. A small opening provided access to the hot room – now demolished, except for an immersion pool – and to a side room with a small stairway. A large part of the pavements and overlays of the walls in the baths made of tiles and stucco have been conserved. Pieces have been discovered during the archaeological interventions that attest to its rich decoration.

The inscriptions found throughout the palace complex belong to two different eras. Those in the *mirador* and in the eastern hall are from the second half of the 14th century, based on the reference made to Muhammad V. In the eastern hall, there are other inscriptions very similar to those in upper balconies in the Torre de las Damas and in the middle of the Generalife that hark back to the early 14th century. Their similarity to the part of the Generalife dating from the last third of the 13th century is apparent, so that – given the lack of any other information – it is assumed that the original palace must have been built during that period. There are indications that in the 16th century different materials — especially columns — from this palace were used for remodelling and reconstruction carried out in the Patio de la Reja and the Patio de Lindaraja.

Palacio de Yusuf III

Traditionally known as the Palacio de Mondéjar or the Palacio de Tendilla, the Catholic Monarchs ceded it as the residence of the governors of the Christian Alhambra until 1718, when Phillip V stripped the family of this title and ordered them to leave. In retaliation, they ordered its demolition in 1795, selling many of its construction materials, columns and gates, or reusing them for repairs in other places. During the 20th century, some impressive original palace pieces were discovered in private collections. This may be the origin of the well-known Fortuny tile on which the sultan's name appears, and that is preserved in the Institute Valencia de Don Juan in Madrid.

This was the sad end to what must have been an extraordinary palace, both in terms of materials as well as decoration, as seen from testimonials such as that of ambassador Hieronymus Münzer,

who was received here in 1494 and described the palace as "sumptuous." Its construction is attributed to Sultan Yusuf III (1408–1417), though he may have remodelled or redecorated a much older construction built by Sultan Muhammad II (1273–1302), the second ruler of the dynasty. Although the first years of the 15th century are already a late period, the decadence of the Nasrid dynasty had not yet fully begun; however in terms of the decorative styles, it is considered to be a recurrent or repetitive period. The main palaces in the Alhambra from the 14th century must have had some influence at the time it was planned and designed. It is significant that this is the palace chosen by the Christian governors for their personal use, as in the period immediately after the conquest there were many from which to choose.

The location of the palace in the highest area of the Partal defines its strategic importance. Its main tower to the north must have stood out above the gardens and other buildings, and would have had magnificent views that permitted the surrounding area to be monitored and protected.

With the palace stripped of its richest pieces of decoration, the parcel of land must not have been very attractive, and it fell into a state of

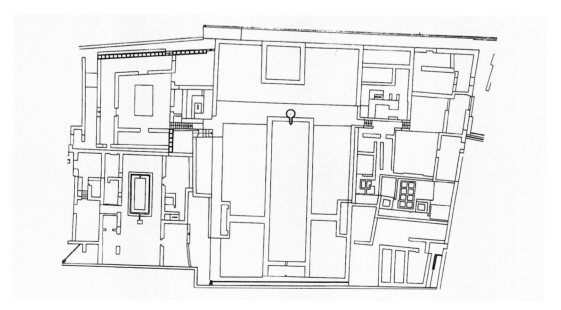

Palacio de Yusuf III. Main layout of the excavated remains: in the centre, the main part of the palace; to the right, the *hammam;* to the left, the two annexed living quarters. Plan Especial Alhambra y Alijares, 1986

The Fortuny tile, whose inscription mentions Yusuf III. Instituto Valencia de Don Juan, Madrid

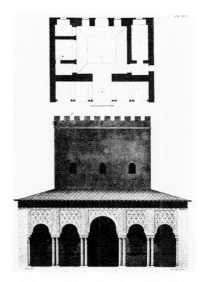

Ground plan and elevation of a building identified with the Generalife, similar to the Palacio de Yusuf III. Engraving by James C. Murphy (1815)

almost total neglect, at the mercy of the weather and nearly buried under its own rubble. In the 19th century it formed a part of the Huerta de Santa María, which was gradually expropriated, as were the majority of the properties in the area. The exploration of its remains coincided with the interest in the recovery of the entire area of the Partal during the first third of the 20th century. Today, the partial anastylosis of its main structural part remains, but almost another third is unexplored. The remains of its walls jutting up from the ground offer a rather approximate idea of the compound, whose main features can be identified to a certain extent: a large rectangular courtyard with a long water tank in the centre that must have imitated — on a somewhat smaller scale — the three-part design of the Patio de los Arrayanes. On the northern side would have been the main bay, laid out round a tower that probably included a porticoed gallery. On the southernmost side, there was another similar

structure, the remains of which may be preserved behind a retaining wall on a higher piece of land and that closes off the parcel of land in this area.

There are remains of walls belonging to the palace structure on both sides of the compound occupied by the courtyard. To the east is the *hammam,* with the boundaries of the majority of its rooms well defined. The water conduits, the hypocaust, and the fountains in the hot room are all easily identifiable. It repeats the typical structure of this type of building, and is similar to those found in other places in the Alhambra.

At the northern end, there are various structures, among which the probable entrance to the palace is worthy of mention, and on the façade of which there is a large door with the recesses for the door frame intact. Behind the door, a corridor leads to an almost square-shaped courtyard that may have been used to dismount from horses, as there is a building next to it that resembles a stable. There are several streets running in front of the door, the descending one connecting the Calle Real Alta of the Medina to the gate of the Torre de los Picos. Another street — running at a right angle — leads to the current gardens, where in the past there were orchards

that extended to the wall. Calle Real Baja also crosses the area, and the remains of roadway near the palace — which it borders at its northern end — can be identified.

The western area of the palace is more problematic, as it was greatly modified so that the entrance to the Christian governors' residence could be installed there. In front of it still remain several wall structures that surround two medium-sized courtyards at different levels which can be identified as large houses. Both are connected to the palace and formed part of its rooms, although they were probably initially separate and then subsequently attached to it at some point, perhaps when it was allocated for use as a residence for the governors.

The house located on the highest terrace has a central water tank with rooms on its sides, except to the north, where remains of pavements and of a latrine are found. The adjacent home — on the lower terrace and of a somewhat irregular shape — also has a water tank in the centre of its courtyard. The remains of another latrine and of smaller rooms that probably belonged to the palace — with which they were connected via a stairway — appear on a higher level. The main room of the house was probably the one opening on to the courtyard; inside are the remains of the traditional side alhamíes, slightly raised. To the north, it is connected to a second courtyard — smaller in size, and perhaps providing access to the house — with a lovely polygonal fountain of glazed ceramic in the centre. To the west, the house was bordered by a gently sloping pebblestone street that may have served as a link between the two royal streets.

In front of the entrance to the governors' palace there was a wide tree-lined road that connected it with the palaces reserved for the kings and, once it was built, with the Palacio de Carlos V. On the wall enclosing the palace there is a commemorative plaque dedicated to the writer and Dominican friar Brother Luis de Granada, who served here as squire to the Count of Tendilla during the first years of the 16th century and later as private tutor to the count's children.

Remains of the entrance portal of the Palacio de Yusuf III

8 Paseo de las Torres

Through a stone roadway linking the interior of the old Medina to the Puerta del Arrabal, visitors arrive at the segment of the wall protecting the area between the Partal and the Generalife, dotted with some of the most emblematic towers of all of the Alhambra: those of Picos, Qadí, Cautiva, Infantas, Cabo de la Carrera and Agua. A landscaped promenade across the rampart of the embankment leads to the eastern part of the compound.

In front of the remains of the portal that served as the entrance to the ruins of the Palacio de Yusuf III, we find the pebblestone section of a street linking the interior of the Medina of the Alhambra with one of its exterior gates, the Puerta del Arrabal. From here, it is possible to see the profile of the general wall of the Alhambra dotted with different towers and continue on toward a large area that connects the Partal with the upper Alhambra and the Generalife. As though they were milestones,

the Torre de los Picos, the Torre del Qadí, the Torre de la Cautiva, the Torre de las Infantas, the Torre del Cabo de la Carrera and the Torre del Agua appear one after the other.

They are connected via an intermediate *parata* or terrace — today covered by gardens — over the rampart of the embankment, which has a continuous railing to protect passersby and allow them to gaze at the surroundings. Below is the lower terrace, also landscaped and filled with numerous species of trees.

Aerial view of the area of the Torre de los Picos and the bastion in front

The Torre de las Infantas on the main wall and Calle de Ronda

Paseo de las Torres

In the area of the Alhambra between the Partal and the far eastern side of the wall, there is a landscaped promenade with archaeological remains that leads to the interior of the wall, towards the Generalife. In this section of the wall are located some of the most emblematic towers in the Alhambra which — in addition to being defensive — were used as residences, and inside they house some of the most exquisite spaces of all Nasrid architecture.

❶ Picos

This is one of the dual function towers as — besides its obvious defensive character — it was also used as a home. It defended the Puerta del Arrabal, along the Cuesta del Rey Chico, which connects to the Albaicín and to the Generalife. Inside, it is divided into three floors and has some decorative remains.

❷ Qadí

Due to its strategic positioning, this tower belongs to the defensive towers that sent and received warning signals. It interrupted the rampart, thus requiring passersby to be inspected by the guards.

❸ Cautiva

Inside this residential tower is one of the most exquisite spaces in all of the Alhambra. The main hall is reached via an access which is bent to maintain privacy. It comprises a courtyard with arches on pillars and three alcoves with double arched windows.

❹ Infantas

Another tower with housing inside, its decorative elements have defined it as a tower-palace. It dates from after the Torre de la Cautiva. Its layout is similar, but its execution — in terms of both design and decoration — link it to a later era.

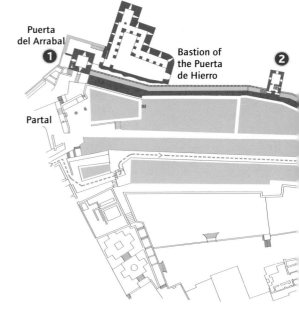

Puerta del Arrabal

❶

Bastion of the Puerta de Hierro

❷

Partal

❶ Picos

❷ Qadí

❸ Cautiva

❹ Infantas

❺ Cabo de la Carrera

❻ Torre del Agua

╌╌╌▶ Direction of the visit

Wall Nasrid architecture Nasrid archaeological remains Christian architecture

Gardens Hydraulic elements Ronda trench or passageway

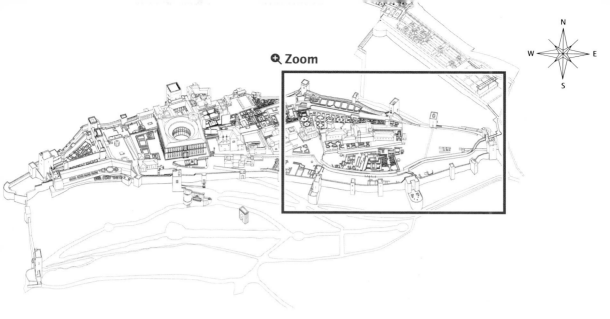

⊕ Zoom

 ❺ Cabo de la Carrera

This is the easternmost tower in the northern part of the Alhambra. At one time there was an inscription, now disappeared, attributing its construction to the Catholic Monarchs, dating it in 1502. It was almost completely destroyed by the Napoleonic troops during their retreat in 1812.

 ❻ Torre del Agua

Having a completely different function from the rest, this tower marked the entrance of the Acequia del Sultán water channel to the walled compound and, therefore, of the necessary water. It was destroyed by the Napoleonic army and reconstructed in the 20th century.

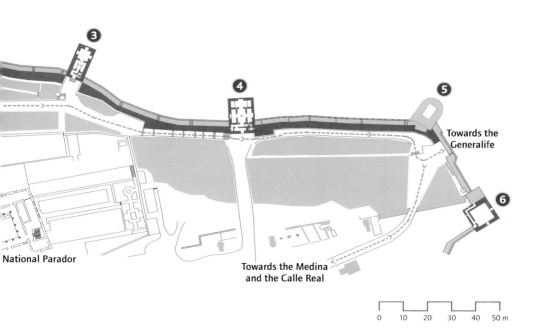

Towards the Generalife

National Parador

Towards the Medina and the Calle Real

0 10 20 30 40 50 m

View of the Torre de los Picos from the lower Partal

Torre de los Picos

This tower is one of the types of towers that – in addition to its obvious defensive function – also served as housing, as shown by the ornamentation inside, primarily plasterwork and paintings. It is also remarkable for its role in the urban fabric of the Alhambra. It defends one of the main entrance gates to the walled compound, the Puerta del Arrabal, which opens on to the Cuesta del Rey Chico and connects the Alhambra with the Albaicín neighbourhood and the old entrance to the Generalife.

Its name comes from the corbels that are found in the upper corners to support the machicolations and to defend the compound from any potential attacks from above. It was built by Sultan Muhammad II, reformed by Muhammad III and, perhaps, also by Yusuf I; after the Christian conquest, it underwent major modifications to its construction and decoration. It is one of the largest towers in the entire compound. Noteworthy inside are its vaults: cloister vaults on the second floor and vaults with four ribs on the third floor. The windows of the main floor – made of stone – have pointed horseshoe arches and Mudéjar-style capitals.

An overall view of the Generalife – with its large terraced orchards in use, separated by large clay rammed earth walls and presided over by the palace's white structure can be seen from different points of the route.

Vault with four ribs in the Torre de los Picos

In the forefront, the Torre del Qadí; to the left the Torre de los Picos. In the background, the Albaicín and the wall of Granada

Facing the landscape, inside the Alhambra is the former Convento de San Francisco, today a national parador. Built on the remains of a Nasrid palace, it has a remarkable lookout point that juts out from the building, inside which the tombs of the Catholic Monarchs were kept while the Royal Chapel — where their remains lie today — was being built in the city.

Torre del Qadí

This tower belongs to the group that — from a structural point of view — comprised the defensive guard towers of the compound. They were tactically important as they served to check, inspect and allocate the guards that carried out the basic monitoring of the city from the upper rampart of the wall, in patrols that combed the different areas in which it had been divided. These sections included the concrete sites located at equally spaced points on the perimeter, with any incident being communicated to the central command. This is why the guard towers are small — seemingly unimportant — however, the basic, immediate defence of the city depended on their functioning.

The Torre del Qadí also monitored the northeastern side of the Torre de los Picos, with the access from below to the Generalife, ascending through the gardens via a street protected by large walls. Halfway up the path is a courtyard with portico and pillar, from which the accesses to the orchards begin, as does the road that descends in the direction of the palace.

The upper part of the wall that encloses the palace-city of the Alhambra has a parapet-covered path — in some sections with battlements known as ramparts — that served as the guards' patrol route. To maintain its independence and to avoid disruption of the domestic life transpiring inside, the rampart was connected via a tunnel at the locations of the towers, as occurs in the Torre de la Cautiva and the Torre de las Infantas. Other towers, such as the Torre del Qadí that do not have a living space inside but are of a purely military nature interrupt the pathway of the guard with a control point.

In addition to the rampart, there is a road that runs along the inside of the wall for more than a kilometre in distance — called the Foso (moat)

Detail of one of the tiles from the Torre de la Cautiva with its exceptional purple-coloured pieces

Outside view of the Torre de la Cautiva, from the Generalife

or Calle de Ronda — which had two purposes: to connect with various sectors of the city near the palace and — in the event of attack — to serve as an impassable compartment, a moat or safety zone around the compound. As with the rampart, tunnels were built so that the towers did not interrupt the route. It covers virtually the entire urban compound — with the exception of the Alcazaba — although its forewall was also connected to it in some way. This street, whose route is identifiable for the most part by the wall, is hidden in some of its sections.

Torre de la Cautiva

The entrance to this tower — built on the wall — is from the inside of the city, crossing over the Foso via a barrel-vaulted bridge reconstructed during the early 20th century. It is for this reason that this is one of the most appropriate sites in the compound to understand how the defensive structure of the fortress worked. The Torre de la Cautiva is called *qalahurra* in the epigraphic poem that appears inside the main room. In fact, it is one of the most impressive buildings in the entire Alhambra complex, and

can be considered an authentic tower-palace. Its construction was attributed to Sultan Yusuf I (1333–1354), who was also responsible for the Palacio de Comares and other important buildings in the Alhambra, such as the Puerta de la Justicia and the Puerta de los Siete Suelos. Because of its architectural structure and decorative composition it may be considered a masterpiece of Nasrid art.

As in other domestic-related structures, after its bent entrance, it opens up on a small courtyard with arches on pillars. The main chamber inside the tower has small alcoves with double arched windows on each of its sides.

One of the most impressive elements in this space is, without a doubt, the tiling on the baseboards that runs across the lower area of the walls; it has love designs with pieces of several colours, the most remarkable being

Interior of the *qalahurra* Torre de la Cautiva

Exterior of the Torre de las Infantas

Vault in the entrance of the Torre de las Infantas

purple, whose use on ceramic architectural elements is considered unique. Also impressive is the epigraphic cartouche that borders the upper part of the baseboards, directly related to those found in the Mirador de Lindaraja, with which they are considered masterpieces. The text is a poem by the grand vizier Ibn al-Yayyab, teacher and predecessor of another grand vizier of the dynasty, Ibn al-Khatib.

The room's plasterwork — originally polychromed — was covered with hangings or tapestries above the tiles, characteristic of Nasrid architectural decoration and found in the more impressive spaces of the Alhambra's palaces. The marble floor and the wooden ceiling date from the restoration of the tower carried out in the late 19th century.

As is typical of the traditional domestic-related structures, the rooms and a terrace on the upper floor are accessed via a narrow door in the bend in the entrance.

Torre de las Infantas

This tower's architectural structure is similar to that of the neighbouring Torre de la Cautiva and, like it, may be considered a tower-palace. However — based on the characteristics of its decoration — it belongs to a later era; specifically, it has been attributed to Sultan Muhammad VII (1392–1408). Perhaps due to this chronology, this tower has been considered to mark the beginning of the decadence of Nasrid art. However, its aesthetic design is a continuation of traditional models, having perhaps a rougher execution and less perfect proportions.

Interior of the Torre de las Infantas

Exterior of the Torre del Cabo de la Carrera.
Current state

The Torre del Agua and the aqueduct in 1862.
Photograph by Charles Clifford

The tower has the typical bent entrance with an impressive little vault of large *mocárabe* designs that still conserve some of their original colour. The inside of the tower is distributed according to the traditional design of the Nasrid house; it gives one the impression of being in any house in any area of the Alhambra instead of in a tower on a wall. The covered space corresponding to the courtyard with a central polygonal marble fountain is surrounded by the main rooms: three alcoves with windows looking outside, the most impressive at the end with the typical alhamíes (low stone bench) on the smaller sides. All the doors to the courtyard have the traditional *taqa* openings at their thresholds.

At the level of the first floor, the central space has galleries on two sides and windows on the others. The ceiling was originally covered with a *mocárabe* vault, which was lost and replaced during the last century with the current wooden frame. As in the Torre de la Cautiva, access to the upper floor and to the terrace is via a bent entrance. This tower is the scene of the well-known legend of the three princesses — Zayda, Zorayda and Zorahayda — mentioned by Washington Irving in two of the stories from his famous *Tales of the Alhambra*.

Torre del Cabo de la Carrera

After visitors have walked along the last section parallel to the wall, they come upon the so-called Torre del Cabo de la Carrera — the easternmost of the the towers on the northern wall — whose construction was commissioned by the Catholic Monarchs in 1502, according to a no-longer existing inscription. Today, the tower is practically in ruins — like most of this section of the Alhambra — due to blasting by the Napoleonic troops upon their retreat in 1812.

Torre del Agua

Most of the towers in the walled compound of the Alhambra — within their obvious differences — can be grouped according to the different functions they carried out. Some have a uniqueness that sets them entirely apart from the rest. This is the case of the Torre del Agua, one of the largest towers in the Alhambra in terms of size located in the southeast, at the far end of the compound.

Despite the fact that in the mid-20th century, only its massive base remained (as a result of the previously mentioned blasting done by Napoleon's troops), its exterior walls were reconstructed. This tower performed an essential role, as the base of its northern side marked the entrance of the Acequia del Sultán water channel which supplied water to the entire Alhambra.

The Acequia Real or Acequia del Sultán
Next to the gardens and promenades of the upper Alhambra, and integrated into the archaeological remains of the entire Secano area, we find various elements belonging to the hydraulic infrastructure of the Acequia del Sultán: anchoring devices for waterwheels, water tanks and a large aqueduct — partially reconstructed — are all witness to a small but surely very active industry in service to the court

in the most elevated area of the palace-city. It is precisely at the end of the promenade where we find an entrance to the Alhambra's water channel: a water distributor that has maintained part of its original materials — despite the Napoleonic blasting — and that is guarded by the Torre del Agua at the eastern end of the walled compound.

This is a highly modified area that today connects different areas of the monumental compound. The Generalife can be accessed directly via a large gate in the wall, in front of which a large bridge extends, all of which date from the 1970s. Visitors may also exit the Alhambra by way of this bridge.

The upper Alhambra can be reached through the inside of the compound; from here one can access Calle Real, and there are connections with the Alcazaba and the palaces made via an opening in an important element of the medieval infrastructure (although reconstructed) — the aqueduct — through which flowed the water of the Acequia Real or Acequia del Sultán into the city.

Torre del Agua. Its base is where the Acequia Real or Acequia del Sultán — which supplied the water needed by the palace-city — entered

9 The Medina

In Arabic, *medina* means city. The Alhambra's Medina comprised the upper part of Sabika Hill, two streets — Calle Real Alta and Calle Real Baja —, and other secondary streets that crossed them. Inside the Medina, houses, baths, industries and all of the typical elements any city needs were built. The Alhambra's Medina, however, was also a court city, a city planned and organised to work in the service of the sultan.

Calle Real Alta

Calle Real Alta (which means Upper Royal Street) is the backbone of the Alhambra's interior urban fabric, a space that has undergone numerous modifications over time, but that offers sites of interest to visitors. From here, visitors may head for both the Palacio de Carlos V and its exhibition areas (Alhambra Museum, Fine Arts Museum, Exhibition Halls, Bookstore/Shop, etc.) or the Alcazaba and the Generalife, all inside the compound. Visitors may also exit the palace compound from this site and, via the woods, visit the compound's surrounding areas or go down to Granada.

The name of this street obviously has its origins in the Christian era, during which the street maintained its important urban role. A Royal Decree of Grace from 1501 refers to it as Calle Mayor (Main Street), evidence of its position within the urban hierarchy.

Currently, this street helps to organise part of the visit to the monumental complex. It is also the only part of the walled compound that may be accessed — with certain restrictions — by motor vehicle.

Calle Real Alta is the main street in the Alhambra's Medina. During the first third of the 20th century, archaeological excavations began to clarify the medieval Alhambra's urban fabric, and this permitted the recovery of another important street with a similar — almost parallel — route, but at a lower level, that was called Calle Real Baja.

Calle Real Alta

It begins at the Puerta del Vino — the main entrance to the Medina — and continues its path east until reaching the Parador de San Francisco, then heads southeast in the direction of the Puerta de los Siete Suelos. Its route was probably determined by the Acequia Real or Acequia del Sultán, discovered thanks to archaeological excavations in the early 20th century. The street ascends gently until reaching the highest point on Sabika Hill where the Alhambra sits, and where the Medina was located. To the left is the area occupied by the 14th-century palaces and some public buildings such as the mosque or its hammam, replaced today by the Palacio de Carlos V and the Iglesia de Santa María de la Alhambra.

Exterior portal of the Puerta del Vino

The Medina

From the 13th to the 15th centuries — that is, the entire period of Nasrid rule — the Nasrids developed a city with all the elements required for daily life. Few traces remain of the buildings constructed there, though a series of archaeological excavations are gradually bringing more remmants to light.

❶ Calle Real Alta

This was the main street of the Alhambra, crossing the length of the compound and facilitating the connection between the different areas of the palace-city. Beginning at the Puerta del Vino and passing by the mosque, the *hammam* and other areas such as this outbuilding, it went as far as the upper *medina*.

❷ Upper Medina

During the Nasrid era, a modest neighbourhood for Nasrid craftsmen was built on the highest part of the hill — known as the Secano —, with a network of houses, workshops and streets, similar to any city in North Africa. Currently, little is left except archaeological remains that are gradually revealing part of its past.

❸ Secano

In the 19th century, the area of the upper Alhambra came to be known as the Secano, after Napoleon's troops ravaged the compound during their retreat. The area was restored over the 20th century through the excavation and repair of archaeological remains and the creation of gardens and a promenade accessing the Generalife.

❹ Tannery

During the 1930s the archaeological remains of a factory dedicated to the production of leather — a tannery — was discovered. It was located next to the Acequia Real channel in order to use the water it supplied.

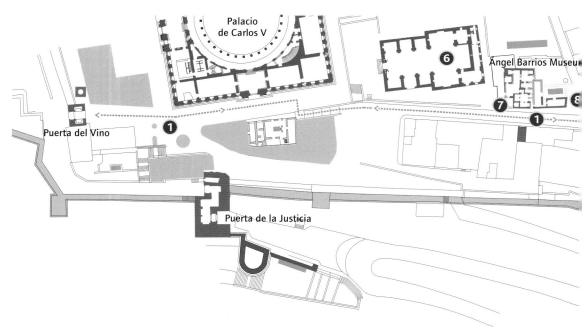

❶ Calle Real Alta   ❸ Secano   ❺ Two Nasrid houses   ❼ Baths of the mosque

❷ Upper Medina   ❹ Tannery   ❻ Santa María de la Alhambra   ❽ Nasrid house

┄┄┄> Direction of the visit

▨ Wall   ▨ Nasrid architecture   ▨ Nasrid archaeological remains   ▨ Christian architecture   ▨ Gardens

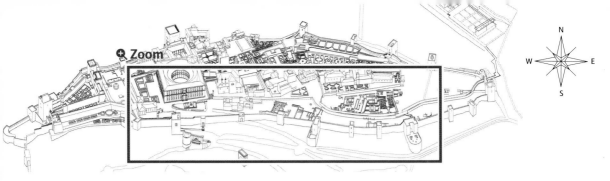

+ Zoom

5 Two Nasrid Houses

At the same time that the ruins of the tannery were discovered, very close by appeared the remains of two Nasrid houses whose design is similar to that of the palaces, one of which had a courtyard with rooms opening onto it, as well as a central water tank.

6 Santa María de la Alhambra

Built between 1581 and 1618 on the parcel of land that had been the site of the Nasrid mosque, this church has a central nave with side chapels and a large Baroque altarpiece presided over by the image of Our Lady of Sorrows.

7 Baths of the Mosque

Like all mosques in the Islamic world, the Alhambra's mosque had its own *hammam* with the necessary facilities. Although it was torn down in the 16th century, it has been reconstructed on the basis of the remains that had been preserved.

8 Nasrid House

Next to the baths of the mosque are the remains of a Nasrid noble's house preserved in good condition; it has an interior courtyard with a water tank and walls decorated with plasterwork.

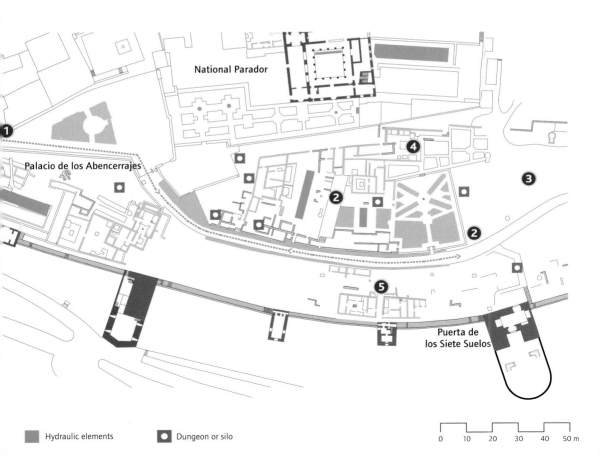

National Parador

Palacio de los Abencerrajes

Puerta de los Siete Suelos

Hydraulic elements   Dungeon or silo

0   10   20   30   40   50 m

Aerial photograph of the upper part of the Alhambra, the main area of the Medina

The area first chosen for the construction of a residential palace in the Nasrid era was located on the highest part of the hill, a typical characteristic of acropolis cities, in which those in power used this elevated position to better dominate the city. The *Dar al-Sultán's* connection to the military compound protecting it and the traditional connection to Granada were most probably achieved via the original route of Calle Real Baja, at least until the early 14th century, when Sultan Muhammad III built the first elements of the Alhambra's urban fabric. He built the Puerta del Vino — at least its western façade — and made it the main entrance to the Medina, where Calle Real Alta begins. The same sultan is credited with the creation of the mosque and the *hammam* located some 100 metres further up, marking the boundaries of the Medina and the area it occupies.

It is probable that the layout of the street depended on the Acequia Real or Acequia del Sultán water channel, which entered from the east through the upper area of the walled compound and then descended to the Puerta del Vino. Today, Calle Real Alta more or less follows its original path, and it is assumed that it would have continued on eastward. Based on archaeological studies carried out, a certain hierarchy in the route can be seen. In the northern area there is a series of installations of a semi-public nature: the mosque, its *hammam*, and a house associated with it, with the remains of other buildings integrated into modern ones currently used for the monument's services — lodging, restoration and small businesses — and to house the offices of the Council of the Alhambra.

On the southern side of the street, starting at the Puerta del Vino, residential buildings are integrated into modern constructions or scattered among the urban reconstruction that has taken place in the area.

Half-way up Calle Real Alta, a Nasrid-era outbuilding has been preserved

Reconstructed façade of a Nasrid house next to the *hammam* of the mosque

The archaeological remains of a Nasrid house discovered in 1922 opposite the southern façade of the Palacio de Carlos V has several rooms around a courtyard with a water tank. This area has undergone a number of modifications since the first third of the 16th century, when it was levelled in order to facilitate the transport of materials for the construction of the imperial palace.

Next, opposite the mosque — today the Iglesia de Santa María de la Alhambra — we find several large constructions that have been recovered thanks to a series of campaigns beginning in the middle of the 20th century. Among the cluster of buildings — whose foundations may date from medieval times — there are also urban elements positioned at a right angle to Calle Real: secondary streets — part of whose routes are still intact — and a curious outbuilding with a small pointed brick arch preserved in its interior.

At the end of the street's current route is the portal of the Convento de San Francisco — today the site of the national *parador* — in front of a landscaped *plaza* under which, in 1963, the remains of a Nasrid house with its own small baths was found, as well as a water tank, gardens and rich flooring that was a continuation of the street. On the parcel of land are remains from the Palacio de los Abencerrajes, the subject of many archaeological excavations since the early 20th century. Along with the Franciscan convent — built over a Nasrid palace — they created an urban crossroad that suggests that the road may have continued towards the southeast in the direction of the Puerta de los Siete Suelos, in a path that today is an archaeological route through the upper Alhambra. From this elevated point there is an excellent panoramic view of the Sierra Nevada, between the cypress trees trimmed into the shape of arches, designed in the 1930s to

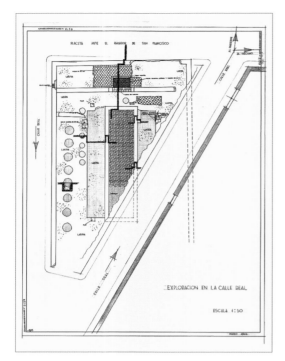

Ground plan drawn up in 1963 of a large Nasrid house on Calle Real, whose remains are today located below the garden opposite the Parador.
Alhambra Archives

Architect Leopoldo Torres Balbás recovered part of the road system of the Medina, planting cypress trees along the edges of the street that imitate building façades. In the background, the Sierra Nevada

imitate (with plants) the façades of the lost buildings facing the street and in order to be able to access the archaeological remains of the area and the adjacent gardens.

The Upper Medina

The upper Medina — located in the area known as the Secano — was probably during Nasrid times the largest area for craftsmen in the palace city, and a more modest neighbourhood in comparison with other areas which featured larger buildings and richer decorations.

Among the network of houses, workshops and narrow medieval streets whose typology coincides with that of the neighbourhoods in many North African cities a small number of constructions are conserved in the Alhambra. Modified over time by Christians their original traits disappeared, hidden in buildings used for diverse purposes for a population of a different culture that progressively eliminated their medieval appearance altogether.

In addition to the tannery, it is possible to identify various other pottery-based industries in the neighbourhood, through the remains of muffles, kilns, and large, undecorated buildings, which suggests they were used as workshops or storage places. It is necessary to remember the importance of the silk industry in Nasrid Granada, which probably had a workshop dedicated exclusively to the needs of the court. Similarly, it is possible that there was also a Nasrid mint in this area that could have survived into the Christian era: next to the remains of the Palacio de los Abencerrajes a coin was found — probably from the last Nasrid period — that was highly debased due to the unstable era in which it was minted; it reads *bi-hamrá' Garnata*, that is, "in the Alhambra of Granada." This coin is now in the Alhambra Museum.

The upper Medina of the Alhambra offers a route in which plants are integrated with the remains of different buildings, mostly from palace-related industries and handicrafts

Secano

Practically all the upper Alhambra was in an advanced state of neglect by the second half of the 19th century as a result of blasting by Napoleonic troops during their 1812 retreat, resulting in it receiving the name of Secano.

During the first third of the 20th century, archaeological explorations and repair of the remains were begun and gardens were planted – a process that culminated in the 1960s when a connection was established between the Alhambra and the Generalife in this area, leading

Secano

The Medina of the upper Alhambra was greatly modified by the new Christian inhabitants after the conquest. Several centuries later – after the retreat of the occupying Napoleonic troops in 1812 that destroyed it with artillery – the entire area was abandoned and converted into a wasteland known as the Secano. An archaeological programme aimed at removing the rubble and repairing the entire area began in the middle of the 20th century, culminating in the 1960s with the design of a promenade in the gardens that currently serves as a link to the Generalife.
Alhambra Archives

Among the remains discovered in the Medina were those of a tannery, that is, an industry dedicated to the tanning of animal skins for use by the Nasrid court

to its urbanisation. Various structures were identified from the fragments of roads, canals and walls.

A building – believed to be a large house or perhaps a palace – was discovered in the highest area; it occupied the land between the Palacio de San Francisco and the promenade of cypress trees trimmed into the shape of arches. Its nucleus consists of a large water tank in the centre of an elongated courtyard, round which several rooms were distributed. The current pergola – located above the level where the wall remains were found – suggests the existence of a perpendicular path or street, where the entrance would have been located. In front of this are the foundations of a portico or pavilion that extended into the courtyard. At the other end of the water tank are the remains of different walls that suggest the presence of a private *hammam*. All the remains identified from the Nasrid era appear hidden in walls that are similar, but from a later era,

evidence of them being reused during Christian times; part of the ovens or kilns and of other hydraulic structures found within the gardens may have belonged to the period after the conquest, or may have been reused at that time.

Tannery

Towards the east, at a somewhat lower level, the structure of a tannery or medieval leather industry was discovered in the 1930s. It was a place dedicated to the tanning of skins for a wide range of uses, a widespread trade in al-Andalus. The remains of the building in the Alhambra are small compared to the tanneries of North Africa; the traditional industries located in the upper Medina area were for the exclusive supply of the sultan's court. The tannery was located next to the Acequia Real in order to take advantage of its large water supply, essential for this type of activity. An open-air courtyard was located in the middle of the building, onto which opened

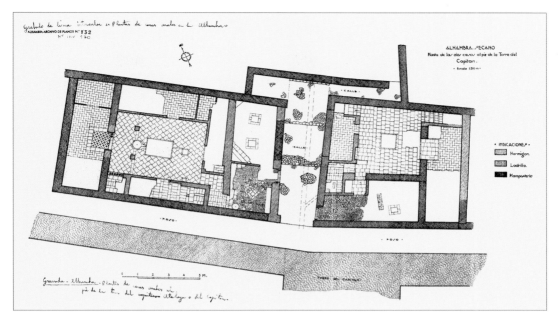

Design of two Nasrid houses located in front of the Torre del Capitán, under the Paseo de los Cipreses, and main street, drawn by Leopoldo Torres Balbás during his time as architectural curator in charge of the Alhambra, between 1923 and 1936. Alhambra Archives

several rooms with two galleries on top of brick pillars. Various water tanks of different sizes and depths and two large clay containers were the elements required for soaking and working the leather. On the ground, numerous holes were found for the distribution of water to the water tanks, whose conduits and drains have been preserved. Other service rooms are located round it, among them a latrine and other constructions possibly built at later dates.

Two Nasrid Houses

Near the tannery – but at a lower level and next to the southern section of the wall – can be identified the remains of two Nasrid houses, unearthed between 1932 and 1933. They are accessed from the steep perpendicular street that begins at the inside lane of the Calle de Ronda near the Torre del Capitán.

The westernmost house has a series of rooms grouped around a typically rectangular courtyard, in the centre of which there is a small water tank with a glazed green decorative border. The

house is accessed via a door with a stone door frame and jamb, and a hall floored with brick laid sideways. At the entrance, separate from the rooms, is a small stable with the remains of two feeding troughs. A bent corridor leads to the courtyard, onto which open the rooms and a portico with pilasters that most likely indicate the main room, at whose middle threshold is a small fountain that supplied the water tank. Part of the original clay floor tiles – some with small pieces glazed in white, green and black – remains. A very deteriorated latrine was found among the remains of the house walls, as well as what appears to be the beginning of a stairway to the upper floor.

The other house – located east of the street – is smaller and made of poorer materials. Its entrance door – located at the lower end of the street – conserves the original door frame recesses. It leads to a hall tiled with stone leading to – as in the neighbouring house – a small stable with a feed trough, which has lost the door that separated it from the entrance.

Nasrid house unearthed between 1932 and 1933 on one of the secondary streets. As usual, the rooms open onto the central courtyard

its *almatraya* (traditional flooring) without glazed floor tiles. These two houses are symbols of the importance of this space in the medieval Alhambra. Along the Calle de Ronda or del Foso, there are other constructions of this type that are still unexplored. The majority of them are domestically-related buildings, and elements of the Alhambra's urban fabric that — although built with less expensive materials and in a poorer state of conservation — are no less important to understand its past.

Alhambra Mosque

Its main description is due to the important work carried out by then architect of the Alhambra Leopoldo Torres Balbás between 1923 and 1936, although the parcel of land it was built on had been previously explored by his predecessor, Modesto Cendoya. His work was a continuation of the research carried out by Manuel Gómez-Moreno at the end of the 19th century. The mosque's central axis is located under the southern side of the current Iglesia de Santa María de la Alhambra and is duly oriented toward the southeast. At that time, only the remains buried outside the church could be explored in detail. Nevertheless, thanks to an old map by Juan de Orea, it was possible to determine the original perimeter of the mosque: towards the exterior of the church, jutting up from the ground was a third of what must have been the building, with the *qibla* wall and the base of the *mihrab*. According to this document, the southern side of the former mosque ran parallel to Calle Real, today

A square courtyard is entered via a small chamber next to the hallway and to the entrance to a latrine. In the centre of the courtyard, the remains of a square mark the site where a water tank was located, although from its small size, it may have been a basin or perhaps a fountain. From the courtyard, two stairways lead to an upper floor with its original floor tile. The remaining rooms — very irregularly shaped — have some of their clay tile flooring. The main room of the house appears to be on the eastern side of the courtyard, as it still has

The street of the Medina

Many smaller streets, alleys, corridors, outbuildings — in general, secondary — branched off from the Alhambra's main street, forming the urban fabric. Removing the rubble from the two Nasrid houses next to the Torre del Capitán — in the image — allowed the path of one of them — the one connecting Calle de Ronda with the Medina — to be recovered. There are still many remains that future archaeological explorations will bring to light, providing us with a more precise view of what the Alhambra was like.

bordered by a parapet that covers the difference between the level of the street and the parcel of land on which church is located. Following this description, the mosque would have had three naves separated by three arches of the *qibla* resting on columns nearly two metres high, "six of them of veined marble and two of white, in addition to the bases and capitals similar in their ornamentation to the style of the Caliphate." The middle nave – wider than the side naves – would have been taller and covered by a ceiling of horizontal carved panels covered with a false frame with beams. According to Torres Balbás, the side naves were covered with hanging reinforcements, while the roof had large glazed tiles. The minaret of the mosque – tall and slender – was located at the western end. According to this description, the building may have resembled the oratory in the Almohad Madraza of Tlemcen. Fourteenth-century vizier Ibn

al-Khatib stated that Muhammad III (1302–1309) commissioned the Alhambra's mosque towards the end of his reign. In 1492, with the Christian conquest, it was converted into a church, and was the headquarters of the diocese while the nearby Convento de San Francisco was being built. With its importance reduced to that of a simple parish, by the end of the 16th century it was practically in ruins and some repair work was undertaken to prevent it from collapsing. The inevitable razing took place in October of 1576, and the construction of a new church was subsequently begun.

Few decorative remains of the Muslim building have been preserved. The most significant is a bronze lamp that belonged to Cardinal Cisneros, whose epigraphic decoration dates the completion of the mosque to 1305. It is currently conserved in the National Archaeological Museum in Madrid with a replica found in the Alhambra Museum.

There are few remains left of the Alhambra's mosque. One of these is the lamp now housed in the National Archaeological Museum in Madrid, a replica of which is located in the Alhambra Museum

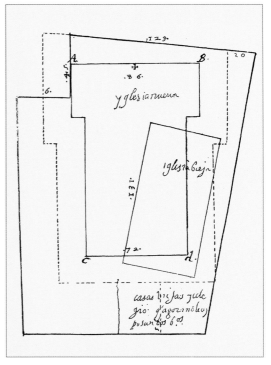

Fragment of a floor plan drawn up by Juan de Orea around 1580 with the location of the Alhambra's new church and the site of the mosque, the latter drawn by **Juan de Herrera.** Archives of the Royal Chapel of Granada

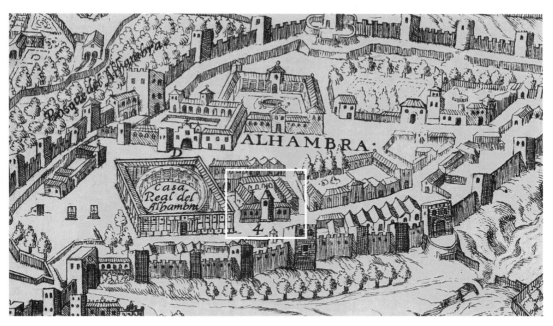

Detail of *Platform* by Ambrosio Vico with the representation of the mosque (ca. 1614). Alhambra Library

Iglesia de Santa María de la Alhambra

This Christian temple was built between 1581 and 1618, with modifications by architect Ambrosio Vico based on the sketches by Juan de Herrera and Juan de Orea. Its nave is surrounded by side chapels highlighting the large Baroque altarpiece of wreathed columns dating back to 1671 that flank the main image — Our Lady of Sorrows — carved by Torcuato Ruiz del Peral between 1750 and 1760. The crucifixion image is also impressive, as are the large images of Saints Ursula and Susan by sculptor Alonso de Mena. The popular image of the Virgin is carried in a procession every year during Holy Week atop one of the most beautiful thrones in Granada, which is a reproduction in embossed silver of the arcades in the Patio de los Leones. Federico García Lorca was a member of this religious brotherhood.

Baths of the Mosque

Steam baths or *hammam* are characteristic elements of Islamic culture. Using them was an act of purification that served as the ablutions required before praying, and so these baths are frequently found near — or even form a part of — mosques; many public baths are incorporated into mosques as a way of maintaining them economically.

The use of these baths, however, is not only for religious purification; they are also places for personal hygiene and frequently serve as places for socialising. They are believed to have positive health properties due to their warm environment that results in perspiration and cleanliness from alternating hot and cold baths.

These baths — whose original entrance was from Calle Real — were built for those worshipping in the mosque adjacent to it, today the site of the Iglesia de Santa María de la Alhambra. Hidden within the walls of a house built between the 17th and 18th centuries, their restoration began in 1934. Although there is evidence that they were demolished in 1534, enough remains were found for them to be reconstructed, such as the bases of the vaults, the lantern (a windowed

Main altar of the Iglesia de Santa María de la Alhambra

Two images of the interior of the *hammam* located next to the mosque

tower built into the ceiling), fragments of tiling, plasterwork and part of the marble flooring. In the preserved structure of the baths it is possible to distinguish various rooms: the rest area — or *bayt al-maslaj* — with its central *lantern* and a layout similar to the baths in the Palacio de Comares. There are also *mastabas* — elevated benches — separated by double horseshoe arches; the transition to a cold room — or *bayt al-barid* — with a truncated vault; a hot room — or *bayt al-sajun* — which is rectangular with side rooms and in which only one bathing pool is currently found, although there probably was another, where a modern water fountain is located; and

The Ángel Barrios Museum

Dedicated to the Granada-born composer and guitarist Ángel Barrios (1882–1964), this museum was created in 1975 on the initiative of the Council of the Alhambra and thanks to a donation from his daughter Ángela Barrios. It is located next to the Iglesia de Santa María de la Alhambra, in the small building also known as Baño del Polinario. It consists of three small rooms in which paintings — signed and dedicated by his friends and members of the social and literary group meetings that took place here — from the musician's private collection are exhibited. There are also personal objects such as correspondence with other writers such as Antonio Machado and Federico García Lorca, several original music scores and other documents by the intelligentsia of the era who passed through the Alhambra and stopped in at the tavern run by the musician's father, who was known as "Polinario." Entrance into the museum is included in the general admission and in the admission to the gardens. In the image, a portrait of Ángel Barrios by Manuel Ángeles Ortiz.

Courtyard of the Nasrid house on Calle Real located next to the baths of the Mosque

finally, the boiler area — *al-burma* — would have been in an area parallel to this, attached behind the hot room, probably adjacent to the storeroom for the firewood and having an entrance that was separate from the rest of the baths.

Like the former mosque, they date back to the era of Sultan Muhammad III (1302–1309), and underwent significant modifications beginning in the 16th century.

The Ángel Barrios Museum

In the 19th century, the baths were part of the structure of one of the neighbourhood taverns — known as the "Casa del Polinario" — which was a meeting place for artists and intellectuals of the era who, after visiting the Alhambra, would stop by to have a rest. Among his many talents, owner Antonio Barrios — popularly known as "Polinario" — was a polyfacetic guitar player and great fan of flamenco music, and father of musician and composer Ángel Barrios. For this reason, the Alhambra has made room for this small museum space dedicated to the musician and to his times.

House Next to the Baths

Next to the baths of the mosque and connected to it via the wall of the façade facing Calle Real, are the remains of part of a Nasrid noble's house. It has an interior courtyard with a water tank, and its façade still features a large part of its original plasterwork decoration. To the south, a room opens onto the courtyard. The entrance to the house no longer exists, although it currently shares the entrance corridor to the baths, and historians believed it to be part of the same structure.

Behind the courtyard are some impressive remains of foundations of what must have been an extension to the building. Next to the parcel of land occupied by both buildings — in the so-called Huerta de Santa María — there is a large water tank oriented similarly to that of the baths and the mosque, suggesting that it may have been part of the same structure.

Archaeological Map of the Nasrid Alhambra

This map by the Council's Conservation Department has been drawn up using documentation obtained over the latest decades of archaeological research in the Alhambra. To create it, the buildings and urban elements built after the 15th century have been eliminated, which allows us to have a more accurate idea of what the Nasrid palace-city might have looked like, as documented by archaeological activities.

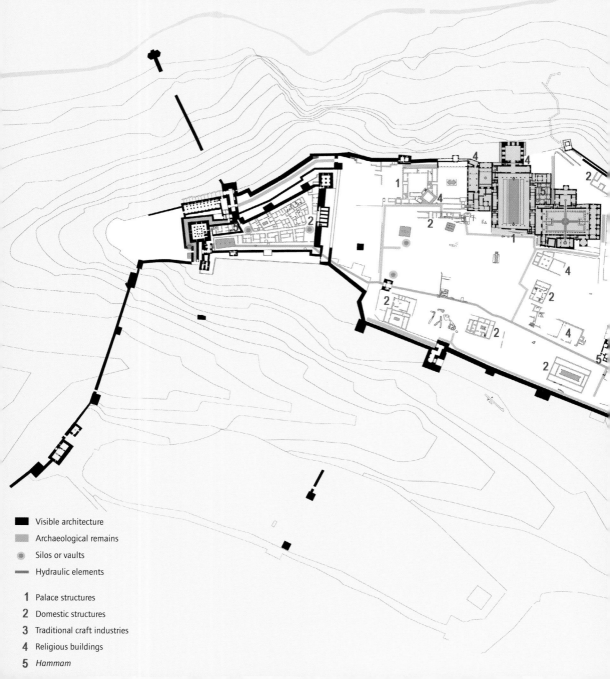

■ Visible architecture

▨ Archaeological remains

◉ Silos or vaults

▬ Hydraulic elements

1 Palace structures

2 Domestic structures

3 Traditional craft industries

4 Religious buildings

5 *Hammam*

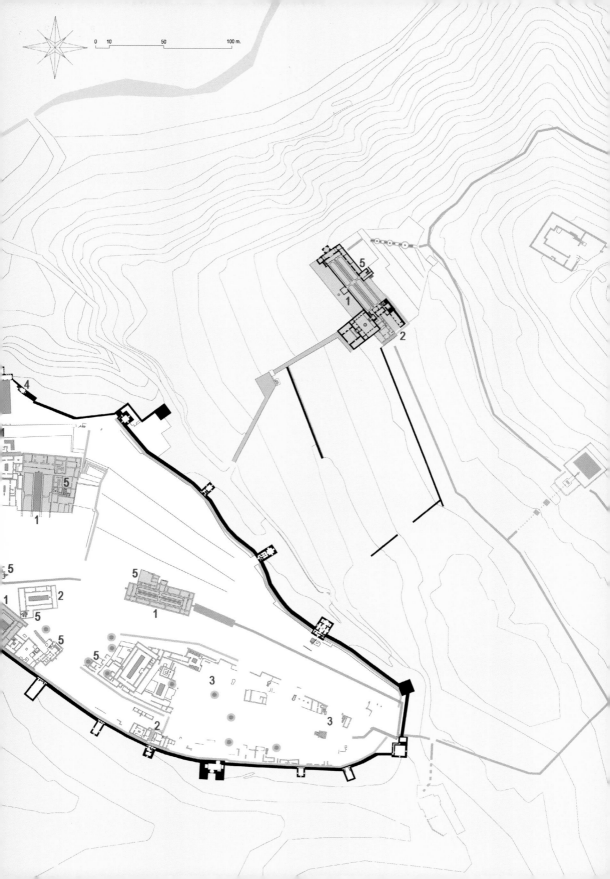

10 The Generalife

Beyond the walls of the Alhambra, to the east on the slope of the Cerro del Sol, lies the Generalife, a country estate belonging to the Nasrid sultans that was also used for agricultural production. During medieval times, it had at least four market gardens; the residence was a palace that vizier Ibn al–Yayyab called the Casa Real de la Felicidad or Royal Palace of Happiness. The relationship between the Alhambra and this country estate has always been close, so much so that the evolution of one cannot be understood independently of the development of the other.

The Nasrid sultans had large country estates — or *almunias* — scattered across their territory. An *almunia* was an estate whose purpose was basically farming and, by extension, raising livestock. *Almunias* always included a house, a cottage or a pavilion used for respite. When the estate was very large and extensive, there was also an outbuilding for the temporary residents or field workers; in Andalusia this model has developed into different types of farmhouses known as *alquerías, cortijos* and *caserías*. The Generalife's *almunia* is the country estate nearest to the palace-city of the Alhambra and, therefore, perhaps the most important. In medieval times, it contained at least four large market gardens and a large building that more than a residence is a palace, called by poet and vizier Ibn al-Yayyab in his Arabic ornamental inscriptions the *Dar al-Mamlaka al-Sa'ida*. The entire estate is irrigated by the Acequia Real, the same channel that provides water to the Alhambra.

The relationship between both compounds has always been close, so close that the evolution of one cannot be understood without that of the other. Even today, the institution responsible for its conservation is known as the Council of the Alhambra and Generalife.

The *Yannat al-Arif* or "architect's garden" — like the palace-related spaces of the Alhambra — is the result of remodelling and additions carried out by different sultans. Based on its oldest decorative elements, the palace was most likely built around the end of the 13th century by the second sultan of the Nasrid dynasty, Muhammad II (1273–1302), and was remodelled by Isma'il after 1319, and — just as in the Alhambra — there is evidence of work by Muhammad V, the great builder who actually happened to be in the Generalife when he was informed of the conspiracy to assassinate him, allowing him to escape. Lastly, in the 15th century, Yusuf III did the final remodelling in the southern section of the palace.

Located at the foot of a mountainous elevation known as the Cerro del Sol, it is separated from the Alhambra by a ravine and is an independent compound, although its visit is combined with that of the Alhambra.

Legal Dispute over Property Ownership
When the Catholic Monarchs took possession of the city in 1492, they reserved the most outstanding spaces of the Alhambra for themselves and distributed the rest among the nobles of the court, leaders of the army, members of the clergy, and soldiers in general. Something similar happened with the Generalife country estate. After it was ceded to several of the kingdom's commanders, in 1539 it passed as a dowry into the hands of Pedro de Granada Venegas, member of an illustrious family of Moorish converts with historical ties to the Nasrid dynasty. In December of 1555, Phillip II issued Royal Decrees of Graces awarding the governorship of the Generalife and the tenancy of the estate to the family's heirs in perpetuity. The

Patio de la Acequia in the Palacio del Generalife

The Generalife

This country estate or country palace commissioned by Muhammad II at the end of the 13th century is located outside the walled compound, but is close enough to reach on foot. Situated in an area above the Alhambra, it is surrounded by market gardens which are still cultivated using traditional agricultural methods passed down from generation to generation. The palace — built at various levels to adapt to the land and surrounded by gardens and irrigation channels — is where the Nasrid sultans went when they wanted to rest.

❶ Jardines Nuevos

Since 1930, these gardens were planted in the area connecting the Alhambra to the Generalife with the aim of facilitating travel between the market gardens in the different compounds. There is also an open-air theatre that has been the site of the Granada International Festival of Music and Dance since 1952.

❷ Las Huertas

In addition to being a country estate, the Generalife was used for the production of agricultural products for use by the court. There were market gardens, orchards and pastures for livestock. It is interesting to examine the species that are still cultivated today in these market gardens.

❸ Palacio del Generalife

Referred to as the Casa Real de la Alegría by vizier Ibn al-Yayyab, its structure is similar to that of the other Nasrid palaces in the Alhambra. It has a large rectangular courtyard with a water channel flanked by gardens; on its shorter sides are arched porticoes leading to the palace's rooms.

❹ Patio de la Acequia

This cross platform courtyard with gardened parterres along the sides is presided over by a lengthwise water channel through which runs the Acequia Real and has crossed water spouts that give it a unique appearance. Originally it was a closed courtyard, but a corridor-balcony was installed on its western wall looking towards the Alhambra.

❺ Pabellón Sur

Located on one of the smaller sides of the pavilion is a two-storey building that has been considerably modified from its initial layout. The ground floor has a façade with seven open areas. The middle of the area upstairs has been converted into a balcony opening on to the courtyard.

❻ Patio del Ciprés de la Sultana

Of the initial layout of the Patio del Ciprés de la Sultana, the only thing left is the Water Stairway of the Acequia Real and a section of its path to the palace. Its first Moorish owners tried to eliminate the Nasrid style of the courtyard, adding a U-shaped pool with over thirty water spouts and a number of flower beds.

🔍 Zoom

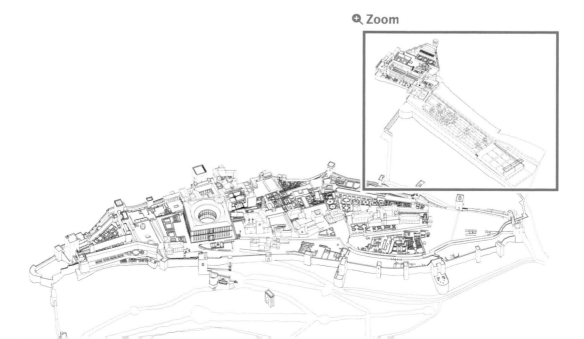

7 Jardines Altos

Facing the gallery that encloses the northern side of the Patio del Ciprés de la Sultana, in the 19th century a wide, steep area was upgraded and arranged in terraces that mark the boundary of the Generalife estate. Its romantic gardens offer breathtaking views of the surrounding area.

8 Escalera del Agua

The Water Stairway is one of the most special elements in the compound. It is a four-flight staircase with three intermediate landings and a laurel vault whose railing consists of a short wall with small channels on top through which water flows from the Acequia Real.

9 Casa de los Amigos

The remains of the guest house adjacent to the palace and connected to the Southern Pavilion belong to a house laid out around two courtyards on different levels. It was named for its similarity to a 14th century text in which it was suggested that a house be built for friends.

10 Paseo de las Adelfas

This lovely plant-lined road running through the upper area of the Generalife has hundred year-old cypresses, oleanders that give it its name and — most importantly — the Moorish myrtle, considered to be a heritage variety native to the Alhambra that has been grown in the Generalife since medieval times.

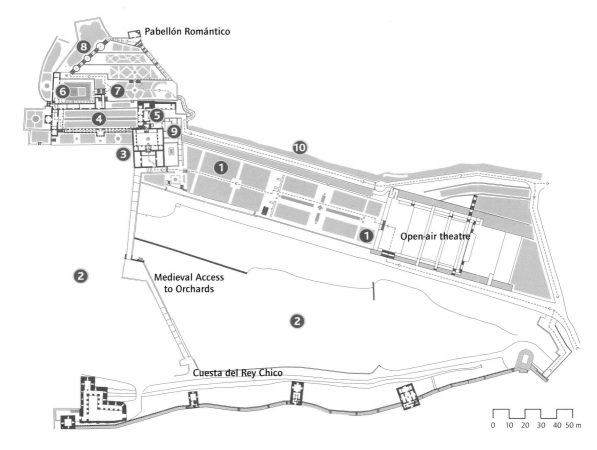

Pabellón Romántico

Open-air theatre

Medieval Access to Orchards

Cuesta del Rey Chico

0 10 20 30 40 50 m

| 1 | Jardines Nuevos | 3 | Palacio del Generalife | 5 | Pabellón Sur | 7 | Jardines Altos | 9 | Casa de los Amigos |
| 2 | Las Huertas | 4 | Patio de la Acequia | 6 | Patio del Ciprés de la Sultana | 8 | Escalera del Agua | 10 | Paseo de las Adelfas |

------ > Direction of the visit

 Wall   Nasrid architecture   Christian architecture   Gardens    Hydraulic elements

View of the Generalife estate from the Alhambra

Crown never exercised its rights to the property, believing that only the use of the palace and its annexes had been granted to the governor, until 1826, when the private property legal advisor to King Ferdinand VII initiated a legal process known as the Generalife Lawsuit. This lawsuit lasted almost an entire century and pitted the Spanish state against the heirs of the Granada-Venegas line — the Marquesses of Campotéjar — to whom the tenancy of the Generalife and its governorship belonged as a result of the marriages and successions of the Italian houses of Durazzo and Pallavicini. They likewise held the title — which was also linked to the Grimaldi line — when the suit began and throughout its duration.

After ninety-five years of numerous proceedings and appeals, the lawsuit came to an end on 2 October 1921 via an out-of-court settlement that established its incorporation into the national heritage and tied its management to that of the Alhambra by means of a Council.

This country estate has been visited throughout its history by authorities and distinguished personalities that have contributed to creating its Moorish legend including Venetian Ambassador Andrea Navaggero in 1526, botanist Carolus Clusius in 1564, fable writer Ginés Pérez de Hita in 1595, diplomat and writer François Bertaut in 1659, English architect James C. Murphy at the beginning of the

19th century, French Romantic writers Théophile Gautier and Alexandre Dumas, Valencia native painter Joaquín Sorolla in the early 20th century, and poet Juan Ramón Jiménez, winner of the 1956 Nobel Prize in Literature, who wrote one of the most lyrical pages about the Generalife – included in his work entitled *Olvidos de Granada* – in which he made clear the fascination produced by his visit during the summer of 1924 with his wife Zenobia Camprubí, hosted by members of the families of Federico García Lorca and Manuel de Falla.

The visit to this section of the monumental complex begins in the so-called Jardines Nuevos of the Generalife.

Jardines Nuevos

When the Generalife was incorporated into the Alhambra, the monument's curators designed a strategy to connect both compounds in a way that would keep the formal relation and facilitate movement between them through the use of gardens integrated into nature. Thus, in the nearest part of the estate – occupied by an old olive grove – they created gardens in the 1930s and 40s that increased the compound's landscaped assets. The sequence encountered upon entering the Generalife is as follows: the open-air theatre, the garden of the water channel and the rosebush labyrinth, whose path to the palace residence allows visitors to observe – from above and from different perspectives – part of the estate's medieval gardens, with the panorama of the Alhambra and Granada in the background.

The open-air theatre was installed among the gardens in 1952 for the Granada International Festival of Music and Dance, celebrated each year at the beginning of the summer. It was recently remodelled so that other performances could take place there. It reopened in July 2005 for the 54th edition of the Festival.

Open-air theatre in the Jardines Nuevos of the Generalife

The nearest garden was created in 1951 by architect Francisco Prieto Moreno, based on the cross-platform gardens of Neo-Islamic inspiration, between walls of cypresses, with a central pool, fountains and a pergola opening onto the Alhambra, as well as other ornamental trees and shrubs. The rose labyrinth — lying between the parterres with seasonal blooming flowers — was created in 1931 by architect Leopoldo Torres Balbás as an antechamber to the palace buildings of the Generalife.

For a better understanding of the context in which these gardens were created and their intelligent relationship with the architecture and the landscape that existed here, see the *Alhambra Manifesto*, a theoretical document written in 1953 by a select group of architects and heritage experts.

Las Huertas

Since the 14th century, the Generalife has continued to use in its market gardens the traditional agricultural techniques applied and transmitted without interruption down the ages, adding an anthropological value to its historical and artistic value and making the Generalife an exceptional compound with a cultural heritage that has remained virtually intact for centuries, something truly extraordinary in this day and age.

The name Generalife — "market garden" or "estate of the architect" — is an indication of the purpose for which the Nasrids wanted to use their *almunia*: farming, focusing on the cultivation of garden products and fruit trees as well as providing pastures for selected livestock. This is why they gave the name Casa de la Felicidad to the country estate — also surrounded by gardens — using the same name for the entire estate, in that duality so characteristic of Islamic culture. The estate, located outside the walls of the city of the Alhambra, was crossed longitudinally by the Acequia Real which, together with a series of water tanks and other hydraulic elements, made possible the maintenance of the large market gardens and numerous fruit and ornamental trees located around the palace, as well as the private gardens inside. Probably around the end of the 13th century, the water channel was partially diverted into a smaller channel (the Acequia del Tercio) several kilometres before it entered the Generalife — in order to irrigate more land. Due to its location on sloping ground, most of the estate's perimeter is enclosed, and it is laid out in *paratas* or terraces by means of large retaining walls that have survived for more than seven centuries since their creation. The buildings are located in the upper part of the property, on the edge of the slope that descends steeply towards

The market gardens of the Generalife

Although it was considered a recreational estate, its rustic style, the availability of irrigation and the need for products for consumption by the court resulted in the areas between the Alhambra and the Generalife palace being cultivated for agricultural purposes. These gardens have been worked with the same system of cultivation from the 14th century until today, passed down from generation to generation, from father to son, maintaining the traditional techniques used in the era of the sultans. It is interesting to examine the different species being grown and their origin. Similarly, the original rammed earth walls have been maintained — virtually without alterations — on the stepped terraces.

Central fountain and water canal of the Jardines Nuevos

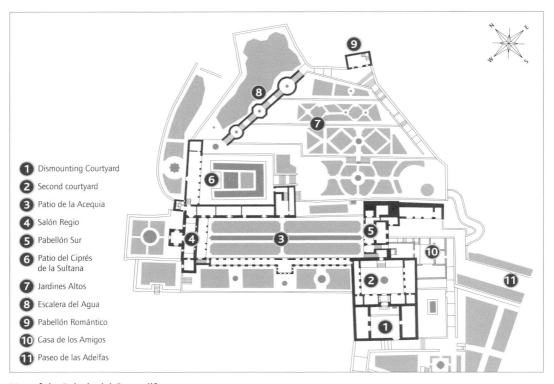

1. Dismounting Courtyard
2. Second courtyard
3. Patio de la Acequia
4. Salón Regio
5. Pabellón Sur
6. Patio del Ciprés de la Sultana
7. Jardines Altos
8. Escalera del Agua
9. Pabellón Romántico
10. Casa de los Amigos
11. Paseo de las Adelfas

Map of the Palacio del Generalife

the Darro River. The channel irrigated an area of over seven hectares of market gardens, which have been named Grande, Colorada, Mercería and Fuente Peña, and which – to a greater or lesser extent – have continued under cultivation since medieval times. In these groves – and in other surrounding lands that were used to supply the court – fruit and vegetables were cultivated year-round in order to avoid dependence on other markets. The varieties that were introduced or spread by the Islamic culture in al-Andalus are indicated with an*:

Vegetables and legumes: chard, spinach*, leeks, carrots, cabbage, cauliflower, artichokes*, fava beans, lettuce, radishes, eggplant, pumpkins, zucchinis, cucumbers, onions, French beans, watermelons*, melons*, etc.

Fruit trees: pomegranates*, fig trees, grape vines, olive trees, apple trees, pear trees, quince trees, persimmon trees, mulberry trees*, loquat trees, Mediterranean medlar trees, Chinese date trees, the so-called "strawberry tree" (*Arbutus unedo*), apricot trees, peach trees*, cherry trees, plum trees, lemon trees*, etc.

Nut trees: hazelnut trees, walnut trees, almond trees*, umbrella pine trees, etc.

Aromatic and seasoning herbs: basil, oregano, fennel, mint, thyme, cumin, coriander, lemon balm, wormwood, etc.

Access

The Generalife *almunia* had various exterior entrances during the Middle Ages. One of them – the Cuesta del Rey Chico – was more important than the rest, as it allowed for direct connection with the Alhambra via a ravine that separated the two. This steep road has maintained its original two-section route – onto which open different gates leading to the gardens – with a courtyard having a watering trough for animals between the sections. It begins in front of the bastion of the Puerta de Hierro, at the foot of the Torre de los Picos and ascends between the market gardens,

Access to the Generalife palace between the market gardens

Portal separating the two entrance courtyards

protected by high walls, until reaching the entrance door to the building, the same door that visitors use today to begin their visit to the palace.

Palacio del Generalife

The palace is entered via two successive courtyards at different levels, reminiscent of the palace area of the Alhambra, with its two courtyards before entering the Mexuar. The first of these courtyards is known as the Patio Apeadero or the Patio de las Caballerizas. Its perimeter is lined with benches used for dismounting from horses after entering via the market gardens. It is for this reason that the bays that enclose the courtyard to the north and south served as stables on the lower level and as living quarters or haylofts on the upper storey. Documents from 1580 mention repair work on the buildings, which must have been in a ruinous state by the 19th century. This was accentuated by the disuse of this access at the expense of the new entrance on the route along the upper

section. With the estate now the property of the government, beginning in the first third of the 20th century, explorations and repairs were carried out that allowed the pillar and most of the main portal to be recovered. This portal is located in the middle of the façade, highlighted by the raised area before it and the cutaway framing the arch whose keystone still displays the ceramic remains of the traditional key and the original wall paint that imitates red brick with white joints. The gate – with benches inside for the guards and a windowed chamber above them, with all probability used to monitor and defend the entrance – leads to a second courtyard. This courtyard has porticoed galleries and a central fountain, along with a steep stairway and a portal framed with pieces of marble and a ceramic lintel that repeats the key motif and indicates the main entrance to the residence. Behind it, a small dark passageway with a bench for the guards serves as the beginning of a steep and narrow stairway leading inside the palace; this

Gallery and northern portico of the Patio de la Acequia
Originally, the Generalife's Patio de la Acequia was enclosed by a wall to preserve the privacy of this unique site, considered to be an "enclosed paradise." However, at the western wall, an outward-facing open pavilion offering stunning views was built over the market gardens. Toward the interior, a small section of the original façade — higher than the others — is preserved, with a portal that still has a large part of its medieval plasterwork. The most radical modification to this side of the courtyard occurred at the end of the 15th century when the entire side wall was lowered and an open passage running along its entire length was added, transforming the medieval closed garden into a belvedere that faced the landscape. In the image, it is possible to see the small part of medieval wall that was preserved where it meets the northern portico of the courtyard.

layout is also reminiscent of the bent access to the Nasrid Palacio de Comares, and is evidence of a deeply-rooted pre-established ritual: an entrance hall with benches for guards whose only opening is the door, an angled and ascending passageway opening on to an open-air courtyard or garden, exactly like the entrance to the Generalife.

Patio de la Acequia
The Patio de la Acequia — also called the Patio de la Ría during the 19th century — is accessed from the

side. It is an elongated space, crossed lengthways by the Acequia Real or Acequia del Sultán in its centre, making it a cross platform courtyard, with four orthogonal parterres on the level beneath the platforms bordering its perimeter. Its original design was discovered and recovered following a fire that occurred in 1958 affecting the houses located to its north. Once rubble was removed from the courtyard, a roundabout-like *plaza* was discovered on the axis of the four original gardens that were irrigated by clay and lead pipes embedded in the

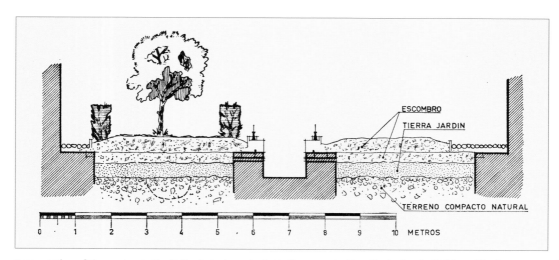

Cross-section of the garden in the Patio de la Acequia that allows one to identify the level of fill found in the excavations carried out following the fire of 1958. Alhambra Archives

Patio de la Acequia and the northern pavilion of the palace

Central pavilion of the palace with views of the market gardens

walls surrounding the channel, through which water entered and rose to the level of the channel in order to flood the parterres. The gardens have been recently restored; analyses of the pollens and the plant beds and comparative studies of the medieval agronomy have been carried out and these have led to their current layout: the hedge of myrtles at the edges on a background of a field of flowers belonging to different small species (rosebushes and aromatic plants), ornamental varieties (laurel, ivy and jasmine) as well as fruit trees (pomegranate trees and orange trees).

The medieval hydraulic system was modernised at an unknown date, using the crossed spouts that have made the courtyard so popular and whose image has been established in the Romantic engravings and through the generalised use of photography beginning in the 19th century.

The Nasrid Patio de la Acequia was closed to the outside scenery, and it was only possible to look out from the small observation balcony located along its axis. The windows in this balcony have a very low ledge so that one may see the view while sitting on the floor, as was the custom in the Islamic culture of the time. The interior decoration demonstrates a curious overlapping of the plasterwork – evidence of the renovations done over the first third of the 14th century – discovered when the chapel that was here was dismantled when the Generalife became public property.

This entire side section of the courtyard was enclosed by a wall with a hanging eave, all of which had been reduced in height except at the ends, which still display some of its original decoration. The narrow passageway that preceded it was added during the Christian era, judging from the emblems of the Catholic Monarch painted on the intrados of the arches built in the walls, converting what had been an interior oasis into a garden that served as a *mirador*.

Open corridor of the Patio de la Acequia leading to the Alhambra

passageway between them, aligned with the cross platform. The houses — severely affected by the fire of 1958 — had a ground and an upper floor, in a layout similar to that of the Palacio de Comares in the Alhambra; during the restoration work after the fire, a stairway was discovered that leads to a lower level that, as in other similar compounds, suggests that it was an access to a *hammam* or steam bath.

The appearance of this courtyard has changed over time as it was adapted to the mores of *ars topiaria* or the art of ornamental gardening. Many drawings, engravings and photographs have been conserved that illustrate this evolution, in which the development of the architectural work with cypress trees is noteworthy.

Salón Regio

In keeping with the Nasrid architectural tradition, the main structure of the residence is located at the front of the courtyard. The Salón Regio is preceded by a portico of five arches, whose middle arch is the biggest. This gallery, covered with *taujel* — an architectural device using strips of wood — filled with small symmetrical octagonal domes, has traditional *alhamíes* (tile-covered stone benches) slightly raised off the floor that owing to their size resemble cupboards. The portico and the hall are connected via a triple arch with columns and capitals of plaster *mocárabe* and with the typical *taqas* — in this case rectangular in shape — in the wall ends. The upper part of the left *taqa* has this epigraphic inscription in kufic-style Arabic calligraphy: "Enter with sense, express knowledge, be frugal with words and leave in peace." The axis of the hall is not centred with respect to the

Under the gallery of the courtyard was the lower garden, terraced, with hexagonal fountains and myrtle shrubs, described by Andrea Navaggero as "an even meadow," confirming its age. It was remodelled in the 16th and 19th centuries.

On the other long side of the courtyard can be seen two houses and a high garden with a

Detail of the overlaying of plasterwork from two different eras in the central pavilion
On the north side of the Patio de la Acequia — as in other palaces of the Alhambra — is a porticoed pavilion with five arches and rooms at the sides, before the entrance to the Salón Regio and the Isma'il I's Mirador. As in other sites in the Alhambra, there are plasterwork decorations, *mocárabes* and *taqas* and — as was typical of this era — each sultan remodelled the palaces in order to adapt them to his own particular likings or needs.

Interior pavilion of the Torre de Isma'il

Southern Pavilion of the Palacio del Generalife

courtyard, probably due to the remodelling done in the second half of the 14th century, although the main remodelling work in this area — the addition of the *mirador* tower in the middle, extending the large hall to the traditional inverted T shape — was carried out by Sultan Isma'il I after the Nasrid victory over the Castilians on 26 June 1319.

This battle — known as the Battle of the Vega or of the Sierra Elvira and vital to the survival of the Nasrid state — was considered by Arab historians as a great Islamic triumph over Christianity that occurred in spite of the difference in the number of Muslim and Christian troops, with the latter having the advantage; in this battle Don Juan and Don Pedro — advisers to King Alfonso XI — were killed.

The Salón Regio is covered with a magnificent interlaced wooden ceiling that appears to be supported by a frilled cornice of *mocárabe* round its entire perimeter. As is typical, the side rooms

enlarge the room at the ends with — in this case — the unique characteristic that the arches on pillars and half columns dividing it do not reach the floor, perhaps indicating the height of their corresponding platform. The upper floor was added to the medieval building — enlarged by the Catholic Monarchs in 1494 — along with an extensive open gallery that altered the entire complex and gave it its current architectural appearance.

This transformation meant the destruction of the *mirador* pavilion that jutted out from the western end, an oft-repeated architectural device in Nasrid architecture like the one that can be seen — among other examples — in the Palacio del Pórtico del Partal in the Alhambra.

Pabellón Sur

The area directly opposite the courtyard — known as the Pabellón Sur — has been considerably altered by many remodelling projects. On

Inside the palace's Salón Regio

the ground floor, its façade has a symmetrical composition with seven open spaces and a portico or pavilion that may originally have had a single arch, in consonance with the front pavilion. Today, it is divided into three arches that had been reused and have disproportionate capitals that may have come from the palace's *hammam*. The open spaces surrounding it lead to the back section, while the ends are used for the doors that led to the stairways, one leading to the upper levels and the other leading down to the entrance courtyards that today are used to access the palace. The middle pavilion must have had a building above it, similar to the two in the Palacio de los Leones in the Alhambra. It was converted during the first third of the 20th century into an open *mirador* above the courtyard, extending the wide hall of the floor above it, the result of the early 15th-century remodelling carried out under Yusuf III.

Patio del Ciprés de la Sultana

The remaining annexes of the palace have been significantly modified. Beginning in the 16th century, the property was remodelled to suit the tastes of the rulers — from Moorish converts to Renaissance lords. This can be seen especially in the Patio del Ciprés de la Sultana, which is accessed via a recently-recovered stairway that had been hidden by the last renovations of the 19th century.

The scene of late-16th century Romantic legends about love by Ginés Pérez de Hita, the courtyard has a very different appearance from

Patio del Ciprés de la Sultana at the end of the 19th century. Photograph by Ayola (1863-1900)

how it must have looked in medieval times, with only the cascade from the Acequia Real and a section of its path in the direction of the palace surviving from that era. A large water channel located at this point — along with other evidence — encouraged the hypothesis that the palace's *hammam* may have been located here

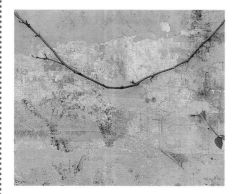

Detail of the remains of a wall painting from the Patio del Ciprés de la Sultana

The Patio del Ciprés de la Sultana is the area in the original palace of the Generalife that has undergone the most modifications. Currently, it stands more than three metres higher than its oldest level on record, and this was done in order to install in it a garden that is as different to the nearby Nasrid garden as it is to the architecture surrounding it. The wall at the eastern side of the Patio de la Acequia was reconstructed during the early 16th century. After the fire of 1958, it was restored and two coins from 1604 — the era of Phillip III — appeared from among the materials that had been used to build it. Some remains of a wall painting with *Costumbrista* images of gardens also came to light.

and been torn down by the new Moorish owners in order to hide this symbol of their Islamic past. This may be why the courtyard was decorated with a garden and a U-shaped water tank with over thirty water spouts; this is the setting which in 1526 served as the meeting place for Catalonian poet and translator Juan Boscán and Venetian ambassador Andrea Navaggero. To the north, the courtyard is closed off with a wide gallery having an upper floor similar to a gazebo, built between 1584 and 1586. The side of the courtyard bordering the Nasrid palace was the most affected by the fire of 1958 and, when it was repaired, the remains of wall decorations came to light, perhaps evidence of remodelling done around 1604.

Jardines Altos

Opposite the gallery, a portal was designed in the 19th century with a steep stairway used to reach what are known as the Jardines Altos del Generalife, a large, sloping area distributed across *paratas* that was landscaped in the style popular during the 19th century. Its lower terrace – perhaps containing fruit trees – may have originally looked out over the Patio de la Acequia. These gardens complete the residential area of the Generalife, where they serve as a boundary

in its most elevated area and have the most remarkable orientation and panoramic views in the entire estate.

Escalera del Agua

Despite all the modifications, one of the most unique and celebrated elements in the Generalife has been preserved among the terraces: the Escalera del Agua. Laid out in four sections, with three intermediate landings, the stairway gradually ascends upward under a vault of laurels, between walls on top of which flow water channels from the Acequia Real, creating with its murmuring sound an environment of tranquillity and meditation. The stairway ends at the highest point of the estate where, in 1836, its administrator erected a Romantic balcony, probably on top of a Muslim oratory. Thus, the path of the stairway would provide the Believer – perhaps the sultan himself – with both the symbolic and ritual ablutions.

The lower area of the gardens is separated from the Generalife's palace by a narrow alley – practically a trench – that possibly served as access for providing firewood to the *hammam*. The separation between the residential zone and the adjacent market gardens is marked with a simple rammed earth wall adapted to the

The Escalera del Agua from the Nasrid era, which probably led to an oratory

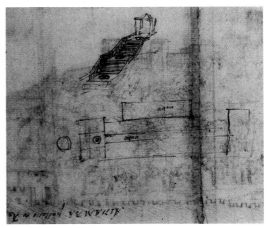

Detail of the drawing by Anton van der Wyngaerde with the representation of the design of the Palacio del Generalife and the Escalera del Agua (1571). ÖNB, Vienna

Courtyard of the Casa de los Amigos in the Generalife

(Book of Agriculture), established the way in which labourers' houses should be constructed — came to light. It describes — with a surprising resemblance to the Generalife — the different structures that these compounds should include: "[...] on the lower level shall be built a room for friends and guests, with a separate door and a small water tank hidden by trees from the view of those above [...]." Ibn Luyún visited the Nasrid court during an era when the Generalife was already established as a farm, and on whose remodelling he may have had some influence, because the Casa de los Amigos was probably built or remodelled at the same time as the palaces in the Southern Pavilion, with which it was directly connected and that was remodelled during the last part of the 14th century. The Casa de los Amigos is distributed around two courtyards at different levels, with the house structured in a way similar to that of the Nasrid houses in the Alhambra. The entrance is located in the southern wall, and is accessed from a sloping stone street that also connected the alley of the *hammam* with the Generalife's intermediate market gardens.

descending hillside, the edge of which is the Puerta de la Mercería, also referred to in ancient documents as the Puerta de los Carneros. Currently, it leads to an esplanade adjacent to the residential building created to facilitate the arrival of carriages at the back part of the palace.

Casa de los Amigos
In front of the gate and at a lower level are the remains of the guest house which is contiguous to the palace. It received its name when a text by the 14th-century agronomist from Almería Ibn Luyún who — in his work *Kitab al-Filaha*

Paseo de las Adelfas
This promenade — named after the ornamental vault formed by the Oleanders covering it — was planned as a direct access to the upper area of the palace. It runs through the area that is the consequence of one of the large

Patio de la Acequia of the Generalife
It has been said that the Patio de la Acequia is the oldest garden in the western world. Although there are few gardens in existence that have continued their function as gardens without interruption, the truth is that the tastes popular at a given time have fashioned its ephemeral changing nature: cypress arches, pruned topiaries, creeping plants, pergolas, fences and plant species have changed in the courtyard over the years despite its strict geometry. The water spouts that have made it famous — until recently believed to be from the 19th century — apparently have their roots deep in the medieval pipes embedded in the walls of the water channels used to water the meadows bordering it. Photograph by Garzón, unsigned. Alhambra Archives

Paseo de las Adelfas

walls separating the market gardens and the path of the Acequia Real after it passes through the palace. At this far edge of the promenade – located among hundred year-old cypresses and other trees and shrubs – is a unique botanical specimen of great importance that has been on the verge of extinction, avoided through a painstaking gardening process aimed at its recovery. It is the Moorish myrtle, named *Myrtus baetica* *latifolia domestica* in the 16th century and – according to documentation – cultivated in the Generalife since medieval times. It is characterised by its height, reddish flaky bark and curled leaf – larger than the common species – and its intense fragrance. This promenade connects to the Paseo de los Cipreses and was planned as an extension of the latter in 1862 in preparation for Queen Isabella II's visit to the estate.

Moorish myrtle

The most characteristic plant in all the Alhambra is the *Myrtus comunis* – myrtle – whose Spanish name – *arrayán* – is derived from the Arabic word *al-rayhan,* meaning "aromatic," for the fragrance of the essential oils its leaves emit when rubbed together. Its cultivation as an ornamental species is due to fine texture and quick growth, its delicate and perfumed white flowers and its ability to adapt to being pruned into different shapes and topiaries. Among its varieties, one of the most remarkable is the Moorish myrtle *(Myrtus baetica)* which has larger leaves, mentioned in texts from the 16th and 17th centuries and widely used in the gardens of Granada. There are some examples remaining in the Alhambra, some of which are hundreds of years old. Currently, their recovery as a species is one of the Council of the Alhambra's primary goals.

Moorish myrtle, according to botanist C. Clusius in his *Rariorum aliquot stirpium per Hispanias observaturum Historia* (1576).

11

The Acequia del Sultán and the Lost Palaces

This complex hydraulic system carrying water from the Darro River about six kilometres upstream from the Alhambra was built during the Nasrid period to supply water to the palace-city. The archaeological remains of this network of pipes can be seen throughout the monumental complex. It supplies both the Generalife and the Alhambra and, although the current dam is modern, its location is probably not very for from that of the medieval dam.

Acequia Real or del Sultán

The Nasrid Alhambra is a complex containing buildings and other constructions that were defined and planned at a particular time, and it was essential for them to have a reliable water supply. It is likely that there was an inhabited settlement on the site before the arrival of the Nasrids, who would undertake the construction of a series of buildings and make adaptations that – though barely recognisable today – were typical of a segmented society from which arose a population that eventually spread beyond the boundaries of the territory of the Alhambra and the Generalife.

To provide this much-needed water to the two sites, the Nasrids designed and built a complex hydraulic system comprising a network of pipelines that began at a high point on

the mountain and which, to a large extent, has survived to the present day. This is the Acequia Real or del Sultán. About six kilometres upstream from the Alhambra, this channel carries water from the Darro River along the hillside on the left bank until it reaches the top of the *almunia* (country estate) of the Generalife, which it supplies with water and then subsequently enters the Alhambra via an aqueduct.

The channel gets its water directly from the Darro River near the farm called Jesús del Valle located 6,100 metres from the Alhambra. The current dam is modern and, although its location is different from that of the old dams that have been documented, these were probably not far from that of the current dam. Located at an altitude of 838 metres above sea level and built of concrete, the current dam has a spillway that provides

Aerial image of the path of the Acequia Real or Acequia del Sultán

View of the Pozos Altos complex in the foreground, with Granada in the distance

Detailed view from around 1940 of the dam where the Acequia del Sultán originates. This site (empty so it can be cleaned) is known as Jesús del Valle and is upstream on the Darro River. In this historic photograph taken after a flood, one can see the dam that channelled the water to the Acequia del Sultán. Alhambra Archives

protection for the supply tunnel. It carries water some 625 metres along the right bank of the river to the Molino del Rey, where the aqueduct crosses the channel, following the slope of the Loma de la Perdiz in the direction of the Alhambra.

After continuing on some 2,840 metres, the water channel branches off into two sections. The first, which runs on higher ground, is called the Acequia del Tercio, and the second is called the Acequia del Generalife. The upper branch reaches the Pabellón Romántico, where it continues on and supplies the water tanks known as Los Albercones. From there it flows to where the Alhambra's car parks are located, after branching back to the south and joining another lower water distributor, probably the so-called Partidor de los Frailes.

After breaking away from the upper branch, the lower branch of the channel descends 4.21 metres then flows on to the Palacio del Generalife, supplying it with water, and then crosses the famous Patio de la Acequia, continuing east to the Partidor de los Frailes and rejoining the branch originating at Los Albercones. The distance from the dam at this point is 5,900 metres. From here, the channel continues to flow in a virtually straight line until it enters the aqueduct, near the Torre del Agua inside the Alhambra's compound.

Currently, only one part of the circuit carries water, which is taken from a modern tunnel built in the gorge area near Las Tinajas approximately 2,000 metres from the dam, channelling water to where it splits off and, from

The Acequia del Sultán runs along the length of the Patio de la Acequia in the Palacio del Generalife

Section of the original water channel found recently in the Paseo de los Cipreses

Detail of one of the sections of the water channel as it passes through a tunnel dug in the bedrock

there, continuing on through the lower section, which is in better condition.

In general, the channel passes over the ground with reinforcements at possible erosion points such as ravines and gullies. When necessary, large sections were channelled between "undersetters" or parallel walls of rammed earth. Lime mixed with oil-impregnated linen was used in the joints to prevent water leaking. In some areas, the channel's bed is protected with cobblestones. A significant part of the channel's lower branch

runs through tunnels dug into the bedrock – the Quaternary conglomerate of the Alhambra – making it highly stable in terms of maintenance. It also has random openings in the embankment for construction and cleaning. These tunnels are from 10 to 20 metres long, and from 0.5 to 2 metres high. In its final section as it approaches and enters the Alhambra, it was efficiently channelled via a series of hydraulic structures – no longer extant – which were part of several aqueducts such as the one still preserved from the early

Overground path of the Acequia Real or Acequia del Sultán across the Cerro del Sol

Detail from *Platform* by Ambrosio Vico in which the water channel's path from the Generalife to the Alhambra can be seen (ca. 1614). Alhambra Library

18th century, although it was rebuilt after it was blown up by Napoleon's army.

The repair work recently carried out on the pavement of the Paseo de los Cipreses led to the archaeological discovery of part of the last section of the channel before it enters the Alhambra. The medieval era channel, located 1.5 metres below the promenade, is formed of two parallel walls built with lime mortar that channel the water inside. After the Christian conquest, the Muslim channel was replaced by another dug in the ground and reinforced with stones at its base and sides; the accumulation of silt carried by the water in modern times caused the channel to gradually rise almost to its present level of 0.5 metres from the surface. Finally, the layout design of the Paseo de los Cipreses during the first third of the 20th century meant that it had to be covered by a brick dome so that the water could be crossed over.

Hydraulic Innovations. Los Albercones

After supplying water to the higher areas and the buildings of the Generalife, the Acequia Real runs parallel to one of the walls separating the gardens. A perpendicular underground gallery was built at a particular point in its path; it diverted water to a deep well, a water wheel and a large water tank, so that cultivation could take place in the highest areas. This gallery was dug out of the rock and reinforced inside with a brick vault; it comprises several sections separated by two air vents that maintain the pressure inside. The first air vent is located 20 metres from the Acequia Real and the second is 12 metres beyond the first; the gallery runs another 11 metres from the second air vent to the main well. Both are located among the orchards, though at different levels. The air vents had brick rims – whose remains can still be seen – that protected them.

Upper part of the Torre de las Damas, which protects the main well and, in the foreground, the large water tank from the Nasrid era

The underground gallery ends at the main well 17.40 metres beneath the surface. This well is under a tower known as the Torre de las Damas, built using the *tapial* (rammed earth) construction method at the most elevated spot in order to protect the main well and to serve as a foundation for an animal-powered water wheel which, when driven by beasts would raise the water up to a collection channel. An archaeological exploration led to the discovery and understanding of this hydraulic engineering system as a result of the circular path left by the animals at the wheel in the tower's pavement. A significant number of *cangilones* (clay water buckets) have also been discovered inside the well.

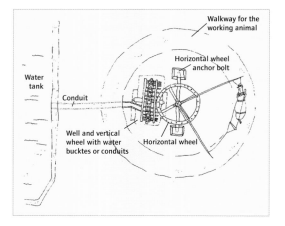

A large reservoir capable of holding 400 cubic metres of water is the final piece of this hydraulic complex. Originally, the water flowed through a channel originating at the upper part of the well and, after passing through a small settling basin, entered the water tank. Rowlock brick platforms surround the reservoir in addition to a wall structure on its north, south and east sides. On the latter there is an arch behind which a stairway begins and provides access to a paved terrace that used to have a parapet — no-longer

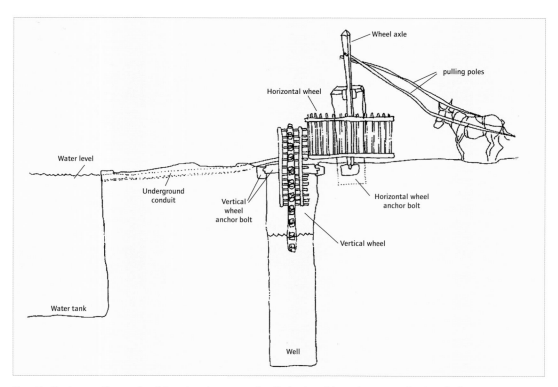

Hypothetical recreation — plan (above) and cross section (below) — of how the water wheel worked. Drawings by María Cullel Muro (*El agua en la agricultura de al-Andalus*, exh. cat., Granada, ed. Sierra Nevada 95 – El Legado Andalusí – Lunwerg Editores, 1995)

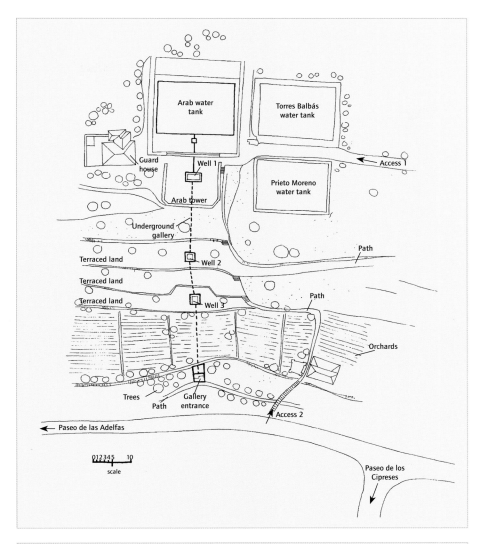

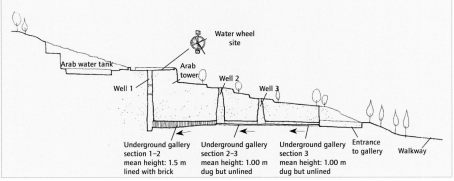

Plan and cross-section of Los Albercones complex. Drawings by María Cullel Muro (*El agua en la agricultura de al-Andalus*, exh. cat., Granada, ed. Sierra Nevada 95 – El Legado Andalusí – Lunwerg Editores, 1995)

Los Albercones hydraulic complex. Right, the Torre de las Damas with the medieval water wheel well and water tank. Left, two water tanks built during different parts of the 20th century

existing — and probably formed an observation point or pavilion over the water tank. The entire structure was made by cutting into the natural terrain, and the largest stones were even used for the masonry walls. Later, when the system was no longer sufficient or the area needing irrigation was expanded, it was modified and the channel was diverted before entering the Generalife through a new direct branch as a replacement for or alternative to the well and waterwheel.

The recovery of the Alhambra's cultural heritage during modern times led to the discovery of how important this element was in the supply and control of water throughout the site. Leopoldo Torres Balbás — the Alhambra's architectural curator from 1923 to 1936 — understood the need to build a new water tank that would make it possible to increase both the amount of water stored as well as the hydraulic pressure throughout the circuit. In 1926, a new tank was built, and its size and technical characteristics doubled its functional capacity.

Years later, in the 1930s, the expansion of the irrigated areas and the repair and entry into operation of all of the water-related elements throughout the complex made building a third water tank a necessity. This construction, built by architect Francisco Prieto Moreno, is located near the tower and is a bit lower and somewhat smaller.

The Dehesa del Generalife and Cerro del Sol Archaeological Site

In an elevated area in the surroundings of the Alhambra are the remains of a large hydraulic and architectural complex linked to it both in terms of space and territory. The different elements brought to light so far are scattered over a wide area of olive groves on whose slopes also grow scrubland species, including some holm oaks — evidence of the presence of Mediterranean forests in this area — and certain species of conifers planted during the first half of the 20th century. This site offers

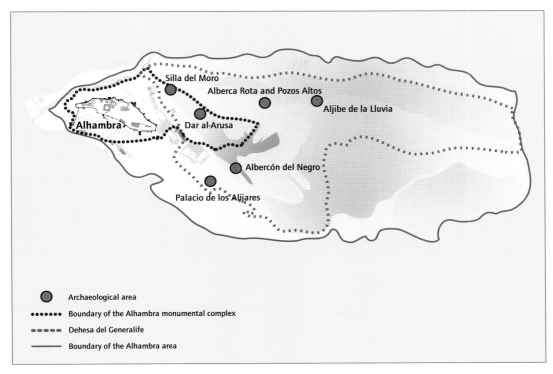

Map of the Alhambra monumental area

a picturesque view of the Darro River valley as it makes its way to Granada as well as an outstanding view of the surrounding landscape. Among the area's cultural heritage elements — all of which are related to their common purpose of channelling and distributing water — are the remains of two palatial residences that are currently considered to be archaeological dig sites: Dar al-Arusa and los Alijares; and there are others whose relationship to them are yet to be clarified but which at a given moment in the Nasrid era formed a hydraulic network either related to or dependent on the Alhambra palace-city: the complex called the Alberca Rota and the Pozos Altos, the Aljibe de la Lluvia, the Albercón del Negro and the Silla del Moro.

In 1494 German traveller Hieronymus Münzer described the plain extending through the mountains as "very tall towers, where the kings of Granada would go to enjoy themselves; their

interiors are well preserved, but the outside is half in ruins." This reference, dated just two years after the conquest, describes how neglected the site was. In the late 16th or early 17th century, these buildings do not appear on Ambrosio Vico's *Platform*, or map of Granada. It shows just the layout of a wall that probably surrounded them, and the tower of the Silla del Moro. The entire system may have been ruined as a consequence of war by the Moriscos, who fought frequent battles in the area.

The Hydraulic Innovation of the Pozos Altos
Part of the hydraulic structure and perhaps related to the water system that supplied the *almunias* of los Alijares, Dar al-Arusa and the Silla del Moro, Pozos Altos forms one of the most important hydrological complexes in medieval Peninsular Islam. It comprises several interdependent components that are subordinate to the operation of the entire system. It has an

Archaeological work on the Alberca Rota (2008)

Part of the water channel's underground structure and its supply channel for carrying water to the surface

enormous tank for collecting and distributing water and one or two wells that enable water to be raised up to its height in order to facilitate supply to the farms and homes scattered around the Cerro del Sol through channels that are still preserved.

Nineteenth-century descriptions called the tank Albercón del Moro, but nowadays its accepted name is Albercón Roto, or broken tank, due to its current state. It used to be filled by one or two water-raising wells – generically called the Pozos Altos del Cerro del Sol – and traces of its channels still remain. The one located to the east – in better condition – retains some of the brick structure on which the parapet was located, while that to the west and bounded by some remaining traces of its structure, currently shows an obvious collapse of materials that fell inside and blocked it to a great degree.

In 1889 Manuel Gómez-Moreno was able to explore some of its galleries, record its dimensions and write an excellent description, thanks to which it was later possible to make a planimetric survey now conserved in the Alhambra Archives.

At one point, water from the Acequia Real penetrated into the mountain via *qanats* (underground conduits) dug in the

ground. It was then channelled to at least one intermediate container excavated at great depth from which it would once again be raised to the surface and collected in the large pool that presumably served as a tank to control the pressure for the country estate of Dar al-Arusa and perhaps that of the Albercón del Negro which, in turn, would do the same thing with the los Alijares farm.

The device used to raise the water was most certainly animal-powered water wheels, perhaps the largest ever designed and built in al-Andalus. The few Arabic sources that refer to these elements describe them as masterpieces of engineering for the times, and Gómez-Moreno stated that it was "the most significant water construction the Moors built in Granada."

The 17th-century Granada-born historian Francisco Bermúdez de Pedraza thought that it might have been built by the Nasrids around 1455 in order to ensure the existence of large extensions of land for crops and pastures since, in the lower areas – especially in the vicinity of the Vega – these were disappearing due to frequent raids being carried out at the time by the Castilian troops, such as the well-known raid led by Henry IV of Castile.

Exterior view of the Aljibe de la Lluvia on the Cerro del Sol. Current state

Detail from Hoefnagel's engraving in the *Civitates Orbis Terrarum* (1575) showing the Aljibe. Alhambra Library

However, in his *Diwán*, the great poet and vizier of the Nasrid sultanate Ibn Zamrak attributed the plan for a major colonisation of these sites – which would have been exploited until the conquest of Granada – to Muhammad V. The new settlers – with different technical concepts and points of view – may have been entirely unaware of these works and their usefulness, and it is possible they abandoned or destroyed them. Since then – and especially after their discovery in the 19th century – they have inspired a whole series of myths and mysteries, pending the opinion of contemporary archaeologists who began digging at the site just a few months ago.

Aljibe de la Lluvia

Cisterns are the most common hydraulic structures in Nasrid Granada. However, this reservoir is – at least so far – the only one known in these latitudes. Its unique dome protruding from the ground makes it easily identifiable in a valley located along the country road leading to the top of Cerro del Sol and the popular spot known as the Parque de Invierno. The Aljibe de la Lluvia or rain cistern is an attraction for Granada locals passing through

this traditional hiking area that winds its way along the hills surrounding the city.

Laid out in a square, two thirds of its structure is underground. It is built of rammed earth, though the roof, the pillars and the pilasters which divide the interior into three areas are made of brick. It still has two ancient, small openings where the water entered from above where the vaults begin, which may indicate where the main source of the supply came from. Although apparently, as its name indicates, the cistern could be filled with rainwater – and, in fact, still is to this day via its centre opening – it may have also been filled by upwelling ground water, since it is located among ravines that drain into the river basins of the nearby Darro and Genil Rivers. Likewise, although not originally, it may at some time have been part of the Pozos Altos hydraulic structure. This, however, cannot be stated with certainly because no related pipeline has been found thus far.

Although there is no known documented date of construction, and the use it was designed for is unknown, it seems clear that this was the work of the Nasrids. The *Diwán* of Ibn Zamrak describes how this pasture was used for cattle in the 14th century, so it may have been employed for

The Albercón del Negro, located adjacent to Granada's current cemetery

this purpose. On the other hand, in al-Andalus it is not unusual to find watchtowers built in strategic areas. These usually had their own supply cistern, although there are no traces of a fortification here.

Its location close to roads leading to and from the city also indicates that it may have served as a way to supply travellers passing through the area with water. In a scene from Hoefnagel's book *Civitates orbis Terrarum*, written in the second half of the 16th century, a character can be seen walking and carrying a container near a reservoir that might be this one, so that it may — at least at that time — have served as a fountain or basin of fresh water. From other liberary sources, we know that its water was very popular in the city due to the belief that it possessed healing properties. Finally, it has been suggested that it may have been used as a reserve for times of drought. In fact, to this day the cistern continues to fill with water and provides important help as a reserve to replenish equipment used to fight forest fires.

Albercón del Negro

This protruding structure is part of the remains of a large water tank adjacent to the park located along the first section of the access road to the Cerro del Sol, above the valley now occupied by the San José Municipal Cemetery and the Rawda or Muslim cemetery in Granada.

Its strange name derives from a traditional local 19th-century legend about the imaginary presence of a burly African character next to the tank, who zealously guarded a legendary palace located under the surface of these remains.

Actually, the purpose of this large container was to store water and serve as a pressure mechanism in the form of a connecting basin for a large quantity of water to supply the *almunia* of Los Alijares. To channel and raise water under so much pressure, it had large siphons made with stone conduits and clay athanors, some of which were found during work done on the cemetery in the first third of the 19th century; these are now in the museums of Granada.

Granada-born writer Ibn 'Asim said in the mid-15th century that the palace tank was fed by means of "some huge conduits carved in hard stone, of which there are enough remaining for it to be rebuilt so that they can once again be displayed in their entirety."

This big tank — one of the largest preserved in the city — retains much of its original structural works, notably an underground tunnel covered by a barrel vault to prevent water draining out. It has, however, lost its related structures linking it to the entire hydraulic circuit.

Arabic texts make mention of when the *almunia* of Los Alijares and the water supply system were founded by Sultan Muhammad V during the last third of the 14th century. However, a series of strong earthquakes taking place between 1431 and 1441 significantly affected the Los Alijares estate and its hydraulic elements, among them the water tank that must, like everything else, have been badly damaged. It was repaired a few years later, although the economic difficulties of a Nasrid sultanate under the increasing pressure of Castilian troops and already aware of its imminent defeat probably led to its gradual abandonment, and it is likely that it was definitively abandoned after the city was conquered, when it became unusable and was forgotten until its rediscovery in the 19th century.

Palacio de los Alijares

This palace was one of many *almunias* and recreational country estates owned by the Nasrid dynasty that were scattered throughout the kingdom. The Palacio de los Alijares, built in the last quarter of the 14th century by Sultan Muhammad V, was a country estate with fields and gardens that covered strips of terraced land descending from the uppermost part of the site where the palace was located. It dominated the entire property and offered extraordinary views.

According to Arabic texts, the palace had a novel quadrangular shape design to which the Sultan himself contributed, with a *zafariche* or pool in the courtyard and four large *qubbas* (square rooms with domed roofs) — one in each corner — oriented to the cardinal points; these were joined by the same number of galleries featuring white marble columns and floors. The *qubbas* had a an outward-facing circular design and must have been covered inside

Large water conduits from the Albercón del Negro.
Archaeological and Ethnographic Museum of Granada

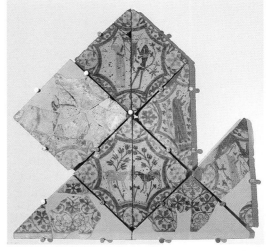

Display in the Alhambra Museum with remains of floor tiles from the Palacio de los Alijares (triangular pieces below) and other similar pieces from the Torre del Peinador de la Reina

Detail of the Palacio de los Alijares in the representation of the Battle of the Higueruela in the Sala de las Batallas in El Escorial (1585–1589). Patrimonio Nacional

with *mocárabe* (stalactite ceiling) decorated domes similar to those in the Palacio de los Leones. It was most likely richly decorated with plasterwork just like the palaces of the Alhambra, and ceramic floors as well. Remains of glazed pieces with motifs similar to those in the Peinador de la Reina, among others, have been preserved.

The estate was surrounded by gardens of trees – some of them unique species – and the sultan's flock grazed in the surrounding area. In order for such a spectacular farm to operate effectively, water had to be brought from the top of the hill by means of a complicated hydraulic system adapted to the rugged terrain, crossing parts of the valley and then raised by pressure requiring – as we saw in the Albercón del Negro – an innovative siphon built of thick stone athanors. Very little has remained of all of this due to the many vicissitudes to which the area was subjected. By the mid-15h century, Arabic texts describe the palace and the estate as ruins, probably due to earthquakes. It was not rebuilt due to the scarcity of resources

brought about by the war. Part of the building may have been preserved and can be identified quite clearly in a reproduction of the Higueruela battle, which took place between the Nasrid troops and those of John II of Castile near Granada on 1 July 14,31. This work of art is housed in the Sala de Batallas in the monastery of El Escorial.

Abandoned after the conquest, they would be occupied as housing or for other uses and were soon forgotten until the early 19th century when, taking advantage of the rubble from the ruins, occupying Napoleonic troops positioned a battery of artillery in front of the water tank that marked the site the palace had occupied. The subsequent construction of the municipal cemetery of Granada and its expansion did away with the remaining vestiges, some of which were used for the construction of the cemetery. Nevertheless, many relics – among which are some tiles and bits of coloured glass that might have belonged to the famous lookout point that dominated the landscape and can be seen in the representation in El Escorial – were preserved and are today in

Remains of the Palacio de los Alijares integrated into the so-called "Nasrid Garden" in Granada's current cemetery

the Alhambra Museum. Currently, only a few traces in addition to part of the tank remain; these were brought together in 2001 in an evocative funerary garden tomb from which one can at least appreciate the archaeological value of the estate.

Palacio de Dar al-Arusa

This term, which means "House of the Bride" — commonly called the Palace of the Bride — is the name given to the remains of a palatial Moorish residence located at the highest point of the Cerro del Sol above the palace and gardens of the Generalife, the Palacio de los Alijares and the defensive structure of the Acequia del Sultán. Although exploration of the building began in October 1924, it was not until pine trees were being planted in 1933 that the central section of the building was happened upon by accident; the next three years were spent in removing rubble from the site.

The residential complex appears to be laid out — as custom dictates in Hispano-Muslim houses — around a large rectangular interior patio

or courtyard with an in-ground tank in the centre that still conserves some remains of its supply and drainage pipes. Remains of pedestals, probably from a gallery or portico, were found along with

Part of the structures that have been conserved from the Palacio de Dar al-Arusa

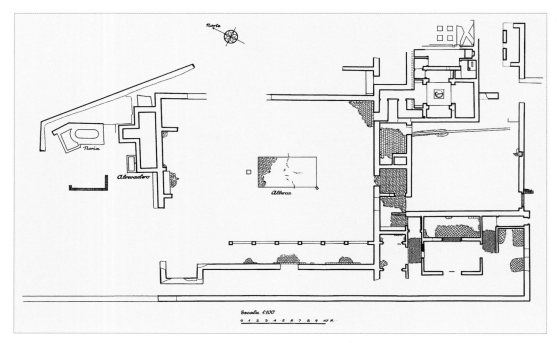

Ground plan of the remains of the Palacio de Dar al-Arusa, on the Cerro del Sol drawn by Leopoldo Torres Balbás (ca. 1936). Alhambra Archives

a few pieces of ceramic flooring. Different rooms, corridors and spaces fill the area around the patio as evidenced by the bottom part of their walls, among which abundant bits of irregular flooring pieces and the small pipes that ran under them have also remained.

At its northwestern end are some unusual structures that at first caused confusion; however, during the exploration they were identified as part of a hydraulic system designed to raise water from a well by means of a water wheel that subsequently poured the water into a basin or tank. A small foundation with a stone basin was also discovered nearby. This well is the only hydraulic device that has turned up in the vicinity of the palace, although several sewer pipes and galleries running on a lower level were also found.

The area in which it appears that most of the buildings were located is south of the courtyard, and this is where the remains of the baths — typical in a house such as this — are found. The *hammam* was accessed from the main courtyard through a corridor

with a double bend that leads to a square room in whose centre the most striking decorative piece in the palace — a circular marble fountain framed by a geometric tile composition — was conserved. Today, it can be seen on display in the Alhambra Museum.

Marble and glazed ceramic basin from the *hammam* in the Palacio de Dar al-Arusa. Alhambra Museum

To the east appeared the incomplete remains of the hot room and the hypocaust. Several chambers, corridors and other material remains, including a sink and the entrance to a latrine, complete the remains of the building.

Other archaeological remains such as drains can be seen as well. These may have been used to irrigate the palace's gardens, which would have been located to the east just before the hill meets the ravine.

Next to the baths are other remains extending to the edge of the building, perhaps indicating that they were joined to a protective wall or fence. The palace must have included more than just the building and adjoining baths and most certainly also had flower or vegetable gardens. The whole site is enclosed by a wall that appears to protect the palace's living area.

The construction of this palace has been ascribed to the 14th century, based on Arabic texts describing the presence of crop fields in the area. It is possible that Dar al-Arusa's water supply system was connected in some fashion to the Pozos Altos system; ongoing research should clarify this in the coming years. What is certain is that the site was most likely abandoned after the conquest, and must have been dismantled, according to testimonials like that of historian Francisco Henríquez de Jorquera from 1632, "for having failed their kings and as a result of accidents occurring during the Moorish rebellions."

Detail of *Platform* by Ambrosio Vico with Saint Helen above (ca. 1614). Alhambra Library

La Silla del Moro

The unusual name by which these archaeological and architectural remains are known comes from the way their ruins looked from the city in the mid-16th century: like a seat or bench — the *silla* or chair — enhanced by the artillery platform installed here by Napoleon's troops around 1810. Beginning in the 17th century, it was also called the Castillo de Santa Elena; by then it was home to hermits dedicated to a shrine to the saint and — according to some authors — it stood on the site of an old mosque, although there is no evidence to prove this theory.

In its original layout, it formed part of the surveillance and protection system for the Dehesa del Generalife and the foothills of the Cerro del Sol, the natural defence rising above the Alhambra to the east. This is an essential function, because it is here where the distribution of water from the channel to the palace-city and its environs, to the orchards and gardens of the Generalife and the whole surrounding area, begins. It must have had a strongly military character in an area replete with country estates and supplies that appeared vulnerable to attack by enemies. Of course, the panorama it offers of its surroundings, with breathtaking views in all directions, shows the importance of its strategic location, which was maintained over the centuries.

The Silla del Moro may have been connected to the adjoining residence of Dar al-Arusa, from which it may have received its water supply, as there is a conduit directed towards it that can be seen in the cut of open land on the hill that was made to build a logging road around 1929

View of the Generalife from the Torre de la Vela, with the Silla del Moro at the upper right in 1871. Photograph by J. Laurent

The Generalife, the Alhambra and Granada from the Silla del Moro in 1871. Photograph by J. Laurent

Engraving by Daniel Meisner (ca. 1623) on which one can see the Silla del Moro (in the upper left) above the Generalife and the Alhambra. Alhambra Archives

and modified at some point afterwards. Remains of the residence's staircase and tower, as well as concrete walls, fragments of vaults and pieces of plasterwork were discovered at the same time.

The history and descriptions related to it that have come down to us date from periods subsequent to the Nasrid era, and provide us with very little information about its layout during medieval times.

In 1942 plans were made to locate a lookout point over the building's remains, based on historical engravings – primarily *Platform* by Ambrosio Vico from the early 17th century – and a model was made. In 1966, a restaurant was planned, which led to the reconstruction of the building with a central tower. This was completed around 1970, but it was never enclosed nor was it put to use. Years later, part of the structure collapsed due to the poor quality

of the construction work, and it was decided to dismantle all the reconstructed part and restore the original remains, upgrading them as part of a project designed to integrate them as a lookout point. In 2001 some underground tunnels located below the building were explored and repaired; the time when these tunnels were built and their intended purpose are unknown. It is thought that they may have been related to the distribution of water for farming in the area. It was suggested that they might have been prepared as mines by Napoleon's troops, who dynamited numerous locations throughout the area during their 1812 retreat. In any event, it appears to have stimulated the 19th century's traditional local fantasy. In his famous *Tales of the Alhambra*, american writer Washington Irving narrates legends of treasures supposedly hidden in the vicinity of the Cerro del Sol.

12 Some Keys to Understanding the Alhambra

The Nasrid kingdom of Granada was the last state in Muslim Spain. This late context has allowed us to detect certain nuances of al-Andalus culture which, had they not been forged in the crucible of the Alhambra's society, might very well have been forgotten. Some of these cultural nuances make the Alhambra a unique place from which to obtain information and knowledge. The following is a brief overview of some of the key concepts for those wishing to gain a deeper understanding of Nasrid culture.

The *Diwán al-Insá'*

Sultan Muhammad II (1273–1302) provided the emirate with new administrative institutions, including a vizierate or *wuzara'*, responsible for, among other things, the Royal Chancellery and the *Diwán al-Insa'*, a kind of official writing department. This office was commissioned to draft correspondence and official documents and headed by the person considered to be both the kingdom's best writer and suitable to hold the post of *Wazir* or Prime Minister. The Nasrid government — which was constantly conducting negotiations and making pacts with its neighbours — needed someone capable of mastering the difficult art of the word to head this office. The fact that his writings also praised the figure of his master the sultan and the greatness of his works would explain the reason why most of his poems adorn the main rooms of the Alhambra. Thus, it is easy to understand why the ambitions of young writers centred on gaining a coveted position as a *kátib* or scribe in the Nasrid court. The *Diwán al-Insa'* resembled a workshop in which writers or *kuttab* worked as artisans of the Arabic language, modelling poetry and rhymed prose under the supervision of the *arráez* or head of the office. The *kuttab* were civil servants who composed panegyrics — known as *qasidas Sultaniyyain* — in honour of the dynasty, for holidays such as the Sacrifices, the Breaking of the Fast or the Birth of the Prophet. They also worked on celebrating family events such as births, circumcisions, marriages, journeys, victorious returns from battles, and funeral ceremonies, including writing epitaphs.

The epigraphic writings in the Alhambra are mainly attributable to three poets who were successively in charge of the Chancellery throughout the 14th century. They describe the most brilliant moments of the dynasty and, in turn, are the most outstanding examples of Nasrid poetry.

The first of the vizier-poets was Ibn al-Yayyab (1274–1349), who managed to serve six sultans, from Muhammad II to Yusuf I:

> The Sultan's greatness shines on this palace of transient beauty. Its beauty shines and the rain from the clouds covers it generously.

His disciple Ibn al-Khatib (1313–1375) served the great sultans of the Alhambra, Yusuf I and Muhammad V:

> I surpass all things with my beauty, my ornaments, my crown, and even the stars in their zodiac houses bow to me, and although [the Alhambra] rides high in its orbit, I [do so even more because] I am its shining diadem and its crown.

He was replaced by Ibn Zamrak (1333–1393), who served Muhammad V and also Yusuf I and Muhammad VII:

> The Sabika is a crown on her hair that she would like to adorn with pearls, but the Alhambra is a hyacinth that rises above this crown.

Painting on the centre vault of the Sala de los Reyes in the Palacio de los Leones

We know of some poems written by Ibn Furkun, who served under Sultan Yusuf III. During the last era:

> The court of the kingdom and its Alhambra have shapes that look like the mansions on the moon.

The Proportional System

In order to understand the complex world of Islamic art and architecture, it is essential to be familiar with one of its key concepts: the proportional system, which is a kind of canon — a basic, abstract law — with which all plastic arts and aesthetics must comply. It is all about adapting the creative work (the building, decoration, etc.) to both the space available for it and, at the same time, to the artistic scheme (which may include one or more designs, depending on whether it is a simple project or a large undertaking like a palace, for example) planned by or entrusted to the craftsman. Medieval Islamic artisans tried to find what other civilisations have called the "golden number," and to do this they used two basic geometric elements, the circle and the square. Using these shapes and their simple design, they went on to develop true mathematical compositions that varied in their level of complexity, depending on the themes, locations and time periods involved.

Typical model of geometric design in Islamic art: it shows the steps to turn a circle into a star-shaped polygon

The decorative motif is created as follows: a square is drawn inside or outside a circle, and this square, when rotated round its centre point, creates a star called a *sino* (centre star): This *sino* has a variable number of points — six, eight, twelve, etc. — and is the basis or starting point for all further development of the decoration. This method is relatively obvious in geometric wall decorations, for example in the creation of a tiled panel in which further developing the star's lines turns them into strip or strand shapes. Continued development of these strips produces what is called latticework or lattice decoration which, in turn, may be of the eight-part lattice, twelve-part lattice, etc. variety, depending on the type of *sino*. To facilitate their work, these artisans had sets of squares, triangles and various templates at their disposal, so not all of them were necessarily masters of mathematics or geometry.

The entire development of the decorative project was based on these basic rudiments, and there are several items in the Alhambra that are considered to be the pinnacle of the evolutionary process of Islamic architecture and decoration, including vaults with *mocárabe* (stalactite ceiling) designs in the Sala de los Abencerrajes and the Sala de Dos Hermanas in the Palacio de los Leones.

However, the basic outline of the circle and square is not confined to decorative developments, but is also present in the architecture: taking into account the space available and the structure to be built, the *alarife* (architect-builder) draws a geometric figure — say a square — in which he draws, for example, an equilateral triangle; through the square root of the triangle's sides he is then able to develop a three-part division for designing and defining the decorative cartouches on a wall, or a rectangle to calculate the dimensions of a pool in a courtyard.

Spatial Multifunctionality

One of the most striking differences between Islam and the Western world is the former's concept of space. In the West, probably due to its classical roots, everything is defined and each space, each element has a function, so

Geometric composition on tiling in the Torre de la Cautiva

that homes have reception rooms, dining rooms, bedrooms, kitchens, etc. In the Islamic world, multifunctionality is the norm and, applied to space, means that all places and all items may be used for any purpose, i.e., there is no specific space dedicated to a particular purpose, for it is believed that useful spaces are those with different uses; any space serving only one function is not practical and, therefore, not useful. This is a general principle that, obviously, has been refined many times over the centuries and has had many

specific variables that depended on geographic influences and local traditions.

One can observe how this principle was applied in the spaces in the Alhambra's palaces. One example is in the Palacio de Comares, where the sultan's throne is located in a room adjacent to his bedroom. This means that the Salón de Comares was not just a place for official "display" but could also be used for other events, and that the Sala de la Barca was not only the bedchamber but was also used as a lounge, etc. That is why the small size of the houses in the Hispano-Muslim neighbourhoods is so surprising, as it is difficult for one to believe that whole families could live in them. In this respect, the spatial layout of the houses that we see, for example, in the Alcazaba of the Alhambra is similar to that of the Moorish houses in the Albaicín that may be seen from any of the Alhambra's lookout points. This is true as well — although on another scale — for the spaces in the Nasrid Palaces.

The root of this feature likely lies in the origins of Islamic civilisation, when the nomadic tribes of the Arabian Peninsula had to move from one place to another in search of settlements for grazing or trade. Bedouin tents and the way they were arranged based on hierarchy and trade had a role in the way space was used. Upon becoming sedentary — which coincided with the dawn of civilisation — many of these tribes' customs were naturally maintained in the new society.

Furthermore, in its rapid process of expansion through the West across the southern Mediterranean basin, Islamic civilisation came into contact with Romanity, where it "recognised" itself in the Mediterranean house with spaces arranged around an inner patio or courtyard containing water elements, cisterns, channels, etc. The Muslims assimilated all that was consistent with their principles, and rejected or modified and adapted other resources. One example is the concept of the *hammam*, or steam bath, and its relationship with the Roman baths, in which the method of bathing was completely changed and transformed over time into one of its signs of identity.

Façades and Entrances

The outside surfaces of Hispano-Muslim buildings are usually smooth, monochromatic and very austere. Instead of windows in the walls, there are just a few ventilation holes, except in the upper floors where there is a tendency to install *ajimeces* or mullioned windows (balconies enclosed by latticework shutters). Neither houses nor palaces — as can be verified in the Alhambra — give any outward hint of what they hide inside. No one

Detail of jaimas during the siege of Vienna by the Turks. Sixteenth-century manuscripti, Topkapi Museum, Istanbul

who walks through an *Andalusí* quarter or neighbourhood and looks at a house can discern the social or economic level of the family living there — or even the size of the house — until he actually enters the place and discovers the splendour of the courtyard around which the living spaces are distributed. This characteristic is reflected in a Moorish proverb that talks of "the ugly ones":

> ... Like the home of the Moors,
> flaking walls on the outside,
> but like a treasure indoors...

The door is the boundary between the public and the private. Despite this, it is always open, but from the street it is impossible to see inside as houses are always designed so that a wall, a corner or another architectural device safeguards its privacy, and this can be seen in the houses of the Alcazaba and the entrance to the Palacio de Comares. In contrast to the traditional Castilian saying "The house with two doors is difficult to keep safe," it is common for the Andalusí house to have more than one entrance.

Spatial layout of the Salón de Comares

Spatial layout in the military district in the Alcazaba

The Partitioning of Space

In terms of the various functions assigned to spaces in the home, the Alhambra also serves the contemporary observer as a "sounding board" of Islamic culture. The arrangement of spaces — apparently spontaneous — in the settlements of nomad camps has somehow survived through time and across the geography of the Islamic world.

Granada's medieval Muslims showed a clear compartmentalisation of the spaces they inhabited. This also occurs in the Alhambra, where the rooms were designed to be integrated into a larger element, while remaining autonomous and independent. Rooms, halls and large, open nave-like spaces were planned as isolated elements, usually separated by a corridor, passageway or recess, but forming a single body, a single structure, with no movement between them possible except through the courtyard. This common layout of Islamic-Andalusian buildings contrasts with buildings having Mudéjar and Christian courtyards, in which the rooms are connected to each other internally. Islamic houses of more than one storey had their own stairway; however, this did not connect the upper and lower floors inside the building, but through the courtyard, a characteristic of Granada's Islamic architecture that strongly influenced the traditional *carmen* (a small walled country house with a garden and orchard).

When the building was large or was part of a palace's structure, the bedrooms were often attached at right angles to the largest architectural element, which could be designed as a large *qubba* (a square room with a domed roof), leaving the corners free. This typical layout also had an important preventive function in terms of dreaded fires, which were encouraged by the large amount of wood found in the roofs of medieval buildings.

Different representations of this practice can be clearly seen, for example, in the Palacio de Comares or in the nave-like space on the eastern side of the Patio de la Acequia in the Generalife.

Space was also compartmentalised inside the rooms of the houses and palaces, probably derived from the internal distribution of the Bedouin tent. Rooms were usually built on one of the smaller sides, or on both, thereby enlarging the main room. When this was done, the bedroom was set off by raising the floor slightly or by changing its geometrical design; depending on the type of building, it may have been further distinguished by an arch and sometimes the ceiling differed as well. Bedchambers replete with restful spaces were thus created on the sides, freeing the central space.

Dungeons

These are very common elements in the Alhambra; to date, a least a dozen dungeons have been discovered in the compound. Several are known to be inside the Alcazaba, two of which are located beneath the Torre del Homenaje and the Torre de la Vela.

Near the base of the Torre Quebrada a third dungeon — a mere hole in the ground — can be seen, protected by a brick enclosure and gate. Adjacent to this dungeon — possibly the most interesting of those that have been conserved due to its structure and the remains that have been preserved — a small spiral staircase was built in the 1930s to provide access to its interior.

The dungeons were used to hold captives, who were dropped down by ropes though the hole in the middle. In general, they were shaped like a bottleneck and most of those that have been found in the Alhambra still conserve inside

Detail of the entrance to the dungeon located in the gardens of the Secano in the upper Alhambra

small radiating spaces dug in the ground and separated by bricks that allowed the captives to lie down as if in separate bunks. The middle area, which was uncovered, usually had a drain and was marked off on the ground. These structures were also used as underground silos designed to store grain, spices or even salt, and several of them have appeared in the area of the Campo de los Mártires.

Taqas

The *taqa* is one of the most characteristic decorative and functional elements in Nasrid palaces. It consists of a niche – usually small – carved into the wall, whose purpose was to hold containers filled with water either for drinking or in washstands.

These niches were designed in proportion with the decorative scheme for the space, and were primarily located in the main walls of the intrados (the surface of the inside curve) of the arches of accessways to important rooms or halls. They were always installed in pairs facing each other.

Its name – of Arabic origin – means "niche, cupboard or opening in a wall," although in the eastern Islamic world *taq* means an "arch" or "arcade" made with a *cimbra* (a kind of formwork).

Taqa in the accessway to the Salón de Comares

In Spanish — a language rich in nuances — it has developed into the word *taquilla*, which means "administrative window or ticket office for issuing tickets for shows or means of transport, etc." Certain kinds of furniture in workshops and offices, pigeonholes for sorting and even the box office receipts from a show — i.e., something related to a small space — are also called *taquillas*.

The niches in the accessway to the Sala de la Barca in the Palacio de Comares are decorated with poems comprising five verses. Their author is one of the two grand viziers — Ibn al-Khatib or Ibn Zamrak — and they describe these curious elements as follows:

> I am like the dais of a bride
>   endowed with beauty and perfection. Look at the
>   water jug and you shall be able to understand
> the real truth of my words. Behold my
>   tiara and you shall see how
> it seems like a crown made of the new moon. [...]
> I am of the prayer time
>   whose *qibla* is the path to felicity. The water jug
>   here can be believed by you
> to be a man standing and fulfilling his prayer [...].

The aesthetics of the *taqa* have lived on in the Maghreb in the embroidered adornment with which brides go to their wedding ceremony.

Latticework Shutters

These structures — mainly found in windows and openings — are common in domestic spaces in Islamic architecture in general. The use of these shutters — made of plaster and stained glass — became generalised beginning in the 13th century under the Mameluk sultans of Cairo. They used other materials to make them, although the most characteristic besides plaster is wood. In Arabic, they are called *qamriyya* (from *qamar* meaning "moon") or *shamsiyya* (from *shams* meaning "sun"), depending on their relationship with the light from outside which they filter or diffuse, allowing just the right amount of light to enter necessary for each room. The way light is received in the interior is of utmost importance. The shutters were usually located high up, so they enhanced the decoration of the walls — which are nearly devoid of any relief — allowing the light

to brush lightly against the walls, emphasising the *chiaroscuro* and imbuing it with a life that nowadays, with horizontal lighting, is lacking. The decorative design on the shutters was always based on geometric shapes with a star-shaped pattern of interlocking strips.

The direct light that now enters the rooms of the Alhambra varies greatly from their original light: with the blinds that once covered the windows and doors they would have looked radically different. Sometimes the shutters were doubled, mounted both on the inside as well as the outside of the wall; between the two, there might also be a section to hold leaded stained glass. The doors to the rooms were nearly always kept closed, thereby managing to maintain a comfortable temperature inside — cool in summer and warm in winter. To do this, two or three small windows covered with plaster shutters — very characteristic of the Alhambra — would be installed

Latticework shutters used for ventilation over the accesway to the Sala de la Barca in the Palacio de Comares

over the doors; their other function – besides softly illuminating the interior – was to provide ventilation. Openings for shuttered windows were also made in the upper part of the walls of important rooms.

A very common architectural element in the Alhambra is the *lantern*, a small, windowed tower on the roofs of these rooms, in which the use of these shutters is essential. These towers consist of a central section, generally with a square base, that rises above the building and lights the room from above.

Patios, Porticoes and General Atmosphere

One of the most outstanding aspects of Hispano-Muslim architecture is its ability to interact with the natural environment, and it takes advantage of this in order to ensure the satisfaction and well-being of its inhabitants, a goal tied to a culture that aspires to sophistication and refinement. Its constructed spaces alternate with cool, shady interior gardens, in which the inhabitants can avoid the strong summer sun and take advantage of the winter sun; they ventilate the interior to cool and clear the air, insulating against and tempering the outdoor variations in temperature through the use of architectural solutions. Thus, we could speak of an architecture with environmental tendencies that is ecological or bioclimatic.

When they settled in a particular place, their architecture adapted to the climate and the environment. For centuries, Hispano-Muslim culture experimented with natural or passive cooling systems and with methods for controlling sunlight. The short, cold winters were solved with braziers and heaters, but the solution was more complicated for the long, hot summers. The intensity of the natural light and the long hours of sunshine contrasted with the diffused lighting of the interiors, where darkness was deliberately sought in order to facilitate meditation, abstraction, relaxation, and this is revealing of aspects of their lifestyle.

Nasrid architecture found a model solution in the interior patio or courtyard, the site where day-to-today household activities took place, regardless of the size of the dwelling or the status of its occupants. Depending on the type of building, a gallery would be located on the shorter sides of the patio, in front of a main room whose multifunctionality – among other aspects – meant that it would be used in different ways depending on the time of the day or season of the year. The inner patio of a house provided light and ventilation to the rooms, creating a natural climate in its environment; it collected rain water, favouring a microclimate that tempered the mid-day sun's rays. Trees and plants in general – with the addition of awnings, pergolas and galleries – helped to moderate the temperature and maintain the humidity, filtering the sunlight and balancing and refreshing indoor environments. Besides helping to lower the temperature, the water and vegetation in the patios helped to provide effective ventilation during the night.

In the Alhambra as in all of their geographic area, the Nasrids tried to build the patios of their residences in a north-south direction so the main rooms would be oriented at mid-day to receive direct sun in winter but not in summer. The 14th-century Almería-born writer Ibn Luyun recommends that: "[...] to determine the site of a house between gardens [...] the building is oriented at mid-day [...]." The orientation of the building – coupled with a well-thought-out architectural scheme with elements such as openings, porticoes and galleries – was the most appropriate method to take advantage of solar conditions. The white exterior surfaces and the thickness of the walls helped to create a favourable thermal environment.

In the palaces of the Alhambra there is a notable presence – usually on the north side – of a *qubba* or tower as the main room laid out in the same direction as the patio, which it uses as an intermediate step or hall, and a portico or gallery with porticoes that protects it from direct sunlight and reduces the temperature. Because of their characteristics, the pavilion or the tower (thanks to the flow of air it draws from the patio) provides continuous ventilation for the room. Much like a chimney; hot air is lighter than cold so it tends to rise by convection, keeping the lower area cooler and ventilated.

Windows situated over large entranceways encourage this air circulation, especially in winter,

that transform them into ethereal, subtle and evanescent elements, one of their most prized aesthetic qualities.

Decoration

From a teaching perspective and summed up briefly, Islamic and Hispano-Muslim decoration – and Nasrid decoration insofar as it represents them – is based on three main ornamental types: geometric, epigraphic and inspired by plants.

Geometry

This is the framework or the basis of all decoration. It regulates the limits, the different spaces that later must be completed with the rest of the decorative items (corbels, strips, arch panels, borders, wall panels, bays, etc.). Proportion plays a fundamental role: the craftsman creates his design taking into account both the space available as well as the characteristics of the assignment or project. To do this, he relies on his technical expertise, skills and abilities, experience and a range of instruments such as triangles, cords, rulers, awls and patterns that serve as stencils, making it easier to decorate the surface. The *alarife*, or architect-builder, does something similar, in this case adapted to the parcel of land, the availability of space, the type of land it was located on or applicable legal regulations or requirements.

All decoration is based on two basic figures: the circle and its accompanying square. The entire decorative scheme is based on these two elements; turning the square round its centre produces a star that – depending on the degrees it is turned – will have eight, sixteen, twenty, etc., points that will make up the entire composition and this can be very basic or very complicated. This star – the axis of all of the decoration, for example, in creating a tiled panel – is called a *sino*. By extending the lines, strips or strands, successive sets of new stars are created, and these can be extended infinitely; this geometric framework is called a lattice composition or latticework and, depending on the centre star, will have eight, sixteen, etc., parts. Among them are multiple geometric images – *zafates, alfardones, almendrillas, candilejos* and others. Sometimes a three-part division is sought by placing inside the square an equilateral triangle for

Drawing illustrating the air circulation inside a palatine space of the Alhambra. The Alhambra for children educational programme. Council of the Alhambra

when the rooms are heated with braziers that fill the air with toxic fumes, creating a need for fresh air and circulation.

The control of light is also a feature of a culture – the Islamic – that came into being in the hot, dazzling desert and which is counteracted with dimly lit, shady rooms; space indoors is for relaxation, meditation, rest, or for observing without being seen. So the windows are covered with latticework shutters which soften the light from the outside while allowing one to see out from the inside, and they used light shining from above, bathing the surfaces decorated with reliefs from sculpted plasterwork, *mocárabe* designs or the play of colours from the polychromatic tiles.

In pools and ponds, Muslim architecture plays with light and the optical effects it produces, reflecting on the walls or on the spandrels of the arches the waves produced on their surfaces

which the square root is found, and then a formula or theorem is applied; this makes the pattern and the design more complex.

All of this is a reflection of the interest in and extraordinary mastery achieved by science and Islamic culture in the field of mathematics and geometry. In these disciplines lies the symbolism — but also the order, the transcendence, the cosmos — in short, Divinity, Creation.

Epigraphic Decoration

As its name suggests, this entails the use of Arabic calligraphy — the letters of their *alifato* or alphabet — in two of its main variants: the Kufic and the Nashki.

The first is named after the new Mesopotamian city of Kufa, a great cultural centre of the Umayyads to where the capital was moved around the year 657; it is considered the cradle of Islamic architecture. The first Qur'anic texts were transcribed with its rigid and straight writing, characterised by the absence of the diacritical marks that distinguish many letters of the alphabet from each other. For this reason, it is considered a cryptic script, to the point that many Arabic-speakers are not able to read it; this gave it — especially in the early days — a mythical character, initially reserved for religious sayings, although over the centuries it evolved into many variations; its angular, straight forms also encouraged its use as another geometric element in strips, to outline cartouches or frame other decorative elements, etc. In many places like the Alhambra it frequently alternated with another kind of writing, the Nashki.

This latter script — also known as cursive — is the most commonly used for writing. Its rounded shapes favour its writing as a spiral-shaped pattern, resulting in numerous local and regional variants. Throughout the history of Islam, common dialects have been recognised: there was an Andalusí Arabic dialect, and yet another from Granada with its own distinguishing features. This is the one we see today on the walls of the Alhambra. The Nasrid dynasty's motto "There is no conqueror but God" is written in this script.

There are also frequent words of praise for the patron of a building: "Glory to our Lord the Sultan," along with religious praise and quotations from the Qur'an. We have already seen that the Nasrids ended up electing their vizier in a poetic contest between the subjects who knew Arabic best, which — besides helping to encourage the vanity of the sultan in power at the moment with metaphors and dithyrambs — was a guarantee of being able to work in the dynasty's famed diplomatic missions. Ibn al-Yayyab, Ibn al-Khatib, Ibn Zamrak and Ibn Furkún were some of the great Nasrid viziers and writers who ended up overshadowing even the sultans themselves; many of the texts adorning the Alhambra are collections or *diwánes* of *qasids* or poems — many of which have yet to be translated — by their own ministers, in which they describe ceremonies or celebrations of the court held in the places they decorate, such as the *Mawlid* or commemoration of the birth of the Prophet in the area where the Mexuar currently is located, the circumcision of the son of Muhammad V in the Sala de Dos Hermanas, or the operation of the water system of the Fuente de los Leones. This is why the Alhambra's epigraphic decoration is considered to be an authentic manual of poetry and literature, in addition to an important source of historical documentation and a valuable descriptive record of the various official areas.

Plant-Based Decoration

Generally known as *ataurique*, as its name implies, it uses elements of nature to develop its decorative scheme. This is, in turn, both very limited with regard to themes, but very varied in

Wall decoration with epigraphic and plant motifs in the Sala de la Barca in the Palacio de Comares

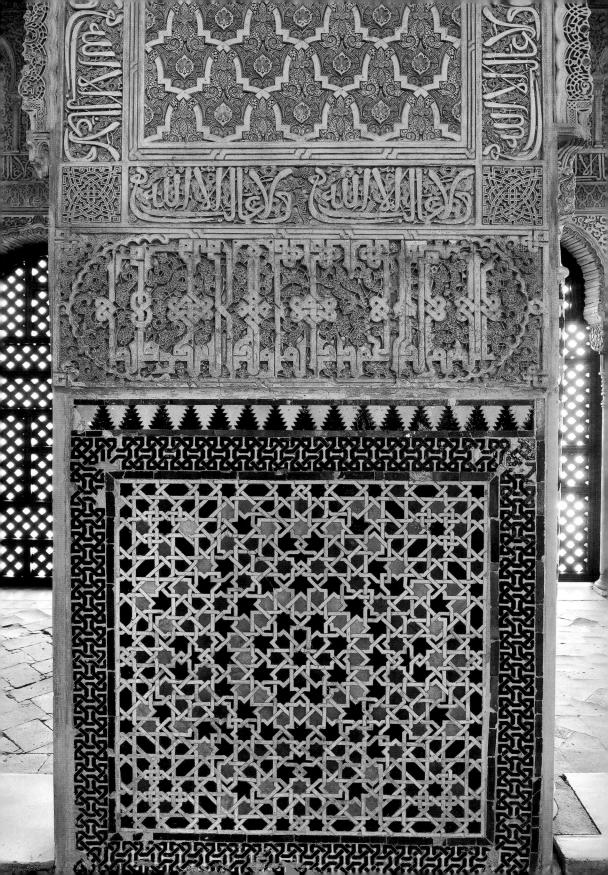

terms of form, something very characteristic of Islamic culture. Probably because of its symbolic nature, the basic decorative element in the early days was the vine, with its design pattern representing woven vines and branches; the acanthus meant development and – above all, as we can see in the Alhambra – so did the palms, shown in a wide variety of forms such as the single palm, double palm, fingered palm, with epigraphy, open or closed, etc. Pomegranates, pineapples, peppers, a few shells and sometimes even flowers instead of grapes, together with stems, leaves, scrolls, etc., complete – in a way that is denatured but very rich in nuances – the decorative scheme.

Stalactite Ceilings

This decorative work was based on the geometric combination of juxtaposed and hanging prisms and was used to decorate buildings. Traced over a pattern of squares and diamonds, the modules or prisms were carved at the bottom where the colour would be applied, while the upper part – resting on a face of another prism – was hidden; their bottom points were cut into a concave surface. One of the rules in the design of this decoration required that the lines where the two juxtaposed pieces were joined be oriented in the same direction.

With *mocárabe* or *muqarna* – also known as "stalactite ceilings" – Muslim art reached the pinnacle of perfection in mathematical calculation and knowledge of geometry rooted in the designs of the ceramic tile panel, in this case, however, represented in three dimensions. The *mocárabe* prototype appeared in the squinches that are the transition from a square space to the circular shape of a dome, resulting in a figure-eight. It appeared at the beginning of the tenth century and expanded rapidly from Turkestan to Andalusia, but debate is ongoing regarding whether it actually originated in Persia or in North Africa. Islamic art applied *mocárabe* designs to a multitude of elements such as cornices, arches and capitals, and did so using different materials

including stone, brick or wood. Without a doubt, however, the most spectacular constructions were those made with plaster domes because of the material's malleability, which allowed them to move away from the strict geometry required when using wood.

In carpentry, *mocárabe* was used for important elements on roofs, from eaves to the entire roof. The prism-shaped strips of wood, called *adarajas,* might have a rectangular, triangular or diamond shape, and were grouped around an octagonal piece to form the so-called cluster. Using a pattern, all of the *adarajas* were cut from one-eighth of this piece, resulting in the "negatives" of the clusters having a domed shape. The construction of plaster stalactite vaulting was not without its complexities and demanded great knowledge of geometry that few *alarifes* ever achieved; those who did were elevated to the class of teachers. Building them began at the corners with the help of wooden slats and metal nails, using black plaster to attach the modules cast with moulds, until it was completely closed and became a self-supporting – and at times even gravity-defying – structure.

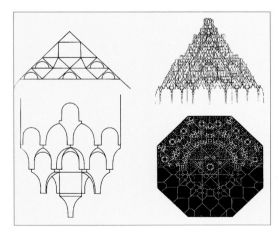

Analysis of the *mocárabe* dome in the Sala de Dos Hermanas. Drawings from the book by Owen Jones and Jules Goury, *Plans, Elevations, Sections and Details of the Alhambra,* London, 2 vols. (1836–1845)

Decoration with plant motifs, cursive and Kufic epigraphic strips and geometric tiling in the Sala de Comares

Detail of two small domes with *muqarnas (mocárabes)* in the Sala de los Reyes

The juxtaposition of the modules generated constructions with thousands of prisms, as in the Sala de los Reyes, the Sala de los Abencerrajes or the Sala de Dos Hermanas, whose vaults may contain more than five thousand prisms. The result of this geometric precision during the Nasrid period is that after five centuries of history, on Sabika Hill one may still enjoy contemplating these domes in which the sense of lightness achieved with the plaster creates an ethereal atmosphere in which the multitude of earthly elements manage to float, closely approaching the infinite multiplicity of the heavenly vault never achieved in the enclosure of a roof.

Water

For Ibn Khaldun, a Tunisian sociologist from al-Andalus (14th century), the first condition that land should meet in order for a city to be founded was that it should have access to a river or source of water. There is no water on the Alhambra's hill, so it had to be brought from a distance over different levels and then distributed through a flawless system of water pipes. A complex hydraulic engineering structure using connecting basins, large pools, cisterns and a multitude of conduits in a perfectly embedded network was devised.

Water is a fundamental element of Islamic civilisation and is the subject of symbolism and traditions. The Qur'an — the Muslim holy book — describes Paradise as a haven of lush greenery filled with gardens where water flows ceaselessly. In a mosque there can be no shortage of water, which — in the Islamic world — possesses an abundance of meanings: it is the origin of life; a symbol of purity as purifier of body and soul; it is considered as pious alms insofar as it facilitates purity to people and animals. It is the cleaning tool of choice for both personal hygiene and household cleaning, and it also has poetic connotations.

Water was considered to be public property. Public water fountains abounded in Andalusian cities. Decorated with polychromatic tiles, they supplied water to pedestrians and anyone who needed it. They were installed next to the mosques in order to facilitate ritual ablutions or near the gates of the city to quench the thirst of travellers.

Many homes in al-Andalus had access to water through wells or cisterns, sometimes located in the house's interior patio, or piped in. These tanks, which were equipped with filters, stored rainwater that flowed from the terraces and flat roofs through athanors or clay pipes, which were cleaned frequently. It was rare for an Andalusian patio — no matter how humble the home's residents were — not to have some kind of central water-related element, whether this was a pool, fountain or sink. Most of the houses had latrines with running water to keep them clean and to prevent an unpleasant odour. Many of these — simple holes in the floor with sewer pipes running underneath — can be seen in the Alhambra.

For Islam, cleaning the body is a socio-religious principle. Arabic literature offers a multitude of books devoted to hygiene. The 14th-century Granada-born vizier and polyfacetic writer Ibn al-Khatib himself wrote on taking care of one's health during the different seasons of the year. In addition to ritual ablutions prior to prayer, carrying out personal hygiene with water was especially recommended for the hands before eating, once the meal had finished, and after having sex. A large variety of containers was available for washing. Most were ceramic, though some were made of metal, such as water jugs, hand basins, etc., and, of course, there was the steam bath. The *hammam* were located in central areas of the city, close to the gates, but they were also installed in some homes that, due to the owner's social status, could afford them to entertain guests.

They were public gathering places, with shifts for women and men. The groom used to reserve the baths for his friends before the wedding, and historic public uprisings have been plotted in their rooms. It is a rare inland Andalusian town in which a street or town square related to the baths does not still exist.

The early Muslims learned irrigation techniques from the Persians, and during their expansion across the southern Mediterranean basin to the Iberian Peninsula they discovered Roman hydraulic works. In Persia, Mesopotamia and Syria there were underground conduits or *qanats*.

In Granada, the rules for distributing water for irrigation were controlled by the *Sahib al-saqiya* — the Albaicín's *zabacequia* or water master for the *cármenes* — until not long ago. Working under the *qadí*, who was in charge of the regular courts, he would mediate between the irrigators, ensuring that they met the supply for each shift, overseeing the water in the channels and making sure that users kept them clean. Islamic law — *Fiqh* — distinguished between "pure" and "purifying" water, "pure" (but not "purifying") water, and water contaminated by impurities, establishing lists of "pure" and "impure" materials, ways to purify water, or defining its functions.

As in many parts of the Maghreb today, until not long ago in Granada one could see water being sold by water carriers in exchange for a few coins. Their activity was regulated by city ordinances inherited from the medieval *hisba* (rules regulating public morality) treaties.

Countless devices were devised to channel and distribute water, with the names of many of them having endured to this day. The Spanish word for diversion dam, *azud* (from the Arabic *al-sudd)*, is the name given to the dams that divert the flow of rivers; water distribution tanks or water distributor boxes distributed the smaller circuits. The water wheels (Spanish *noria,* from the Arabic *na'ura)*, raise the water, sometimes to a great height.

The Palacio de los Leones in the Alhambra can be considered the epitome of Hispano-Muslim art. The fountain in the middle of its courtyard is the synthesis and symbol of

its decorative wealth, while at the same time it is a prototype for the compound's entire hydraulic system. The fountain in the Patio de los Leones is an example of technical traditions that were the result of the construction-related studies and experiences taking place over many centuries of inspiration that led to the creation of the Alhambra.

Water Tanks

The Alhambra's *albercas* are genuine elements that represent the different uses and functions that a structure or element can have in Islamic culture, in this case the Nasrid culture.

These tanks play an essential role in the city's hydraulic system — whose operation is based on a network of connecting basins strategically located throughout the site that took advantage of different heights and uneven terrain — by means of which water pressure was adjusted and distributed across all sectors. This is a reflection of the profound understanding that the Nasrid builders had of the land, as well as their mastery of hydraulic engineering, something we have not yet completely managed to decipher even today. The large Albercón de las Damas, for example, located on the slopes of the Cerro del Sol between the Alhambra and the Generalife, shows the importance of these elements for the first rural and then urban settlement and its evolution over time. The troops capturing the Alhambra in the late 15th century were largely unfamiliar with how this hydraulic system worked, which, together with the different concept of and needs for water, caused them to neglect and modify the system's installations. When the monument was recovered during the 20th century, the fountains and gardens once again began to work and Los Albercones complex was recovered, a similar one was built adjacent to it (in the 1920s), and another at a lower level (in the 1950s).

The second important function of the Alhambra's water tanks is to decant the water from the channel. The channel gets its water from the Darro River, more than six kilometres away, through various channels and conduits, so it collects silt and impurities as it flows through them. The ponds are supplied with water at their highest point by fountains and dispensers, and are emptied from the top as well via drains located almost on their edges in order to maintain the water level. This achieves a perfect circuit that maintains the pressure but promotes the settling of sediment in the bottom of the tank, interestingly enough in a way that is similar to modern water treatment plants in cities today.

The tanks are also open cisterns, since they hold a large amount of water that, if necessary, can be used as an alternative resource. All we must do is recall how important the water, cisterns and tanks were in the siege of Granada. Thanks to these reserves, its inhabitants were able to hold out for months.

The water tank is also perceived as another aesthetic element integrated into the whole of the building's complex. Its location and size are part of the design scheme for the building or compound for which it is devised. The tank's surface functions as a mirror that reflects the architecture and its surroundings; it probably reached perfection in the palaces of the Alhambra, for example in the Patio de los Arrayanes and in the Palacio de Comares, where it creates a three-dimensional visual effect without which the court would seem too horizontal. At midday, the light reflected from the surface is projected onto the plasterwork of the southern façade, resulting in a play of light and the illusion of twinkling light that helps make the surrounding architecture seem less heavy.

Recent microclimate studies show the importance of the assets of humidity, light and temperature to the architecture of the Alhambra, for which the body of water located in the courtyard — the tank — together with the landscaping that it nourishes, is crucial.

Water, an essential element in Nasrid palatine architecture. The Palacio de Comares, facing south

José María López Mezquita, Patio de los Arrayanes (1904). Fine Arts Museum of Granada, Palacio de Carlos V, Alhambra

Water Basins and Fountains

Water-holding elements are integrated into the Alhambra as a complement to the architecture and its interior spaces; they represent an intermediate step or link with nature, with the garden, an advance interpretation of what awaits the Believer in Paradise. For this reason, Granada's Muslims felt a genuine veneration for water. It is hard to walk through the Alhambra without coming upon a pool, fountain or basin filled with water and noting its refreshing coolness and sound.

The water from the Alhambra's fountains flows. A dynamic element, it enhances the effects from its reflection of the different kinds of light that appear throughout the day, shining on the flat surfaces as if they were a mirror, seeking out another dimension for the architecture, to which it lends an ethereal quality, brightness, a natural environment, coolness, a microclimate.

In the origins of Islam, the desert nomadic culture had a very marked appreciation of water as a resource. This culture internalised the image of the oasis and when it became sedentary, it adapted this image by developing a science of hydraulics whose main objective was to avoid at all costs the loss of even a single drop of something that was so precious. That is why Islamic architecture is lacking in the demonic image of the European Gothic or Romanesque gargoyles that projected far from the building water so abundant that it became superfluous and even a hindrance. The Alhambra's few gargoyles are simple and straight; what is more, they are associated with the gutters and form the spouts for the fountains, as in the Palacio de Comares. Only a few have been found decorated with stylised plant motifs and wedge-shaped segments.

For the Nasrids, having fountains in their courtyards and gardens was not enough; instead, they adapted them to doorways and the inside spaces of the main rooms. They applied the Qur'anic reference to streams and rivulets winding among the feet of the Believers by linking these indoor fountains with narrow gutters that carry water — flowing sometimes quickly, sometimes slowly, but always transparent and murmuring — into the garden. The sultans of the Alhambra sat next to low fountains when conversing with a group of people or when deep in thought, just as did the medieval European kings round a fireplace or bonfire.

The arrival of the Christian kings to the Alhambra, with their different concepts, customs and needs regarding the use of space, was particularly evident in the domestic or residential areas and led to the modification of numerous spaces, including those related to the fountains. Accustomed to the spatter and splash of water — which can be quite noisy — they raised the low fountains and installed new water dispensers with tall spouts that made ripples in the smooth surfaces of the water in fountains and basins. They made the water pour into and then spill over the edges of the containers, in comparison to the Nasrid subtlety — contrived but clever — of maintaining the water level, calculated so as to cause the water to circulate but never overflow except when as part of an artful device, in which case it would slide by gently with a murmur or whisper, but never with strident — or even guttural — sounds.

Small clay athanors and lead pipes made up a pipeline network that when laid above ground used any kind of material: pieces made from cut marble or ceramic, sometimes glazed; simple brick-lined conduits that could be attached to the edges of stairways or run down the centre of their steps; even the tiles that protected the pipe circuits — once they were glazed and turned upside-down — made excellent conduits.

A kind of fountain called a "schematic fountain" can often be found in the Alhambra. Set into the pavement, their edges are flush with the floor of the room or slightly raised. Very shallow, they tend to maintain the water — which gushes forth from a wide pipe — at a low level. A correctly-proportioned drain allows the water to slide by smoothly but quickly, creating subtle ripples that, when they reflect the light, "shine like a dinar" according to the Arabic text.

These basins composed of stylised wedge-shaped elements are shaped like a kettle drum

Schematic fountain in the Comares Courts

or half an orange half and have fluted edges that favour the rippling movement resembling ocean waves inside the basin. Carved in marble of different thicknesses, the number of wedge-shaped segments varies widely and may have regular or alternating forms, sometimes with wedge shapes of different radii and at other times with a protruding edge or angle. They are usually medium-sized, but the larger ones can exceed two metres in diameter. There are also some that are quite small; these are made of ceramic and richly decorated. They owe their development — like many aspects of Hispano-Muslim art and aesthetics — to the Caliphate of Córdoba, of which the Alhambra is a continuation. Although they may be raised from the floor, they are usually slightly recessed with respect to the surfaces they drain into and which may have a polygon-shaped layout.

Gardens

As an inseparable part of palaces and compounds, the gardens and cultivated areas — decorative, sophisticated and symbolic elements — dot every corner of the Alhambra and the Generalife and bring a transcendent component — both in terms of territory and of space — to its landscape. The traces that the passage of time have left on the Colina Roja have multiplied and enriched the variety of gardens in the compound. In addition, the number and uniqueness of the plant species found here are clear examples of the varied tastes and different kinds of gardens that have existed in the Alhambra, and these are, in turn, a reflection of different times and attitudes.

It is true that the medieval gardens created during the Nasrid period are the most important given their far-off origin, the refined style in which the plants, the water and the buildings themselves that frame the gardens are integrated, as well as the close relationship they kept with their conception of the yearned-for Paradise of the Qur'an.

Arabic texts distinguished between different types of landscaped or cultivated spaces, and these names — though sometimes rather imprecise — are still used today to describe them. True to the heritage from earlier Mediterranean civilisations, the *riyad* (*rawd* in the singular) are the landscaped courtyards, pleasure gardens, the deepest reflection of the Hispano-Muslim garden, sometimes divided into four parts — like the courtyard of the Acequia del Generalife, or the courtyard that used to be called the Patio del Jardín and which later became the Patio de los Leones — and sometimes magnified by a large pool, such as the one in the Patio de los Arrayanes in the Palacio de Comares or the one near the courtyard in the Torre de las Damas in the Partal. In the courtyard — as the centre and expansion of the palace, private, safeguarded from observation from the outside, yet sometimes wisely open to the landscape — water takes on special importance as an essential foundation of power and prosperity, as an element whose reflections can "reconstruct" volumes, bring light to shadowy areas and evoke the presence of perfection, of the sublime.

In the monumental complex, it is not unusual to find gardens in which the presence of different types of vegetable species is obvious. As in the Andalusí period, here the flower/vegetable garden has a certain orderly arrangement and structure aimed at reconciling the aesthetic and productive functions, so that both the irrigation systems and the arrangement of ornamental plant species allow for the presence of fruit trees and other classic vegetables in spaces where what is "flower garden" and what is "vegetable garden" merge in a unique way. This way of using plants, water and buildings, in which flowers, herbs, fruit and vegetables are combined with channels, pools and summer houses offering a place of respite, was used in particular outside the city on farms called *munya* or *bustán*. These farms tended to be quite large in terms of surface area and usually belonged to the aristocracy. They generally had multiple purposes — aesthetic, economic and experimental — but, depending on the circumstances, one of these might predominate. The Generalife would be, in this context, a classic *almunia*, a country estate with sophisticated palaces, private spaces reserved for

Basin in the *hammam* in the Palacio de Comares

Gardens of the Partal with the Generalife in the background

recreation and other spaces obviously meant for productive purposes.

Another term – *yanna* – also refers to a farm that is outside the city, but exclusively used for producing irrigated crops; it also had housing and could be divided into parcels for use by small-scale farmers. In a nutshell, *bustán* refers to the current concept of vegetable/flower garden and *yanna* to a cultivated vegetable/fruit garden with vegetable species and fruit trees.

Lastly, Granada's *carmen* (from the Arabic *karm*, "vine" or "vineyard") has also been inherited from the Andalusí system of cultivating vegetables and flowers. It refers to small (in general) farms that extend along the hills that descend to the Darro and Genil Rivers, arranged in what was long ago a group of subdivided plots shielded from the view of passers-by by the walls that surround them, and where a garden and orchard for growing seasonal species and fruit trees are arranged adjacent to the houses in a manner both useful and harmonious.

Among the most modern examples of the wide variety and number of gardens in the Alhambra are the Renaissance-era gardens in the Patio de la Reja or the Patio de Lindaraja – this latter undergoing changes in the 19th century – those of the 17th century (the gardens in the Adarves and the Alcazaba), of the 19th century (the upper gardens of the Generalife), of the 20th century (the gardens in the Partal and the new gardens in the Generalife) and even of the 21st century (in the theatre area).

The complex's plant life has also changed over the centuries, not only in terms of the number and variety of species, but also with regard to cultivation and maintenance techniques and styles. The traditional species used in the Nasrid era – such as the wallflower, jasmine, cypress, bitter orange or varieties of lily – have been joined by many others from other regions and continents that nowadays are considered to be fully integrated into typical Granada gardens, species such as boxwood, Japanese allspice, geranium, aspidistra, wisteria and pompom.

Emperor Babur's Garden of Loyalty. Mogol miniature (1590). London, The British Library [OR. 3714, f. 173b]

From among all of these, if there were one species that could represent the gardens in this compound, it would certainly be the myrtle. This shrub — considered in the Arab world as a plant with *barak* (a blessing, hidden and invisible) — having dense, fragrant foliage, planted individually and trimmed as a hedge, has been used during all eras and in almost every one of the Alhambra's gardens, although the variety known as "Moorish myrtle" — which has a larger, curled leaf and a tradition dating back to the medieval era — goes almost unnoticed in some of the more private areas of the Alhambra and the Generalife.

Construction Materials and Methods Used in the Alhambra

The Nasrid kingdom was founded during a political era that was as difficult as its survival would always be. Excepting a few brief periods, it never enjoyed abundant economic resources, so its builders had to find ways to take the utmost advantage of their imagination, with refined construction techniques and an excellent use of modest materials, in order to achieve such brilliant results, often sacrificing very important — even vital — aspects to this building requirement. In this regard, let us recall the verses in which Ibn al-Khatib — the enigmatic Prime Minister of Muhammad V, the great builder and reformer of the 14th-century Alhambra — warns him about what could happen should he overspend on the priorities, while at the same time reminding him of what, in his judgement, they are:

> [...] You, Muley, you are ignoring me, because you walk under scaffolding and ropes, among sacks of stucco and brick and carts bringing slabs of stone to a barren wasteland, while facing enemies who, greedy and cruel, are harassing us. [...] like someone gathering myrtles for planting on a rundown plot of land with an uninhabited house! [...] Do not abuse your power; awaken, save and, for your own benefit, make the troops and the treasury grow.

The most important of the modest materials used by these great *alarifes* to make the Alhambra a reality appear below.

Muslim masons building a wall in the traditional manner (ca. 1850). Alhambra Library

Rammed Earth

Most of what makes up the structure of the monument — the buildings, towers and walls — was done using a building solution widely used in its surroundings: the *tapial,* or rammed earth construction. Its elegance lies in the fact that it is the best technical solution to a pressing need: the builders of the Alhambra needed — in a relatively short time — to erect a large number of constructions of modest economic cost. To do this, they extracted the clayish material of which the hill itself is made, processed it and corrected its granulometry, added a binder (lime), mixed everything thoroughly and then added water to moisten it. This was used as abuilding material by pouring it inside wooden moulds with two side caps made of boards and a whole host of ancillary parts that made the mould undeformable and able to withstand the pressure of the material when it was poured in and compressed. It was compacted by using a wide range of wooden rammers of different weights and shapes, depending on the area of the mould that was to be built (bottom, surface, corners, etc). Each mould — or *tapial* — built this way produced a construction module which, once filled, compacted and turned out, was called a *tapia* (rammed earth wall segment); a wall built in this way comprised a set of successive wall segments.

This construction system might vary depending on the part of the element being built, or according to the element's intended use, and the terminology varied from one area to another, as usually happens with all traditional systems' techniques. Most of the Alhambra's towers and walls were made using a *tapial*.

Lime-based Concrete

This consists of a mixture of aggregates (gravel and sand) and lime used exclusively as the binder; mixed with water it yields a very strong and durable material. Its manufacturing technique must have been very refined, to judge

from how well-preserved the elements built with it are. In the Alhambra, it is found mainly in those parts of the buildings where more weight had do be borne, such as the lower parts of walls, foundations, etc.

Brick

These were a fundamental part of the interior architecture of the Alhambra, and were made by firing clay from the area in Granada near the Vega and not far from where tile kilns exist to this day, since the manufacture of ceramic products is an activity that has continued over time in the area. They were also used as decorative elements, as seen, for example, in the archway of the Puerta de las Armas or the inside façade of the Puerta de la Justicia. Their measurements tended to vary around 19.5 x 14 x 4 cm. Fired in wood-heated kilns, their degree of firing — and therefore their quality — varied, since the temperatures inside these kilns were not constant. Traditionally made bricks not very different to those used by Nasrid

Detail of the Alcazaba fort where one can see the "boxes" of the Nasrid rammed earth wall, with its layers and putlog holes, indentations and brick reinforcements

architects to build the Alhambra's palaces are still being used today in the complex's ongoing maintenance activities.

Plaster

Plaster was the basic material used for most of the Alhambra's decorative elements. It can be seen in the *mocárabes* that make up part of the vaults, on many of their walls in the form of openwork plaster panels or *sebkas* above the columns framing large porticos, or as an effective means of praising God in the Qura'nic suras used in the epigraphic decoration appearing in many parts of the complex, to praise and flatter the sultans, or to describe – precisely but poetically – some of the more beautiful spaces. Nasrid architect-builders were masters in working with this material, using it where – theoretically – it should least likely perform well, that is, outdoors. However, their refined techniques for mixing the paste made from this material have allowed it to remain intact over time.

Plaster is used in a wide variety of ways in the Alhambra. In the most secluded and private of domestic spaces, it can be found as a fine stucco to cover the baseboards of the walls, serving as a base coat for their tempera-based decorations, or covering walls in the form of a simple gypsum-water plaster.

Lime

Lime was one of the Alhambra's essential building materials. It was used throughout the Nasrid period and was part of the composition of the *tapiales* and of lime-based concretes as an essential part of the mortar used to build walls. Hydraulic lime was used to make mortars for lining pools, cisterns and water tanks, since its waterproof mass could set and harden under water, or by simply using aerial lime to produce exterior finishing mortars – now mostly gone – but that constituted a real "skin" for the buildings, and were noted for their perfect compatibility with the building material on

which they were applied. This technology has been rescued and is commonly used in the renovations carried out in the monumental complex.

Stone

Stone is used in two different ways in the Alhambra: ornamentally and functionally. In the former category, it can be found as symbol of power, covering and forming part of the great gates, the best example of which is the Puerta de la Justicia or the Puerta de los Siete Suelos – the latter was once lost but has been rebuilt – and on others that are less spectacular but of great beauty such as the Puerta del Vino, and even in others that are hardly noticeable, such as the Puerta del Arrabal or the gate to the upper area of the Alcazaba. These gates were usually

Detail of one of the fountain's lions, where one can appreciate the stone's texture

Inside wall of the Torre de Comares with plasterwork decoration covered with stone – limestone or sandstone – obtained locally from the areas around Loja or the Temple. This same ornamental use can be found associated with water, as it is the element used to build the fountains, the best example of which is the Fuente de los Leones, carved in Macael marble. In terms of its functional use, it can be seen employed as flooring – sometimes of spectacular dimensions as in the Sala de Dos Hermanas – or as a structural material in the form of columns in the Patio de los Leones, both in Macael marble. However, in order to see the best example of stonework – both in terms of construction (the stone skeleton) as well as decoration – we should make a stop at the Palacio de Carlos V.

Wood

An essential and ever-present element in the monumental compound, it can be seen supporting its roofs as crossbeams or rafters and collar beams, or serving as a framework

A Muslim carpenter and the tools of his trade (ca. 1850).
Alhambra Library

for supporting the floor as large beams, joists and planking, etc., mostly made of pine. It is also in evidence in apparently modest elements such as latticework shutters or windows, as well as elements of spectacular size, such as the large doors of the Puerta de la Justicia, Puerta de las Armas, Puerta del Arrabal and the Puerta de los Siete Suelos. It may also be found on breathtakingly lovely interior doors such as those in the Sala de la Barca, the Sala de las Aleyas, the Sala de Dos Hermanas and, of course, in what is the pinnacle of Nasrid woodwork, on its ornately carved panelled or coffered wooden ceilings, the finest example of which is in the Salón del Trono in the Palacio de Comares.

The "Alhambra Formation"

For those who spend their lives working in construction, the primary – and perhaps most important – building material is the land itself, considered as the foundation upon which their edifice will be erected. The Alhambra was built in an area especially suited for its foundation. Comprising a reddish conglomerate that includes variable-sized boulders, this very ancient and compact geological formation was responsible for the fact that – despite the passage of time and the many vicissitudes suffered – the monument's compound has done so well in terms of its structure. This geological formation – also present in other elevated areas of the city and its environs – was named the "Alhambra Formation" by geologists, as a tribute to the monument located on it.

The Alhambra's Plasterwork

One of the most commonly used materials in the Islamic world is plaster, used to cover the walls of most of its buildings, both inside and outside the rooms. The ability of Muslim craftsmen, coupled with how easily plaster can be mixed with water and its excellent qualities as a building and decorative material led to a rapid expansion of its use throughout the Islamic world, but it is in the Alhambra where the largest variety of delicately crafted motifs can be found. When gypsum is subjected to temperatures

Detail of the Alhambra's conglomerate with a vein of red earth

between 120° and 1,000 °C, the heat causes all or part of the water of crystallisation to be lost, turning it into semi-hydrated calcium sulphate ready to be mixed with water.

Such an important plaster industry required nearby quarries from which to obtain gypsum and, according to historical documents, a geological exploitation – currently in operation – was located 11 kilometres from the Alhambra in the area of Monte Vives in the municipality of Gabia la Grande. Here, varieties of *lapis specularis* and alabaster that yield a very pure white plaster optimal for fine decorative work can be obtained. It was in the Alhambra where a change took place that revolutionised workshops and working methods; this consisted of using moulds to make a large number of castings. This forced them to develop a new technique for attaching the panels, a technique that had not existed previously, since carvings were done directly on the plaster wall. The Nasrid period combined direct carving with the use of moulds, and this

new technique – not without complexities – greatly reduced the time factor, allowing more space to be decorated in less time. The utmost care was taken in carving the single mould used and, in the final Nasrid period (which can be considered "naturalist"), artisans achieved examples of diminutive motifs that – as if they were authentic pieces of stitched lace – were combined with ornate plant, geometric and epigraphic shapes, as seen in the succession of decorations in the Torre de las Damas.

The plasterwork – very far from the present state in which it is today as the result of having lost most of the expressiveness from its vivid colours – was polychromatic, using a small palette of primary colours along with a clever combination of black, red and blue, alternating with a white background and gold leaf that was reserved for Qur'anic texts.

Until now, no one could understand how it had survived, given its known capacity for absorption of and high solubility in water. However, the latest research activities on this material have yielded information on the presence of a white top layer composed of calcium sulphate and organic additives that covers all the carved motifs, making them more resistant to the external agents that could cause them to deteriorate, and facilitating the adherence of the final polychromatic finish. The presence of this white layer and of other substances applied to the motifs obtained from moulds – a technique unknown to today's artisans – makes the Alhambra's plasterwork unique in the world.

Restoration in the Alhambra

"Restoration" refers to all operations, materials or interventions carried out on a monument or work of art needed to repair damage and to preserve it. From the mid-19th to the early 20th century, the Alhambra was restored in general along the lines of the theory established by Viollet le-Duc (1814–1879) who, in his *Dictionnaire Raisonné de l'Architecture Française du XI au XVI siècle* (Paris, 1854–1868), defines it thus: "The word and the thing are modern. To restore a building is not to preserve it, repair

GRANADA. 1114. — Templete de levante del patio de los Leones. (Alhambra). J. Laurent Madrid.

Eastern pavilion of the Patio de los Leones with the 1859 roof. Photograph by J. Laurent, 1871

it or rebuild it; it is to return it to a condition of completeness that may never have existed at any given time." This kind of restoration is known as "stylistic restoration."

Based on this declaration, 19th-century Alhambra restorers – primarily Rafael Contreras – were determined to give the Alhambra an image that corresponded not so much to its particular historical reality and the vicissitudes suffered over the centuries, as to the ideal of "Arabic style" that they had created, so they added some elements and altered others during restoration to emphasise the monument's "Oriental" aspect. Thus, under the direction of Contreras, in 1859 work was begun to restore the roof of the eastern pavilion of the Patio de los Leones, replacing it with a dome covered in glazed ceramic. Similarly, in the north gallery of the Palacio de Comares, the roof was covered with glazed tiles and decorated with a small dome. From 1843 to 1866, the plasterwork decoration in the Sala de las Camas in the baths was finalised and its polychrome was freely restored. To emphasise that image, many of the plasterwork decorations were recreated, and gaps and missing panels were filled in. Since the aim was simply to create an overall effect absent of any rigour whatsoever, copies cast from fragments located in other parts of the monument were placed on undecorated walls.

Leopoldo Torres Balbás (1888–1960), architect and curator of the Alhambra from 1923 to 1936, introduced scientific criteria that superseded 19th-century stylistic restoration and were consistent with the principles that were emerging in Europe with regard to the conservation and restoration of monuments as reflected in the Athens Charter for the Restoration of Monuments (1931). Basically, these principles are: to understand conservation largely to be the work of regular, ongoing maintenance of historic buildings; an absolute respect for the historical and artistic work of the past, without banning the style of any era from this work; the legitimacy of the use of modern techniques and new materials, provided that they are recognisable; and

the need to provide legal protection to the area around the monument, recommending the removal of all advertising, poles, cables, etc., as well as any noisy activities that might disturb the tranquillity necessary for contemplating the monument. Perhaps the most significant aspect of this document, however, is the recognition that the best way to ensure conservation depends not as much on material restoration activities, as on the feelings of affection and respect that people have for their monuments.

Torres Balbás applied and enriched these principles in the Alhambra. The monument's current conservation is rooted in his management, which he carried out according to a vast plan of restoration activities for which he established the criteria. New experiences and documents have enriched and clarified what the culture of restoration was like around 1930. Its most significant contribution is the value attached to the land on which the monumental complex sits and the need to include it as part of the building's restoration. Coupled with this is the emphasis on the need to undertake protective measures and regular maintenance in order to avoid restoration activities, with these being understood as activities of extensive intervention.

The Alhambra Manifesto
In October 1952, architect Fernando Chueca Goitia convened a group of intellectuals – mostly architects – at the Alhambra to ponder the Nasrid monument through the eyes of modernity. From that event emerged a document – *The Alhambra Manifesto* – that for decades has provided several generations of professionals with food for thought about the ongoing lesson in contemporaneity demonstrated by the Alhambra and one of the most interesting episodes of 20th-century artistic culture in Spain. Looking at the Alhambra through the eyes of modernity was an exciting and committed effort within the context of a critical review of the national and international trends through which contemporary architecture was passing at that time.

The Alhambra is, therefore, a real meeting place and intellectual reference, where many of the ideas underpinning the leading edge of the discipline of architecture converge and remain in effect: an open floor plan adapted to its geographical environment; the intelligent relationship between architecture and landscape; balanced measurement and proportions in space and volume; the dialogue between forms and decorations; the link between art and nature; the geometric abstraction of its profiles and elevations; the constructive rationality of its spaces; and the intelligent refinement of its concept as the enclave of a monument — in short, values that were in line with the main concerns of those scholars.

There can be no doubt that the meeting of this group of architects in the Alhambra was a critical experience and, in itself, innovative. It was the first attempt — from a contemporary vantage point — to think about the monument as a heritage legacy and from the perspective of the lesson it teaches about what history can contribute to the present and the future, not only as a historicist type of model, which was the model that had always been assigned to it perhaps because of the influence of the romantic Alhambresque revival.

The Alhambra of the 21st century continues to maintain its validity as a meeting place upon which the eyes of contemporary art — in all its aspects, without limits or conventions of any kind — are focused. It continues to bring light, shadow and colour to the space of creative freedom. It continues to offer us a lesson on what Dewey called the "experience of art," an experience that makes the understanding of universal values part of being human.

Upper pavilion of the Palacio del Partal. The Observatory

13 The Alhambra's Historical Stages

The Alhambra is a monumental complex housing one of the richest cultural landscapes in the world. From the perspective of time, these cultural treasures have been built through an intertwined series of historical events that, taken together, constitute the essence of its meaning. The Alhambra is a living monument, forged over more than seven centuries by the Muslim culture that invented it, the Renaissance culture that adapted it, the romantic culture that recreated it in its imagination and the scientific culture that continues to interpret it day by day.

The Alhambra before the Alhambra

The name of the Alhambra is inextricably identified with the Nasrid dynasty (13th–15th centuries). There were, however, chronologically much older buildings built on Sabika Hill. Some ashlar stones that were reused because of their size and strength for reinforcing strongholds may be associated with the Roman period. It is not yet possible to determine the presence of Roman remains with certainty, but historians and archaeologists specialising in classical antiquity say there are remains of walls from this time which could have been occasionally used as the foundation of medieval buildings. Watchtowers, roads or land divided into farming plots survived on the Iberian Peninsula into the time of the Visigoths and the early stages of al-Andalus, and were subsequently altered or finished. Currently, research groups are working on land surveying dating from the Roman era and its possible survival in medieval gardens, as well as in the areas around roadways and mines, for which the setting of the Alhambra can be a decisive factor.

The 11th century provided the Alhambra with its design, which coincided with that of the castle-residence of the Banu Nagrilla, viziers of an independent Zirid *taifa* (Muslim-ruled principality), whose sultans sited their palace over the old Roman forum located on the hill of the current Albaicín. Both compounds, separated by the gorge of the Darro River, were the stage for the clashes that took place alternately between the local supporters of al-Andalus and successive invaders from North Africa — the Almoravids and the Almohads — whose goal was to reunify Islam in the Peninsula and whom those living in Granada — despite being Muslim as well — considered to be foreigners. The old Zirid military outpost — one of whose main walls has survived in the current Alcazaba — must have remained in a severely damaged condition until the Nasrid dynasty chose it as the foundation for the Alhambra's compound.

The Banu Nasr or Nasrids

The Nasrid sultanate of Granada (1232–1492) was the last of al-Andalus' Muslim states. Its founder, Muhammad Ibn Ahmad Ibn Yusuf Ibn Nasr, al-Ahmar, a member of a family of Arab origin who ruled the town of Arjona (Jaén), extended its borders along the Andalusian Mediterranean coast from Tarifa to beyond Almería. Strangled in the south by North African sultanates and in the north by Christian kingdoms, and coveted by both for 260 years, Granada alternated between asking for help from one or the other in exchange for heavy taxes or territorial concessions.

Muhammad I joined with Ferdinand III to conquer Córdoba in 1236 in exchange for the city of Granada, ruling over Málaga and Almería in the

future and participating in the conquest of Seville in 1248. On Ferdinand's death in 1252, he struck a deal with the North African Marinids. The Nasrid state's practise of entering into state alliances continued throughout its history. If their foreign policy constantly alternated between diplomacy and military action with one state or another, internally, the situation was no less volatile: there were frequent uprisings by governors along with dynastic struggles and intrigues reflected in the list of sultans who ruled, many of them killed by treachery, deposed or restored to their position in short periods of time. The loss of Gibraltar in 1462, the increasingly heavy taxes, the marriage of Ferdinand of Aragon and Isabella of Castile and the union of their kingdoms in 1479, marked the fall of the Nasrid sultanate. Beginning in 1481 Sultan 'Ali (Muley Hacén) made some gains but, between his subjects' discontent and uprisings while his wife and his Christian favourite fought for their respective son's rights to the succession, he ended up ceding power to his viziers. In the end, the throne was occupied by his wife's son Abu 'Abd Allah Muhammad (Boabdil). He was captured during an expedition and later released in exchange for 400 Christian captives, twelve thousand pieces of gold and the promise to recognise Ferdinand of Aragon's authority over Granada.

After regaining power, Boabdil could not maintain his state's position and one after another, its major cities — Alhama, Ronda, Loja, Málaga, Baza and Almería — fell, until only overpopulated and besieged Granada remained. Given the finality of the situation, the city surrendered on 2 January 1492.

From a cultural and artistic perspective, four different periods can be identified during the reign of the Nasrids. A first phase — from 1238–1314 — of affinity and harmony with their Almohad predecessors that lasted for the reigns of the first four sultans. During the second stage — from 1314 to 1354 — a particular, already-evolved style was developed, with two notable palace-building sultans: Isma'il I and Yusuf I. The third period corresponds to the sultanate of Muhammad V

— the great builder — especially during his second term from 1362–1391, the Golden Age of the Nasrids, aesthetically naturalist and contrived. The last stage — which could be considered repetitive or reiterative and lacking in the brilliance of the previous period — covered the entire 15th century. There were, nevertheless, noteworthy sultans such as Muhammad VII or Yusuf III.

The Alhambra as a Royal Palace

In 1492 the Alhambra became part of the Crown's property as a royal palace and was assigned important military functions, such as the Captaincy General and its own jurisdiction separate from that of Granada, so that it was incorporated into the Catholic Monarchs' modernisation programme, which was designed to introduce innovative administrative structures and policies into the new state with which the Modern Age was being inaugurated in Spain. From then on, the palatial residence of the Alhambra was called the "New Royal Palace" in order to distinguish it from the "Old Royal Palace" or Nasrid Palaces. Its new functions were an indication of the alterations made to the Alhambra's compound. The entrances to the palace city were changed. The entrances that had been habitually used by the Nasrid inhabitants were no longer used, being replaced by the Cuesta de Gomérez entrance,

Charles V's imperial coat of arms on the Pilar de Carlos V in the Alhambra woods, adjacent to the Puerta de la Justicia

Detail of the pictures on the middle ceiling of the Sala de los Reyes in the Palacio de los Leones

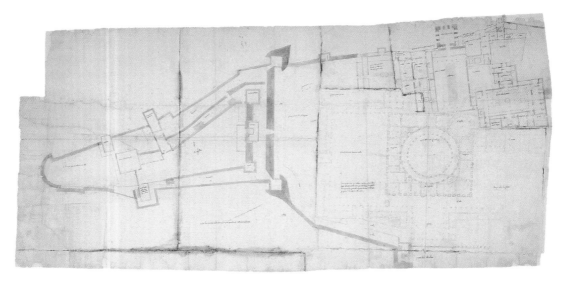

Map of the Alhambra, unsigned and undated, attributed to Pedro Machuca and thought to date from prior to 1542, now conserved in the Royal Palace in Madrid

especially once the Puerta de las Granadas was built as a triumphal arch. The defensive system was reinforced with circular bastions that were more effective against the artillery, the most feared military innovation in the war for Granada. A large cistern was built to supply water to the site, crowded to capacity by a military population with different customs and needs. The spaciousness of late 15th-century Christian palaces when compared to the small houses of Granada's Muslims and Moors resulted in the new occupants joining two or more adjacent houses in order to adapt them to their basic needs. Similarly, the Catholic Monarchs, who divided the Alhambra up between the court and its knights, reserved the most outstanding Muslim palaces for themselves and their royal residence. Already familiar with Muslim buildings — which they accepted and even admired — in other locations, they decided that the repairs to these buildings would be carried out based on the Mudéjar decorative style, summoning artists from the Levante, Zaragoza, Seville and, later on, Córdoba, thus making it possible for their Islamic heritage to be maintained in a subtle fusion with the Mudéjar style in a number of sites in the Alhambra. Nasrid decorative themes were

combined with western Renaissance designs, especially in the entrances to the Casa Real, the Mexuar and the Cuarto Dorado, where the Nasrid cross-bar coat of arms alternated with the emblems of the Catholic Monarchs; the repair of the plasterwork thus became a symbol of respect for Hispano-Muslim culture. The Alhambra's former mosque was turned into a church and the old palace on Real Street became the Franciscan convent. The queen herself asked that her remains be laid to rest there until the construction of the Royal Chapel in Granada was finished. All of these acts point to the royal will that was part of the conquest of a city of fundamental importance in the context of the times.

After Emperor Charles V married Isabella of Portugal in Seville in the spring of 1526, he decided to stay on at the Alhambra until autumn. Living quarters were improvised for him and — in addition to it supposedly being the site of the conception of future King Philip II — he showed how much he admired his grandparents by deciding to build a grand imperial palace and to turn the chancel of the cathedral of Granada into a pantheon for the Spanish Crown. In a way, it was designed to bring legitimacy in the last Islamic bastion in the West to the lineage of the greatest defender of the Christian world. His decision led to the court relocating to Granada, which would play host for a few months to nobles such as Germaine de Foix (the widow of King Ferdinand), the Count of Nassau, ambassadors such as Andrea Navaggero, Baldassare Castiglione (an apostolic nuncio), and writers such as Boscán and Garcilaso de la Vega. At that time, Charles V enjoyed the support of Pope Adrian VI – his former tutor – and of Henry VIII of England through the 1522 Treaty of Windsor, which was decisive in finalising the campaigns on several fronts. The end came in 1525 with the capture of King Francis I of France at the Battle of Pavia and his transfer to Spain, which seemed to signify that a lasting peace had been achieved. However, despite his affection towards the Alhambra, deeply flawed decisions were taken there that would determine the future of the nation, such as increasing the taxes on the Moors – who were in constant revolt – or his willingness to sign the Treaty of

Madrid and free the French king, which meant returning Burgundy and withdrawing from the Duchy of Milan in return for a friendship sealed by the marriage of Francis I to the emperor's sister, the Princess Leonor. After he crossed the border, the French parliament forced Francis I to repeal the agreement, appealing to his royal duty to protect French territory, so the king voided the treaty on the grounds that he had agreed to it under duress.

The discovery in the early 20th century of a floor plan of the Alhambra's Casa Real drawn during those years – now preserved in the Library of the Royal Palace in Madrid – provided valuable information for understanding and recovering the Nasrid Palacio de Comares, the Palacio de los Leones and other alterations of the Alhambra that explain the transition of a medieval city to a royal palace.

A Separate Chapter in the Story: the Tendilla-Mondéjar, Governors of the Alhambra

Any approach to post-Reconquest Alhambra or attempt at understanding the following three centuries of its history would be impossible without knowing who the Tendilla family were and what their family saga represented to the Alhambra. Some of its members were chosen for their connection to the royal location at a given moment in time, because of their relationship with its transformation, or simply because they were born there and grew up in an atmosphere of Renaissance tolerance and erudition that was part of their family tradition, which was not the case for all of them. Until its departure, the Tendilla family lived in the Alhambra in what had been the palace of Yusuf III in the Partal.

Tendilla and Mondéjar: both lineages coexisted in the family, with the oldest being the Tendilla lineage. The Mondéjar lineage was added by Don Iñigo López de Mendoza y Quiñones, the first of this illustrious family originally from Guadalajara – where the family's estates were – to arrive in Granada in response to the war.

Iñigo López de Mendoza y Quiñones (1442?–1515), second Count of Tendilla – a title he inherited from his father, Iñigo López de

Coat of arms of the Counts of Tendilla and Marquises of Mondéjar, located on the Pilar de Carlos V

Mendoza y Figueroa — was the grandson of famed poet Don Iñigo López de Mendoza, Marquis of Santillana. Along with the Catholic Monarchs, he took part in the campaign against the kingdom of Granada, distinguishing himself in the defense of Alhama when Muley Hacén tried to retake it. After a short period when he served as King Ferdinand's ambassador to Rome, he rejoined the war until Granada was conquered, and was part of the king's entourage when Boabdil turned the keys over to the king. Ferdinand then gave him the keys and appointed him Governor of the Alhambra and Captain-General of Granada. For almost twenty-four years, significant changes aimed at adapting the fort to the new tactics of attack and defence based on the intensive use of artillery were implemented under his direction. All of the artillery bastions — Siete Suelos, Cabezas, Justicia, Olivo and Torres Bermejas — designed by the great royal architect Ramiro López were built, and passive defense was improved by building a large water cistern (buried in front of the Alcazaba) that bears his name. Unconditionally loyal to King Ferdinand, he did not hesitate to oppose the monarch when he tried to requisition most of the artillery and gunners (leaving the Alhambra unprotected) for the fleet in his African campaign. Part of the royal burgh of Mondéjar became his property, and in 1512 he was awarded the Marquisat of Mondéjar, a title linked to his family ever since.

Luis Hurtado de Mendoza y Pacheco (1489–1566), third Count of Tendilla and second Marquis of Mondéjar, was governor of the Alhambra from 1515 to 1543. During the Revolt of the Comuneros, he stood unconditionally with Charles V, earning the trust of the Emperor who became a personal friend, and whom he accompanied in the conquest of Tunis. During his tenure, the Alhambra lived moments of great splendour coinciding with the emperor's nearly six-month (June to December 1526) visit during his honeymoon, in which Charles V was captivated by the Alhambra and by Granada and decided to build the splendid palace.

Iñigo López de Mendoza y Mendoza (1512–1580), fourth Count of Tendilla and third Marquis of Mondéjar, was governor of the Alhambra from 1543, when his father was appointed viceroy of Navarre, until 1580. It fell to him to quell the rebellion of the Alpujarras and the African possessions of Oran and Bougie. Though he had a difficult character, he was learned and a good organiser. In the Alhambra, work continued on the Palacio de Carlos V, the ramparts of the Torre de la Pólvora and the compound of the Nasrid palaces. Significant investments were made, work progressed at a satisfying rhythm, and the project enjoyed support from Pedro Machuca and, when he died, from his son Louis, master craftsman Francisco de las Maderas and others who reported to him.

Luis Hurtado de Mendoza y Mendoza (1543–1604), fifth Count of Tendilla and fourth Marquis de Mondéjar, was born in the Alhambra and helped his father during the Moorish Revolt with logistical support from the rearguard. He had a difficult character, did not get along with John of Austria, and was dismissed as warden of the Alhambra by Philip II in December 1569. His departure from the Alhambra marked the start of this family's decline (from this time on the title of Governor of the Alhambra would be honorary), and the beginning of the neglect that would immerse the entire complex in a state of decline that lasted for more than two centuries.

José de Mendoza Ibáñez de Segovia (1657–1734), twelfth Count of Tendilla and tenth Marquis of Mondéjar, coincided with a complicated period as well as the no less complex War of Succession (1701–1713). He chose the wrong side, swearing allegiance to the Archduke Charles, thereby falling out of favour with Philip V, who confiscated his property. On the death of his father in 1708 and that of his mother in 1718, the properties he inherited from them were confiscated, including what had been the family residence in the Alhambra — the palace of Yusuf III in the Partal — for nearly 326 years. Since he was no longer able to make use of the palace — which was in a poor state of conservation — he had it torn down. José de Mendoza regained royal favour after the 1725 Treaty of Vienna between Philip V and Charles — who was by then Holy Roman Emperor — and although he was allowed to keep the purely honorary title of Governor of the Alhambra,

Gustave Doré, *Tile Robbers in the Alhambra* (1862).
Alhambra Library

the title died with him, as did the relationship the Tendilla family had with the Alhambra.

The Governors' Alhambra
(the Saddest Century in its History)

The middle of the 18th century brought with it the darkest period in the history of the Nasrid compound. The Marquises of Mondéjar and Counts of Tendilla were stripped of the governorship of the Alhambra by King Philip V because they refused to support the Bourbons in the War of Succession for the Crown. According to Gómez-Moreno González, "in 1750 the Crown appropriated resources allocated for construction works [...]. After that — and despite the constant complaints they received — they showed not the slightest interest in the palace, and a disastrous period of neglect began." The Alhambra thus entered into a phase of decline, reaching its lowest point with the invasion of Napoleon's troops and the pillaging carried out during their retreat in 1812, and continuing until mid-century: one hundred years that marked an era of

devastation. It was taken over by a large number of unworthy and self-interested individuals who used it for their own purposes, plunging it into a period of authentic mismanagement. Without its Captaincy General and having only the scarcest of resources, its governors no longer exercised any authority; instead, they left the Alhambra in a state of almost total neglect. In 1792 Bartolomé de Rada — a judge charged with overseeing the Alhambra — lamented that he had only "2,302 *reales* and 30 *maravedises!*... when what was needed was several million *reales.*"

Under the reign of Charles IV, the governors and their families lived in the Alhambra with their sole concern being personal gain. Complaints about the state of the Alhambra by American writer Washington Irving — who arrived in the city in 1829 — embarrassed the government and led to it taking action. The governor at the time, Colonel Francisco de la Serna, began to evict the palaces' inhabitants and inaugurated the tree-lined promenades but, for Ford, "his main goal was to give work in the Alhambra to the galley slaves [...] turning [...] much of the Alhambra into storage areas for the fish-salting facilities belonging to the rabble who worked for him."

When Richard Ford visited Granada in 1831, he recounted — with critical irony — that "The Governor, one Savera, [...] removed all vestiges of Arab taste. He put his kitchen and dirtiest belongings in a Moorish lookout point, where the marble and gold still lie among unspeakable abominations [...] this mob was in control over what could be moved or sold." The wife of Governor Ignacio Montilla "penned her donkey in the beautiful chapel and converted the Patio de la Mezquita into an enclosure for her sheep." Workshops were installed in the palaces and pieces of their decoration were sold: "They tore off much of the tiled base surrounding the courtyards around the water tank and others as well, selling them to bakers and cooks [...] finally turning the Sala de Dos Hermanas — the jewel of the Alhambra — into a silk factory, full of looms."

In 1830 Ferdinand VII allocated 50,000 *reales* a year for conservation work — a sign of greater interest in the Alhambra's problems — although the general condition of the premises was not

A LA MEMORIA
DEL
CABO DE INVALIDOS
JOSE GARCIA
QVE CON RIESGO D PERDR LA VIDA
SALVO D LA RVINA LOS ALCAZARES
Y TORRES D LA ALHAMBRA EN MDCCCXII
EL CVERPO D INVALIDOS

Commemorative plaque in the Plaza de los Aljibes
According to oral tradition, when Napoleon's troops withdrew from the Alhambra in 1812, they left a barrel of gunpowder in each tower and set alight the fuse that linked them; the towers fell one by one until Corporal José García risked his life to disable the fuse, which was approaching the area where the Nasrid Palaces were. This plaque is in remembrance of his brave deed, which saved humanity from an irreparable loss. It can be found on the wall that encloses the southern part of the Plaza de los Aljibes.

much better. Among other comments, Ford said that the Puerta del Vino "is used as a rubbish tip", the Patio de Carlos V "has been used for the galley slaves' workshop" and the Alcazaba "is now being used as a prison for galley slaves," although at no time did he mention his own signed graffiti that he left everywhere (Salón de Comares, the Fuente de los Leones). In 1839, in order to "beautify" the monument, the columns and fountain itself in the Patio de los Leones were cleaned using a method involving scraping. In 1840, under the regency of María Cristina, larger amounts of funds were allocated, and there was even a suggestion that the Palacio de Carlos V be finished, but this did not mean that the abuse of the monumental compound ceased: between 1840 and 1848 the Torre de los Siete Suelos was turned into a tavern; shortly after, it was enclosed within the wall around the hotel that was built in front of the tower. Though repairs were made, it continued to be neglected, as mentioned by architect Rafael Contreras with regard to the Patio de los Arrayanes: "During the entire 18th century and the beginning of this century, most of the tiles in this courtyard, the door of the Sala de la Barca and its *comarraxias* or Moorish plasterwork were lost and, finally, its pond was turned into a public laundry room, and its cloistered areas became a tavern serving the people that still, in 1833, came up from the town to play cards under its beautiful coffered ceilings." Named "restorer of ornaments" in 1847, this representative of the saga of the Contreras family not only took charge of all of the compound's nooks and crannies, but also flooded half of Europe with reproductions of Alhambra-style decorative motifs from his own workshop. With him, the

"period of one hundred years, from 1746 to 1847, during which the saddest page in the history of the Alhambra was written," ended.

Napoleon's Troops and Their Occupation of the Alhambra

The expulsion from the Alhambra of the House of Mondéjar — stripped of its governorship title and with its properties confiscated — marked the beginning of the unfortunate period of neglect and decay of the monument that, chronologically speaking, began in 1718 with the abolition of the Captaincy General, and culminated in nearly three years of occupation by Napoleon's troops, who arrived in Granada on 28 January 1810. Leading them was Count Horace Sebastiani, Corsican general of the Fourth Army Corps. Once French rule throughout the kingdom of Granada — except in Almería — was fully established, Sebastiani took up residence in the city, introduced strict ordinances on cleanliness and hygiene for both the city and its inhabitants, and set about undertaking major urban transformation projects.

The Alhambra became a barracks and although some interesting contributions were made — such as the main layout of the tree-lined avenues that would eventually become the Bosque de Gomérez — the fact is that the outcome was disastrous. Many houses were destroyed and some of the finest areas of the monumental complex were converted into warehouses. Some 1,500 soldiers were distributed throughout the compound, including the Convento de San Francisco and the Palacio de Carlos V where, to fight the cold, fires were lit and fed with wood from anywhere: coffered panelling, doors and other wooden items. The Patio de los Arrayanes was used to stack the firewood and its water tank was used for storing gunpowder and cannon shells. There were also alterations, such as the one in the Patio de los Leones, where Sebastiani ordered the pavement to be removed and had a garden of roses, jasmines and myrtles planted; and in 1812 even the courtyard's roofs were worked on. The consequences for one of the Alhambra's most emblematic sites were so disastrous that they sped up its deterioration, which soon after, in 1846 led Alexandre Dumas himself to exclaim: "Pray for the Patio de los Leones, pray that the Lord keeps it standing, or at least pray that, if it does fall, it is not re-built. A corpse is preferable to a mummy!"

Well-versed in the strategic power of artillery, the French placed batteries of guns at vital points in the vicinity of the Alhambra, such as the Silla del Moro, the ruins of Palacio de los Alijares and the Cerro del Sol; mining activities were carried out in the latter, using newly-built galleries or prolonging those already in existence in search of suspected veins of gold. With a reputation for plundering, Napoleon's army became a focus for all possible charges of stripping the Alhambra bare. In fact – as Richard Ford mentioned – after the French withdrawal it was the new local leaders who "plundered the Alhambra, pulled out the locks and bolts, carried off glass objects, selling everything for their own profit and, then, as good patriots, reported that the French had left nothing behind."

When the French abandoned the Alhambra on 17 September 1812, in order to make sure that a well-defended fortress could not be of service to Spanish rebels in the event of a Napoleonic counter-offensive, they mined the towers with barrels of gunpowder, blowing up eight of them, which fell one by one in anti-clockwise order beginning with the Torre de la Barba adjacent to the Puerta de la Justicia. Despite the risk to his life, Corporal José García from the Regiment of Invalids – who had lost a leg in the Battle of Bailén – managed to stop the chain of explosions by disabling the remaining fuses, saving the Alhambra from certain disaster. This heroic act was forever immortalised in a memorial plaque in the Plaza de los Aljibes.

Orientalism and Romanticism: Alhambrism

With its occupation by Napoleon's troops, the Peninsular War converted the Alhambra into a desolate place that gave it the appearance of a romantic ruin in the eyes of the travellers who began to visit and admire it, and it quickly achieved international recognition. Its unique, evocative character favoured its transformation into an artistic and literary myth that in some way still survives and that modern historiography has taken care to glorify.

The neglect suffered by the Alhambra after the first decade of the 19th century coincided with a series of circumstances that led to it being converted into a prison but – unlike

Alhamí in the Patio de Comares. Drawings from the book by Owen Jones and Jules Goury, *Plans, Elevations, Sections and Details of the Alhambra*, London, 2 vols. (1836–1845)

Oil painting by Manuel Gómez-Moreno González, done in 1880, representing *Boabdil's family leaving the Alhambra.*
From the collection of the Granada Provincial Government

in the past – it no longer held important personalities, just common prisoners. After the liberal revolution and a series of subsequent exclaustrations, the community of Franciscan friars gradually decreased until it disappeared from the compound, while the civilian population found itself giving way in the face of a motley settlement of unranked soldiers. The governor of the Alhambra himself no longer lived there, leaving it in the care of a family described in contradictory fashion by Washington Irving and Richard Ford. Among the ruins, semi-desertified landscapes, prisoners, disabled soldiers and marginal population, the romantic perspective allowed one to contrast the neglect and misery of the palace-city with its past grandeur.

Romanticism as a cultural concept originated in Germany in the late 18th century, although its name comes from the Spanish expression "a thing of romance," an expression used to describe all that existed outside reality. Canvasses, watercolours, novelised stories, travel guides and books extolled the mind – the power of reason – in contrast to what is concise and limited, a consequence of the Enlightenment. The description and representation of the architectural, decorative and landscape elements of a monument like the Alhambra coincided in time with 19th-century Europe's interest in everything Oriental. Thus, romanticism and orientalism melded into one in the Alhambra, chosen as an exotic prototype of the Arab world of which Andalusia would be its closest European expression. Just saying the word "Alhambra" in any language evoked unconscious feelings that wove together dream-like fantasy and reality.

During the first half of the 19th century, European artists and writers took uncustomary trips to Italy, the Middle East and – after the Peninsular War – Spain, in particular Granada and its Alhambra, which became places of pilgrimage. Chateaubriand, on his return to Paris after a jaunt around half of the world, brought with him as relics a stone from the River

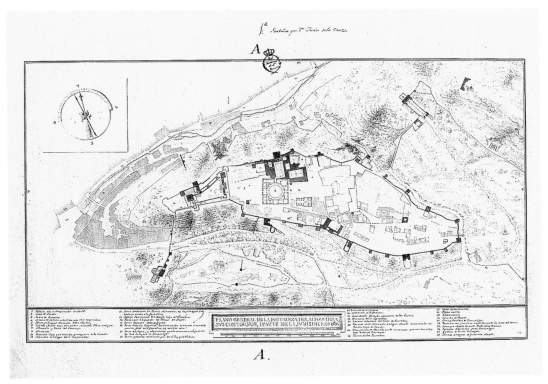

José de Hermosilla, map of the citadel of the Alhambra in 1766.
Museo de la Real Academia de Bellas Artes de San Fernando, Madrid

Jordan and a piece of bark from a cypress in the Generalife; British officers returning to the islands after supporting the rebels against Napoleon spoke wonders of the treasures to be discovered in Spain; the liberals themselves that were exiled in England helped to encourage interest in all things Spanish. Fiercely individualistic, with no classically-based rules or guidelines, these travelling artists believed that they could recognise in it the synthesis of the civilisation and traditions of the peoples of the Orient.

The world-wide attention paid to the Alhambra owes much to the ruin's evocative character as presented by Washington Irving in his *Tales of the Alhambra*, the first edition of which appeared in London in 1832. The efforts of 18th- and 19th-century travellers and enlightened individuals such as Dutailly, Laborde, Swinburne, Roberts, Ford, Lewis, Girault de Prangey, Owen Jones, etc., to transmit these spatial and stylistic values, made the Alhambra an icon of the era's aesthetic renewal. The Alhambra became a model or object of admiration and emulation for a generation of intrepid precursors of a new nomadism that would evolve into today's cultural tourism.

Architect-Led Management

The Real Academia de Bellas Artes inaugurated the 19th century with a series of inspection visits of the Alhambra carried out by architects, resulting in the 1804 publication of the book *Antigüedades árabes de España* by J. Hermosilla, J. de Villanueva and P. Arnal, which included the very first "official map" of the Alhambra. In March 1847 architect Domingo Gómez de la Fuente was commissioned with visiting the Alhambra to resolve differences on the conservation of the monument, and on 18 September 1890, following a fire in the

Sala de la Barca, Ricardo Velázquez Bosco was commissioned with issuing a report (1903) and, later, the Report on the General Plan for the Conservation of the Alhambra (1917). As a result, the architect become *de facto* the actual director of the complex.

Over the centuries, many architects have carried out construction work aimed at conserving the Alhambra, and several administrative agencies have worked to oversee these activities and to determine the correct criteria for each intervention. Never more than during the time in which the responsibility for conserving the monument fell upon an architect could the influence of his training and personality be seen more clearly in his vision of the whole and in his reading of the historical and architectural treasures.

From the mid-19th century to the early 20th century, the Alhambra was restored following, in general, the so-called "stylistic restoration" theory established by Viollet le-Duc (1814–1879), who defined it thus: "The word and the thing are modern. To restore a building is not to preserve it, repair it or rebuild it; it is to return it to a condition of completeness that may have never existed at any given time."

The early part of the 19th century saw the beginning of a period (from 1828 to 1907) during which a family saga of architects and restorers — the Contreras (José, Rafael, Francisco and Mariano) — would take charge of the monument. Their work stood out as a result of a decidedly stylistic restoration focused on the decorative elements. This period coincided with the turmoil within European thought on the debate between conservation and restoration as criteria for intervening in monuments (John Ruskin, Camillo Boito, etc.). In Spain, this debate mostly took place between intellectuals and technical specialists related to the institutions responsible for national monuments. Thus, the restorers of the Alhambra — primarily Rafael Contreras (1824 or 1826–1890) — devoted themselves to creating an image of the Alhambra that corresponded not so much to its particular historical reality and the vicissitudes suffered during modern times, as to the ideal of "Arabic style" that they had created: they decided to add elements or alter others to emphasise the monument's "Oriental" aspect. With this intention, in 1859 Rafael Contreras and Juan Pugnaire repaired the roofs in the Patio de los Leones, replaced the roof of the eastern pavilion with a spherical glazed ceramic dome, and adorned the roof of the northern portico of the Palacio de Comares with glazed tiles and a small dome. Between 1843 and 1866 they completed the plasterwork decoration and freely restored the polychrome in the Sala de las Camas; many of the plasterwork decorations were recreated, gaps and missing panels were filled in and copies cast from fragments located in other parts of the monumental compound were installed.

From 1907 to 1923 Modesto Cendoya focused his management efforts on the idea of a "global Alhambra" based on trying to discover hidden areas via a frenzied search for archaeological finds. This was a faltering period, marked by unfinished attempts that led to the digging of trenches and the removal of debris, but that yielded meagre results in terms of maintaining its architecture, despite his capacity for observation and drawing (he left behind a magnificent notebook).

From 1923 to 1936 architect Leopoldo Torres Balbás — trained in archaeology and art history and very active in the debate on historical heritage — carried out his highly intense work in the practical application of conservation criteria. Today, his work can be seen in a large percentage of the Nasrid buildings. His work was based on the principles of the 1931 Athens Charter for the Restoration of Monuments: conservation through the work of regular, ongoing maintenance of historical buildings; an absolute respect for the historical and artistic work of the past, without banning the style of any era from this work; the legitimacy of the use of modern techniques and new materials provided that they were recognisable; and the need to provide legal protection to the area around the monument.

The long period that followed — which ended with the implementation of the current democratic government — was closely related to the country's political circumstances. From 1942 to 1970 the architect in charge of the monument, Francisco Prieto Moreno, continued the work undertaken by his predecessor and introduced many of the urban and landscape elements on which current tourist itineraries are based.

Detail of the commemorative plaque placed over the door to Washington Irving's room by the Council of the Alhambra in 1914

Plaque commemorating the Alhambra being included on the UNESCO's World Heritage Sites List in 1984

New experiences and documents on conservation have enhanced the value of the area where the compound is located and the need to include this area within the overall interpretation of its structure. It is also necessary to take precautionary measures and to carry out ongoing maintenance, with the understanding that restoration activities should only take place as last-ditch measures. There should not be a single person with a vision in charge, but rather multi-disciplinary technical teams equipped with the appropriate scientific and technological capacity.

CHIEF ARCHITECTURAL CURATORS OF THE ALHAMBRA IN THE 19TH AND 20TH CENTURIES:

José Contreras, who was appointed in 1828 to be in charge of defense and security construction works

Salvador Amador, appointed Architectural Director, 17 July–7 November 1847

Rafael Contreras, Director and Curator beginning in 1869 (Restorer of Ornaments since 1847)

Francisco Contreras, appointed in 1850

Juan Pugnaire, Director, 1851–1858

Ramón Soriano, Colonel and Commander of the Alhambra beginning in 1856; appointed Chief Architect in 1858

Baltasar Romero, Chief Architect, 1872

Mariano Contreras, 1890–1907

Modesto Cendoya, 1907–1923

Leopoldo Torres Balbás, 1923–1936

Francisco Prieto Moreno, 1936–1970

Conservation Service of the Alhambra, since 1986

A Council for the Alhambra

The 1868 revolution resulted in Isabella II losing the throne and marked a significant change in the status of the Alhambra, since after the government seized all the royal family's assets, the Alhambra passed from the Crown to the public domain. The Alhambra was declared a National Monument in 1870, and a fixed amount from the national budget was allocated to adequately meet its conservation needs. During the last third of the 19th century the government exercised its custody and control through the Provincial Commission of Monuments. However, due to the Alhambra's uniqueness, in 1905 a specific commission for it was created within the main commission; while originally not intended to assume the latter's responsibilities, it soon caused significant friction, making it impossible for it to continue. To complicate matters further, in 1913 the Council of Friends of the Alhambra was founded. Its legality was questioned at the outset. One year later after having assumed its duties, it was disbanded, mainly because of tensions with then architectural curator Modesto Cendoya. Beginning in 1915, the original committee was linked — using the name "Council" — to the Directorate-General of Fine Arts of the Ministry of Public Education, later the Ministry of National Education.

After the Civil War — during which the Alhambra fortunately suffered only minor skirmishes — the new, strongly centralised government assumed responsibility — with a

Group of images that illustrate the Palacio del Pórtico del Partal at different stages of architectural restoration, in 1835, about 1920, about 1930 and currently

markedly symbolic gesture – for the conservation of the site. On 9 March 1940 a Council was set up to install residential facilities in the Palacio de Carlos V and on 13 August of the same year a decree was issued that expanded the Council to the entire Alhambra. From 1942 to 1970 architect Francisco Prieto Moreno was at the forefront of the conservation of the Alhambra. A follower of and assistant to Torres Balbás, he carried on his work, preparing the Alhambra for the increase in tourism in the 1960s, an enormous challenge he had to face during that period. The monument enjoyed influence in the government from distinguished Granada-born professor Manuel Gómez-Moreno Martínez and, later, from another Granada native, Antonio Gallego Burín, who was appointed Director of Fine Arts in 1951. Also important were the creation of the Archaeological Museum of the Alhambra in 1942 under the direction of Jesús Bermúdez Pareja and,

one year later, the declaration of the Alhambra and the Generalife as Historical Gardens. With the Council established as the monument's trustee, it located its corporate headquarters in the Palacio de Carlos V, which also houses its offices, the Library, the Archives and, since 1958, the Fine Arts Museum. The infrastructure and restoration work carried out during those years led to an administrative process that culminated in 1962 with the publication of the Statutes of the Council of the Alhambra.

Years later, the German Friedrich von Schiller Foundation awarded a gold medal to the Alhambra in recognition of the conservation and restoration of European buildings, and this was formally presented to the Council in the Salón de Comares on 8 November 1980.

The 1978 Constitution restored democratic and decentralised legislation in Spain by means of its Autonomous Communities, and this also had an influence on the evolution of the Alhambra with the drawing-up of the 1981 Andalusian Statute of Autonomy. In terms of cultural administration, the process of transferring culture-related responsibilities from the central government to the Andalusian Community Government was completed in 1984, and this led to the adoption on 19 March 1986 of the new Statutes of the Council of the Alhambra and Generalife.

It is important to highlight the main legal instruments that were created to protect the management of cultural resources – among which the Alhambra is an outstanding example – during this institutional democratisation process: the Spanish Historical Heritage Act of 1985 and the Laws on the Historical Heritage of Andalusia of 1991 and 2007. As a result of this legislation, the first territorial planning document applied to a monument in Spain – the Special Plan for the Alhambra and Alijares – was created in 1986.

Since 2008 the development of the new Master Plan of the Alhambra has become a strategic tool for managing the Monumental Complex of the Alhambra and the Generalife as a first class heritage asset for the 21th century. The more than two million visitors who see the Alhambra and its surroundings each year claim their right to have access to cultural assets while at the same time insist on guarantees that they will be preserved for future generations.

THE FOLLOWING ARE OR HAVE BEEN RESPONSIBLE FOR MANAGING THE COUNCIL OF THE ALHAMBRA AND GENERALIFE:

SPECIAL COMMISSION
Manuel Gómez-Moreno González, President, 1905–1914

COUNCIL OF FRIENDS OF THE ALHAMBRA
Santiago Stuart y Falcó, President, 1913–1914

COUNCIL OF THE ALHAMBRA
Manuel Gómez-Moreno Martínez, Secretary, 1914–1915

Directly Dependent on the DIRECTORATE-GENERAL OF FINE ARTS 1915–1940

COUNCIL OF THE GENERALIFE
Benigno de la Vega-Inclán y Flaquer, President, 1921–1925

COUNCIL OF THE ALHAMBRA
AND OF THE PALACIO DE CARLOS V
Joaquín Pérez del Pulgar y Campos, Vice President, 1940–1944

Antonio Gallego Burín, Vice President, 1945–1951

COUNCIL OF THE ALHAMBRA AND GENERALIFE
Antonio Marín Ocete, Vice President, 1951–1970

Emilio Orozco Diaz, Vice President, 1970–1973

Juan de Dios López González, Vice President, 1973–1978, and Director, 1978–1981

Antonio Gallego Morell, Director, 1981–1985

Mateo Revilla Uceda, Curator for the Alhambra and Generalife, 1985–1986, and Director, 1986–2004

María del Mar Villafranca Jiménez, Director since 2004, and Director-General since 2010

Patio de los Arrayanes in the Palacio de Comares

Sultans of the Nasrid Dynasty*

1 Muhammad I (629–671/1232–1273)

2 Muhammad II (671–701/1273–1302)

3 Muhammad III (701–708/1302–1309)

4 Nasr (708–713/1309–1314)

5 Isma'il I (713–725/1314–1325)

6 Muhammad IV (725–733/1325–1333)

7 Yusuf I (733–755/1333–1354)

8 Muhammad V, first reign
(755–760/1354–1359)

9 Isma'il II (760–761/1359–1360)

10 Muhammad VI ("the Redhead")
(761–763/1360–1362)

11 Muhammad V, second reign
(763–793/1362–1391)

12 Yusuf II (793–794/1391–1392)

13 Muhammad VII (794–810/1392–1408)

14 Yusuf III (810–820/1408–1417)

15 Muhammad VIII ("the Small"),
first reign (820–822/1417–1419)

16 Muhammad IX al-Aysar ("the Left-handed")
first reign (1419–1427)

17 Muhammad VIII ("the Small"),
second reign (1427–1430)

18 Muhammad IX al-Aysar, second reign
(1430–1431)

19 Yusuf IV Ibn al-Mawl (Abenalmao) (1432)

20 Muhammad IX al-Aysar, third reign
(849/1432–1445)

21 Yusuf V ("the Lame") (849–849/1445–1446)

22 Isma'il III (849–851/1446–1447)

23 Muhammad IX al-Aysar, fourth reign
(851–857/1447–1453)

24 Muhammad X ("the Small"), first reign
(1453–1454)

25 Sa'd, first reign (1454–1455)

26 Muhammad X ("the Small"), second reign
(1455)

27 Sa'd, second reign (1455–1462)

28 Isma'il IV (1462–1463)

29 Sa'd, third reign (869/1463–1464)

30 Abu l-Hasan'Ali (Muley Hacén),
first reign (869–887/1464–1482)

31 Muhammad XI (Boabdil),
first reign (887–888/1482–1483)

32 Abu l-Hasan'Ali (Muley Hacén),
second reign (888–890/1483–1485)

33 Muhammad XII al-Zagal
(890–892/1485–1487)

34 Muhammad XI (Boabdil), second reign
(892–897/1487–1492)

* The charts marked with an asterisk are taken from María Jesús Viguera Molins (coord.). "El reino nazarí de Granada (1232–1492): política, instituciones, espacio y economía," in J. M. Jover Zamora, *Historia de España Menéndez Pidal*. Madrid: Espasa-Calpe, 2000. Vol. VIII–III.

N.B.: The dates appearing next to each sultan refer firstly to the Muslim calendar and secondly to the Christian era.

Historical Events during the Nasrid Reign*

1232 Proclamation of Muhammad Ibn al-Ahmar in Arjona (Jaén). Beginning of the Nasrid dynasty

1236 Cordoba is conquered by Ferdinand III

1237 Muhammad I enters Granada, Almería and Málaga and is recognised as their sovereign

1243 Murcia comes under the rule of Castile

1246 Jaén is conquered by Ferdinand III. Muhammad I becomes a vassal of Castile

1247 Seville is conquered by Ferdinand III

1262 Niebla is conquered by Alfonso X

1266 Revolt of the Banu Ashqilula in Málaga

1274 Beginning of the Marinid intervention in al-Andalus (first expedition)

1279 Recovery of Málaga by Muhammad II

1287–1288 End of revolt by the Banu Ashqilula

1292 Conquest of Tarifa, under Marinid control, by Sancho IV

1295 Marinid withdrawal and transfer of Algeciras and Ronda to Muhammad II. Conquest of Quesada and 22 more castles by the Nasrids

1300 Conquest of Alcaudete by Muhammad II

1303 Three-year truce with Castile

1306 Conquest of Ceuta by Muhammad III

1308–1309 Allied offensive by Castile and Aragón against Granada. Siege of Algeciras and Almería. Loss of Ceuta to the Marinids. Loss of Gibraltar to the Castilians. Transfer of Algeciras and Ronda to the Marinids

1312 Conquest of Alcaudete by Ferdinand IV. Recovery of Algeciras and Ronda returned by the Marinids

1319 Victory in the Battle of the Vega with the deaths of Princes Don Pedro and Don Juan, Regents of Castile

1327–1328 Alliance of Muhammad IV and the Marinid Abu Said Utman

1333 Recovery of Gibraltar, under Castilian control, by the Marinids

1340 Defeat, along with the Marinids, in the Battle of Salado or Tarifa, by Castile

1344 Conquest of Algeciras by Alfonso XI. Ten-year truce with Castile

1369 Recovery of Algeciras by Muhammad V

1372 Break with the Marinids. Muhammad V establishes relations with Tlemcen and Tunis and wrests Gibraltar from the Marinids, who will not return to al-Andalus

1373 Recovery of Gibraltar, under Merinid control, by Muhammad V

1392–1406 Offensive against Castile

1410 Conquest of Antequera by Prince Ferdinand of Aragón, Regent of Castile

1431 Severe defeat in the Battle of the Higueruela by John II of Castile

1462 Conquest of Gibraltar and Archidona by John II. Truces

1479 Castile and Aragon unite under Isabella I and Ferdinand II

1482 Conquest of Alhama by Ferdinand the Catholic. Victory of Abu l-Hasan in Loja

1483 Overwhelming victory in the Axarquía of Málaga. Defeat in Lucena and captivity of Boabdil, who signs a treaty of vassalage and takes up residence in Guadix. Civil war in Granada

1485 Siege and surrender of Coín, Cártama, Ronda and Marbella

1486 Siege and surrender of Loja, Íllora and Moclín. Civil war in Granada's Albaicín

1487 Siege and surrender of Málaga

1489 Siege and surrender of Baza. Transfer of Almería and Guadix by Muhammad XII al-Zagal

1491 Siege and surrender of Granada

1492 Transfer of the Alhambra (2 January) and of the city (6 January). Boabdil exiled to his principality of Andarax

* Source: María Jesús Viguera Molins.

Genealogical Chart of the Nasrid Dynasty*

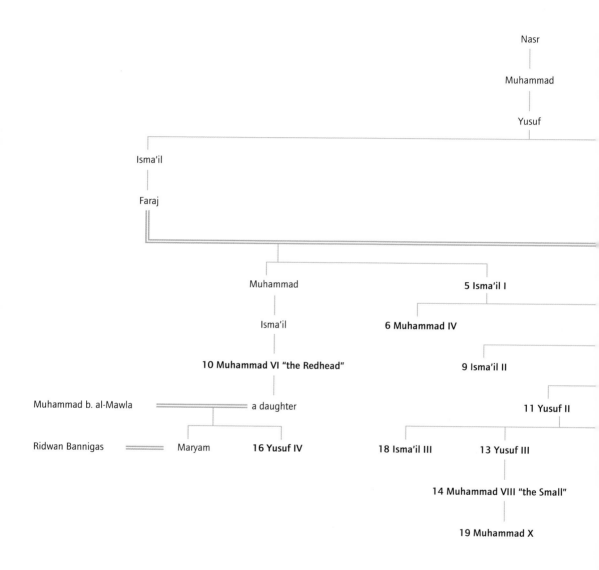

——————— offspring

═══════ marriage

Bold and Number: Sultan

* Source: María Jesús Viguera Molins.

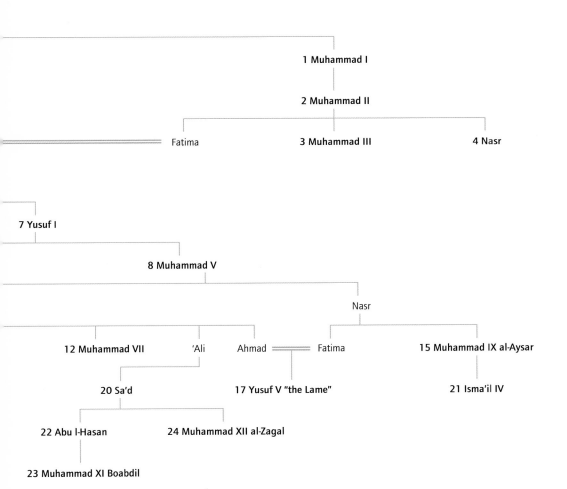

Comparative Table of the Rulers of Granada, Castile, Aragon and the Maghreb Al–Aqsa (Marrakech and Fez)*

Granada	Castile
Muhammad I (1232–1273)	Ferdinand III the Saint (1217–1252)
	Alfonso X "the Wise" (1252–1284)
Muhammad II (1273–1302)	Sancho IV "the Brave" (1284–1295)
Muhammad III (1302–1309)	Fernando IV "the Summoned" (1295–1312)
Nasr (1309–1314)	
Isma'il I (1314–1325)	Alfonso XI "the Just" (1312–1350)
Muhammad IV (1325–1333)	
Yusuf I (1333–1354)	
Muhammad V (1354–1359) (1st)	Peter I "the Cruel" (1350–1369)
Isma'il II (1359–1360)	
Muhammad VI (1360–1362)	
Muhammad V (1362–1391) (2nd)	
	Henry II Trastámara (1369–1379)
	John I (1379–1390)
Yusuf II (1391–1392)	Henry III "the Ailing" (1390–1406)
Muhammad VII (1392–1408)	
Yusuf III (1408–1417)	John II (1406–1454)
Muhammad VIII "the Small" (1417–1419) (1st)	
Muhammad IX al-Aysar (1419–1427) (1st)	
Muhammad VIII "the Small" (1427–1430) (2nd)	
Muhammad IX al-Aysar (1430–1431) (2nd)	
Yusuf IV Ibn al-Mawla (1432)	
Muhammad IX al-Aysar (1432–1445) (3rd)	
Yusuf V "the Lame" (1445–1446)	
Isma'il III (1446–1447)	
Muhammad IX al-Aysar (1447–1453) (4th)	
Muhammad X "the Small" (1453–1454) (1st)	
Sa'd (1454–1455) (1)	Henry IV "the Impotent" (1454–1474)
Muhammad X "the Small" (1455) (2nd)	
Sa'd (1455–1462) (2nd)	
Isma'il IV (1462–1463)	
Sa'd (1463–1464) (3rd)	
Abu l-Hasan 'Ali (Muley Hacén) (1464–1482) (1st)	
Muhammad XI (Boabdil) (1482–1483) (1st)	Isabella "the Catholic" (1474–1504)
Abu l-Hasan 'Ali (Muley Hacén) (1483–1485) (2nd)	
Muhammad XII al-Zagal (1485–1487)	
Muhammad XI (Boabdil) (1487–1492) (2nd)	

* Source: María Jesús Viguera Molins.

Aragón	Maghreb al-Aqsa
James I (1213–1276)	ALMOHAD
	Al-Rashid (1232–1242)
	Al-Rashid (1242–1248)
	Al-Murtada (1248–1266)
	MARINIDS
	Abu Sa'id I (1217–1240)
	Abu Mu'arraf (1240–1244)
	Abu Yahya (1244–1258)
Peter III "the Great" (1276–1285)	Abu Yusuf Ya'qub (1258–1286)
Alfonso III "the Liberal" (1285–1291)	Abu Ya'qub Yusuf (1286–1307)
James II "the Just" (1291–1327)	Abu Tabit'Amir (1307–1308)
	Abu l-Rabi (1308–1310)
	Abu Sa'id II (1310–1331)
Alfonso IV "the Benign" (1327–1336)	
Peter IV "the Ceremonious" (1336–1387)	Abu l-Hasan (1331–1351)
	Abu 'Inan (1348–1358)
	Al-Sa'id I (1358–1359)
	Abu Salim (1359–1361)
	Abu 'Umar (1361)
	Abu Zayyan (1361–1367)
John I of Aragón (1387–1395)	'Abd al-'Aziz (1367–1372)
	Al-Sa'id II (1372–1374)
	Abu l-'Abbas (1374–1384)
	Abu Faris Musà (1384–1386)
	Abu l-'Abbas (1387–1393)
	'Abd al-'Aziz (1393–1396)
Martin I "the Humane" (1395–1410)	'Abd Allah (1396–1397)
Ferdinand I "of Antequera" (1412–1416)	Abu Sa'id III (1397–1420)
Alfonso V "the Magnanimous" (1416–1458)	
	Abd al-Haqq (1420–1465)
John II (1458–1479)	
Ferdinand II "the Catholic" (1479–1516)	Muhammad b. Imran (1465–1472)
	Muhammad al-Shaykh (Banu Watt) (1472–1504)

Islamic Dynasties*

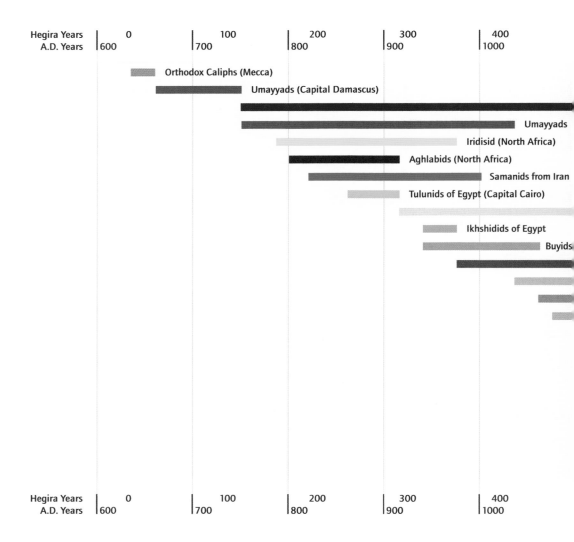

* Chart based on Alberto Canto and Tawfiq Ibrahim (curators). Exhibition Catalogue *Un resplandor del Islam.*
Los dinares del Museo de la Casa de la Moneda. Madrid, 2004.

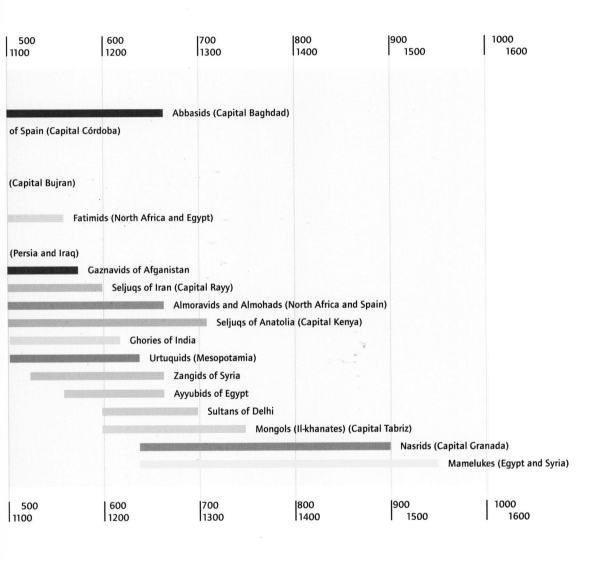

500	600	700	800	900	1000
1100	1200	1300	1400	1500	1600

Abbasids (Capital Baghdad)

of Spain (Capital Córdoba)

(Capital Bujran)

Fatimids (North Africa and Egypt)

(Persia and Iraq)

Gaznavids of Afganistan

Seljuqs of Iran (Capital Rayy)

Almoravids and Almohads (North Africa and Spain)

Seljuqs of Anatolia (Capital Kenya)

Ghories of India

Urtuquids (Mesopotamia)

Zangids of Syria

Ayyubids of Egypt

Sultans of Delhi

Mongols (Il-khanates) (Capital Tabriz)

Nasrids (Capital Granada)

Mamelukes (Egypt and Syria)

500	600	700	800	900	1000
1100	1200	1300	1400	1500	1600

14

Appendices

To complement the information contained in this guide, on the following pages we offer additional data showing the impact this monumental site has had throughout history. Firstly, there is a set of rules and tips that should be kept in mind in order to make the most of your visit. This is followed by a section with a selection of historical figures who have left their mark on the Alhambra's history and its conservation and distinguished travellers who have visited it, an index of the names of people appearing in the guide, a glossary to help you understand the meaning of some of the words used and, lastly, a selection of books that can help you to better understand the Alhambra. On the last page, a list of equivalencies in Spanish and English of the place names in the Alhambra could help visitors to understand their meanings.

Practical Information

The Alhambra and the Generalife are a Heritage Site, and have been included on the UNESCO's List of World Heritage Sites since 1984. The Council of the Alhambra and Generalife — an independent body under the Ministry of Culture of the Andalusian Regional Government — is responsible for ensuring its management and care and, in that respect, for taking the necessary steps to make the protection and conservation of the monument and public access to it compatible.

The reality of the site and its complexity and richness have led us to offer a series of recommendations to help you to fully enjoy and understand your visit. For the same reason, we have indicated certain limitations that have been established to ensure both the preservation of the monument as well as the safety and enjoyment of visitors.

Tips for Planning your Visit

It is important that you pay attention to the information contained in this section and to the information offered along the recommended routes on signs or through touch screens, Bluetooth connections, information centres, sites where reading material is available, the web site, etc.

We recommend that you carefully plan your visit, taking into account the time available, prioritising the places to see based on your interests and avoiding excessive fatigue.

There are four main areas that may be visited: the Alcazaba, the Nasrid Palaces, the Partal and the Generalife. The order in which you visit them should be determined bearing in mind that the Nasrid Palaces have set access times listed specifically at each entry point. After this time period has ended, the right to enter this space will be lost.

The visit lasts around three hours, so we recommend a 15-minute break after exiting the Nasrid Palaces in the rest area located in the gardens in the Partal.

After visiting the Generalife, it is sensible to take another break in the area set up for this purpose at this palace's exit, as this area is somewhat distant from both the complex's way out as well as from the accesses to the other three sites where visits are allowed.

We recommend the use of appropriate, comfortable footwear and, in the summer, sun-protection gear.

The Alhambra is closed on 25 December and 1 January. If, for conservation or organisation purposes, the Alhambra should remain closed to visitors at other times, this information will be made available through the web site and information points set up for this purpose.

Buying Tickets

The Council of the Alhambra reminds visitors to the site that daily capacity is limited for conservation purposes.

Arched entrance to the Salón de Comares

Individual Tourism

Tickets can be purchased by using the systems identified on the Council of the Alhambra and Generalife's web site; we recommend that tickets be reserved and purchased in advance. Tickets may also be purchased at the ticket offices in the Alhambra.

Ticket office hours:
- Day visits:
  - From 15 March to 14 October:
    from 8:00 am to 7:00 pm.
  - From 15 October to 14 March:
    from 8:00 am to 5:00 pm.
- Evening visits:
  - From 15 March to 14 October:
    from 9:00 pm to 10:30 pm (Tuesday to Saturday).
  - From 15 October to 14 March:
    from 7:00 pm to 8:30 pm (Friday and Saturday).

The Alhambra is closed on 25 December and 1 January.

Group Tourism

The purchase of tickets for organised groups can be done through the Council of the Alhambra and Generalife's web site (www.alhambra-patronato.es) under "Ticket sale/organised tourism (professional)."

Types of Tickets

The general visit to the Monumental Complex of the Alhambra is organised in two shifts, one in the morning and another in the afternoon. There is also an opportunity to visit some parts of the complex at night. The Council of the Alhambra and Generalife offers you the opportunity to combine your visit with other cultural events held in collaboration with other institutions; updated information regarding these activities will appear on the web site and information points set up for this purpose.

Ticket Times

General Visits

- Morning tickets:
  - From Monday to Sunday from 8:30 am to 2:00 pm.
- Afternoon tickets:
  - From Monday to Sunday from 2:00 pm to 6:00 pm.
    (from 15 October to 14 March)
    and from 2:00 pm to 8:00 pm
    (from 15 March to 14 October).

This tickets allows access to all the areas that may be visited in the Alhambra and the Generalife.

Visits to the Gardens, the Alcazaba and the Generalife

- Morning tickets:
  - From Monday to Sunday from 8:30 am to 2:00 pm.
- Afternoon tickets:
  - From Monday to Sunday from 2:00 pm to 6:00 pm.
    (from 15 October to 14 March)
    and from 2:00 pm to 8:00 pm
    (from 15 March to 14 October).

This tickets allows access to all the areas that may be visited, except the Nasrid Palaces.

Evening Visits

NASRID PALACES:
- Friday and Saturday from 8:00 pm to 9:30 pm
  (from 15 October to 14 March).
- Tuesday to Saturday from 10:00 pm to 11:30 pm
  (from 15 March to 14 October).

GENERALIFE:
- Friday and Saturday from 8:00 pm to 9:30 pm
  (15 October to 14 November).
- Tuesday to Saturday from 10:00 pm to 11:30 pm
  (from 15 March to 31 May
  and from 1 September to 15 October).

For other ways of visiting the monument, please consult the web site (www.alhambra-patronato.es).

Special Visit Programmes

The Council of the Alhambra and Generalife organises a series of educational, informational and cultural events of many types that take place throughout the year.

You can check the schedules for these activities at the monument's information points, on the Council of the Alhambra and Generalife's web site (www.alhambra-patronato.es), and in the city centre, in both the office the Council has at the Corral del Carbón, Calle Mariana Pineda, 12, 18009 Granada, as well as the store located at Calle Reyes Católicos, 40, 18009 Granada.

Education in the Alhambra Programme (Corral del Carbón)

Aimed at schoolchildren.
- The Alhambra for children
- The Alhambra for adults
- Summer in the Alhambra
- Draw and get to know the museum (International Museum Day, 18 May)

*A Closer Look at the Alhambra Programme
(at the shop in Granada)*
For the general public. Information in the shop in Granada.
- Tours guided by specialists
- Programme for families
- Activities for Granada residents

Alternative Routes

Guided Tours of the Landscape and Urban Surroundings and other Combined Tickets
The Alhambra offers other routes which aim to raise awareness of the key factors involved in the relationship between the monument, the city and its landscape and urban surroundings through their historical memory.

Its programmes are constantly being updated, so those interested can obtain more information at the information points set up throughout the complex, or on the Council of the Alhambra's web site.

Compulsory Rules for Your Visit
The purchase of any of the types of tickets mentioned means that you agree to the following rules for visiting the monumental complex:

- Pick up your reserved tickets at least one hour before the time scheduled for your entry to the Nasrid Palaces.
- Carry one barcoded ticket per person, including children under twelve, whose entry to the area is free.
- Enter the Nasrid Palaces during the time frame indicated on the ticket.
- For safety's sake, please hold children under eight by the hand.
- Drop off backpacks, large bags and strollers at the checkroom (see map).
- Smoke, eat and drink only in the spaces provided for these activities (see map); they are prohibited on the rest of the route through the monumental site. Water fountains with potable water are available throughout the complex.
- Take photographs without using a tripod or flash, unless expressly authorised to do so.

In order to preserve the monument, do not touch decorations, walls, columns, plasterwork, latticework or plants; the entire compound integrates elements from different periods that are extremely fragile and easily damaged.

To help with the complex's maintenance, do not throw away rubbish or waste except in the bins installed for this purpose.

While inside the monument's complex, you may not remove your clothing, your footwear or lie down on benches or railings or in gardens, nor may you enter the complex accompanied by animals, except guide dogs that help people with visual impairments to make the visit more convenient for them.

The Council of the Alhambra and Generalife may make changes to the routes as well as limit access to certain areas or during certain visiting times – even temporarily suspending visits by the public – for security or maintenance reasons or to host other events.

In order to preserve its historical and cultural legacy, and for the sake of the safety of citizens and visitors, the monumental complex is under video surveillance carried out in accordance with the law.

General Services

Management
Council of the Alhambra and Generalife
Calle Real de la Alhambra, s/n, 18009, Granada
Spain
http://www.alhambra-patronato.es

Information Service
There are points where information is provided in five languages regarding schedules, routes, accesses and all of the monument's services, as well for the rest of the city and the province; these can be found in strategic locations in the complex (see map on pages 24–25).
Information telephone: 902 441 221

Visitor Service Points
Any incident or problem visitors may have during their visit to the complex can be addressed here in several languages (see map on pages 24–25).

Checkroom
In the entrance pavilion or atrium and in the service pavilion adjacent to the Puerta del Vino; this service is offered for storing packages, bags and handbags larger than 35 cm.

Guides' Association

The Council of the Alhambra does not offer guided tours of the complex. However, this service is provided by the Associación Provincial de Informadores Turísticos (Provincial Association of Tour Guides), a private organisation that is independent of the Council of the Alhambra and Generalife.

Food and Drink Vending Machines

The Complex offers food and drink vending machines located in the following areas:

- The Alhambra's carpark
- Entrance pavilion
- Service pavilion adjacent to the Puerta del Vino

Rest Areas

The Complex has the following rest areas:

- Jardines del Partal (next to the portico of the Torre de las Damas)
- Mirador of the Casa de los Amigos (adjacent to the Paseo de las Adelfas)

There are also other rest areas where eating, drinking or smoking are permitted:

- Plaza de los Aljibes
- Paseo de los Nogales
- Gardens of Las Placetas, opposite the cannons and in the square of Palacio de Carlos V in the area set aside for this purpose.
- Plaza de la Alhambra (opposite the atrium or Entrance Pavilion).

Alhambra Bookstores/Shops

There are three official Alhambra bookstores/shops located throughout the complex: one in the atrium or Entrance Pavilion, another in the Palacio de Carlos V and the third in the sub-post office on Calle Real de la Alhambra; there is a fourth shop in the city centre at Calle Reyes Católicos, 40.

There is also an online store accessible from the Alhambra's web site. Here you will find specialised publications, CDs and DVDs, stationery supplies and other items related to the Alhambra and the Generalife.

Car Park

The monumental compound has a public car park, which is guarded and open 24 hours a day; there is space for 630 vehicles. There are parking spaces reserved for people with disabilities, coaches and caravans.

Audio Guide

We offer an audioguide service in English, Spanish, French, German and Italian. They may be rented in the atrium or access pavilion next to the ticket office and in the shop located in the Palacio de Carlos V.

Toilets

Toilets are located at:

- The atrium or Entrance Pavilion (toilets adapted for people with disabilities)
- The service pavilion, adjacent to the Puerta del Vino (toilets adapted for people with disabilities)
- The Jardines Nuevos of the Generalife (toilets adapted for people with disabilities)
- The Patio del Ciprés de la Sultana, in the Generalife

Health Care Services

A first aid facility has been set up in the service pavilion adjacent to the Puerta del Vino; it is staffed by health care personnel from the Spanish Red Cross.

Post Boxes

These are located in the old sub-post office on Calle Real de la Alhambra, and in the atrium or entrance pavilion.

Public Telephones

There are public telephones located throughout the Complex.

Lost and Found

In the event personal belongings are lost, visitors can request information at the Visitor Services Centre. (See location of services on map, pages 24–25).

Cultural Offer

Museums

The Alhambra's museums offer the opportunity to experience a wide variety of the monument's heritage elements — ranging from Medieval Islamic archaeology to the fine arts — from the perspective of their historical and cultural environment.

Alhambra Museum

Located on the ground floor inside the Palacio de Carlos V, (see pages 76–78).

Fine Arts Museum of Granada

Located on the first floor of the Palacio de Carlos V (see page 79).

Ángel Barrios Museum

Located on Calle Real de la Alhambra, adjacent to the Iglesia de Santa María de la Alhambra (see pages 214–215).
Information on their opening hours — which do not completely coincide with those of the rest of the complex — is updated on the web site and at information points set up for this purpose. Guided tours of the Alhambra Museum are offered by senior citizen volunteers.

Programme: Museum Piece of the Month

On Saturdays mornings (except holidays) the Alhambra Museum offers free theme tours with specialist guides. Consult the web site and the information points set up for this purpose.

Programme: Area of the Month

Each month visits can be made to a space in the monument that is usually closed due to conservation or security reasons, since its structure and its characteristics cannot withstand a large number of visitors. Information is provided in the atrium or entrance pavilion and in various parts of the complex.
Consult the schedule on the web site and at the information points set up for this purpose.

Temporary Exhibitions

The Council of the Alhambra also sponsors temporary exhibitions — usually installed in the chapel and crypt of the Palacio de Carlos V — in collaboration with museums and other heritage centres, both national and international. Their purpose is to display and share information about the bibliographic, documentary and museum-related assets preserved in the monumental compound.

Alhambra Library

The Library of the Council of the Alhambra and Generalife specialises in Islamic art and architecture, archaeology, gardening and landscaping, architectural techniques and conservation, restoration, the administration and management of the Heritage Site, archival, library and museum sciences, history, Oriental thought and literature, Orientalism, Renaissance art and the Islamic decorative arts.

Its facilities are located in the Nuevos Museos building, located adjacent to the Paseo del Generalife. Access is limited to weekday mornings in accordance with official opening times.

Access to the consultation room is limited to those having a researcher's card issued by the Council of the Alhambra and Generalife; a temporary authorisation may also be requested.

Due to the nature of its resources and collections, access is subject to regulations available on the premises and on the Council's web site.

The Alhambra Library offers its users the following services, among others:

- Researchers' room equipped with computerised resources, with access to the Library catalogue and internet
- Periodicals. One of the Library's most important collections, there is a computerised consultation catalogue available.
- Internal loans
- Interlibrary loans
- Acquisition requests
- Information requests
- Document reproduction. Reproductions — both hard copies as well as digital — may be obtained of the consultations made, subject to the established public prices.

The institution has an extensive collection complemented by several additional collections of monographs, special legacies and an extensive and important collection of periodicals, pamphlets, reprints, and audiovisual materials.

Alhambra Archives

The Archives of the Council of the Alhambra and Generalife, which is integrated into the Sistema Andaluz de Archivos (Andalusian Archives System), collects, preserves and makes available documentation related to the monumental complex and produced throughout its history to Council staff, researchers and citizens.

Its facilities are located adjacent to the Paseo del Generalife, in the building called Nuevos Museos, with access limited to weekday mornings in accordance with official opening times.

Access to the consultation room is limited to those having a temporary authorisation or researcher's card issued by the Council of the Alhambra and Generalife. Given the nature of its resources and collections, access is subject to regulations available on the premises and on the Council's web site.

The Archives offers its users the following services, among others:

- Information on the Archives, its resources and collections as well as related documentation in other archives
- Requests regarding its documentary collections
- Document reproduction
- The opportunity to offer suggestions and register complaints

The Alhambra Archives regularly produces a newsletter aimed at sharing information about the work it does and thus the vast, rich documentary heritage it preserves.

Publications

Publications issued by the Council of the Alhambra basically fall into two categories: the first is for consolidating the Council's classic publication line of scientific works, represented by the *Cuadernos de la Alhambra* journal, a reference in the field of heritage research and information sharing. The second is focused on the annual publication of themed collections, such as the "Colección Plural de la Biblioteca de la Alhambra," the "Colección de Monografías de la Alhambra" and the "Colección Fuentes de Investigación," to mention a few.

Conference Room

In the Palacio de Carlos V there is a room dedicated to the cultural and scientific activities that take place throughout the year in the complex: seminars, courses, conferences, book launches and other events directly related to sharing information about the historical and cultural legacy of the Alhambra and the Generalife. Capacity: 90 people.

Cultural Events

The Council of the Alhambra collaborates with other public and private entities to carry out — both on- and off-site — cultural events and historical and artistic information-sharing activities. Their aim is to promote people becoming acquainted with its image and with the values of the monument and cultures related to it. Similarly, the Council regularly and directly offers a set of educational, informational and cultural programmes and activities.

You can check the schedule for all of these activities at the information points throughout the complex or through the Council of the Alhambra and Generalife's web site: www.alhambra-patronato.es.

Granada International Festival of Music and Dance

The city offers many cultural activities throughout the year. The most established event is the Granada International Festival of Music and Dance, held in several venues scattered throughout the city, including the Alhambra and the Generalife. Every year between June and July, the outdoor theatre of the Generalife, the Palacio de Carlos V, the Patio de los Arrayanes and the Plaza de los Aljibes become stages hosting first-class performances with the finest orchestras and national and international performance companies (www.granada-festival.org).

Lorca and Granada in the Gardens of the Generalife

This programme began in 2001 with the aim of creating a cultural extravaganza for Granada's summer nights. The figure of Federico García Lorca and the universal familiarity of his work is a powerful attraction for all kinds of audiences. His evocative ability provides us with the perfect formula based on our authors and on our oldest cultural roots — such as flamenco — in symbiosis with a multicultural creative language, a reflection of the cultural potential of Andalusia. This event takes place in summer.

The Alhambra, with the Alcazaba in the foreground, and the Palacio de Carlos V and the Iglesia de Santa María de la Alhambra in the background

Personalities Related to the Alhambra

Muhammad I. Al-Ahmar
(Arjona, 1194 – Granada, 1273)

Founder of the Nasrid dynasty, he reigned between 1237 and 1273. In 1238 he settled in the ancient citadel of the Albaicín, but he noticed the ruins on the hill of the Alhambra and decided to begin to rebuild them and locate his court there. He started building the Alhambra we know today.

Yusuf I
(Granada, 1318 – Granada, 1354)

Seventh ruler of the Nasrid dynasty (1333 – 1354). Under his reign, the Palacio de Comares – one of the jewels of Nasrid architecture – was built, and he opened the madrasah (Islamic school) in Granada. He signed agreements with Alfonso XI of Castilla and Alfonso IV of Aragón to keep the peace, but the control of the Strait of Gibraltar led to the resumption of the war.

Muhammad V
(Granada, 1338 – Granada, 1391)

He reigned during the apogee of the Nasrid sultanate (1354 – 1359/1362 – 1391), outstanding examples of whose artistic development are the Palacio de los Leones and the façade of the Palacio de Comares, built to mark the conquest of Algeciras in 1370.

Muhammad XI-Boabdil
(Granada, 1452 – Fez, 1528)

He was the Alhambra's last king, ruling under the name Muhammad XI, though called by Christians "Boabdil" or "Boabdil the Small" and popularly known as "the Unfortunate" (1482 – 1483/1487 – 1492). Son of Muley Hacén and Sultana Aisha, he led a rebellion against his father in Guadix in 1482 and came to the throne through the support of the Abencerrages and his own mother. The era of the Nasrid sultanate came to its end on 2 January 1492 when the Catholic Monarchs took Granada.

Aisha bin Muhammad Ibn al-Ahmar

Wife of Muley Hacén and mother of Boabdil el Chico (Boabdil the Small), she – with the support of the Abencerrages – helped her son take the throne of Granada. She was the heart and soul of the resistance against the Catholic Monarchs. In 1493, she accompanied her son to his exile in Fez, where he died shortly afterwards.

Ibn al-Yayyab
(Granada, 1274 – Granada, 1349)

Poet and politician during the Nasrid dynasty in the kingdom of Granada, he served the court for over fifty years, something unheard of in a court accustomed to the intrigues of power. He began his career under Muhammad II, creator of the Diwan al-Insa' or official government writers' office, which he managed in his role as Wazir-Prime Minister. He wrote neoclassical qasidas (poetry whose subject was kings or nobility), in a series of neoclassical monorhymes with a regular metre. Some of his poems are found in the palaces and in the portico of the Generalife.

Ibn al-Khatib
(Loja, 1313 – Fez, 1374)

He was the greatest polyfacetic Nasrid writer: poet, writer, historian, philosopher and politician, the best of his writings decorate the walls of the Alhambra. He spent much of his life at the court of Sultan Muhammad V, whom he served as minister and historian and with whom he established a close friendship. He held important political offices, and was appointed double vizier, earning him the nickname of "Dhul-wizaratayn" or "Man of the Two Vizierates". Author of numerous books on history as well as chronologies, he wrote his autobiography in 1369. Twice forced into exile in North Africa, he also served the Marinid government. Arrested and tried in Granada for the charge of treason, he was sentenced to imprisonment and the destruction of all of his books, but the government hired professional assassins who strangled him in his prison cell in Fez, in 1374.

Ibn Zamrak
(Granada, 1333 – Granada, 1394)

Politician and, perhaps, the best of the Alhambra's poets, his poems decorate the most important fountains and palaces, such as the basin of the Fuente de los Leones. Of humble origins, he was brought to the court thanks to his teacher Ibn al-Khatib. He accompanied Sultan Muhammad V to the Maghreb and, once restored to the throne of Granada, the Sultan named him as his private secretary and appointed him to the position of court poet. When Ibn al-Khatib was dismissed as vizier in 1371, he was replaced by Ibn Zamrak. Later, Ibn Zamrak himself was imprisoned for nearly two years and was killed on the orders of Sultan Muhammad VII.

Catholic Monarchs
(1492 – 1516)

Isabella I of Castile (Madrigal de las Altas Torres, Ávila, 1451 – Medina del Campo, Valladolid, 1504) and Ferdinand II of Aragón (Sos, Zaragoza, 1452 – Madrigalejo, Cáceres, 1516). The reign of the Catholic Monarchs marked the transition from the medieval to the modern era in Spain. Their marriage brought together, in the dynasty of the Trastámara, the crowns of Castile and Aragón. When they conquered Granada in 1492, the Alhambra became a royal palace. The monarchs named Iñigo López de Mendoza, Count of Tendilla, Governor of the Alhambra.

Iñigo López de Mendoza y Quiñones
(Guadalajara?, 1440 – Granada, 1515)

Second Earl of Tendilla and first Marquis of Mondéjar, and known as "the Great Tendilla", he became the first governor of the Alhambra when named to this position and to that of Captain-General of Granada by the Catholic Monarchs. After the Christian conquest, he had an enormous water tank built under the Plaza de los Aljibes that is a splendid example of vaulting work.

Hieronymus Münzer
(Feldkirch, 1437 or 1447 – Nuremberg, 1508)

German humanist, physician, geographer and map-maker, he arrived in Granada in 1494 – two years after its conquest by the Catholic Monarchs – and was received in the former Palacio de Yusuf III, of which he left written testimony that has been of assistance in determining what the palace was like.

Andrea Navaggero
(Venice, 1483 – Blois, 1529)

Writer and politician, he was the Venetian ambassador to the court of Charles V, residing in Spain from 1525 to 1528. He left his Viaje por España as a testimony. In it, he describes the garden under the Palacio del Generalife as follows: "With ivy-covered walls and a fountain that threw water ten fathoms high".

Pedro Machuca
(Toledo, 1485 – 1550)

Sixteenth-century Spanish painter and architect, he is considered one of the earliest representatives of Mannerism in Spain. He was the architect who designed and built the Palacio de Carlos V, a Renaissance building commissioned by the Emperor as his residence in Granada in the Alhambra, adjacent to the Nasrid Palaces.

Luis Hurtado de Mendoza y Pacheco
(Guadalajara, 1489 – Mondéjar, Guadalajara, 1566)

Third Earl of Tendilla and second Marquis of Mondéjar, he was the second governor of the Alhambra and captain-general of Granada since, at the death of his father, he succeeded him in all of his positions. He was a personal friend of Charles V, ever since the king and his wife, Isabella of Portugal, stayed at the Alhambra for their honeymoon (1526). He also supervised the construction of the Cathedral of Granada and the Palacio de Carlos V in the Alhambra

(Pedro Machuca, the architect, was his standard-bearer) as well as that of the so-called Pilar de Carlos V.

Pedro de Granada Venegas
Third Lord of Campotéjar and Jayena. After the Christian conquest of the Alhambra in 1492, the Catholic Monarchs granted the Generalife a governor for its safekeeping and proper use. In 1631 this governorship was awarded in perpetuity to the Granada-Venegas family until, after a long-lasting lawsuit filed in the 19th century, it was transferred to the government in 1921.

Garcilaso de la Vega
(Toledo, 1498? – Nice, 1536)

He was educated at the court where in 1519 he met Juan Boscán, who would become a great friend and fellow writer. In 1520 he entered the service of Charles I and in 1525 he married Elena de Zúñiga, one of Charles V's sister's ladies, and become part of his entourage. In 1529, he travelled to Rome with the court for Emperor Charles I of Spain's investiture in Bologna. In 1526, Granada was the centre of European diplomacy, where Papal nuncio Baldassare Castiglione and the ambassadors of England, Poland and Venice met together. The meeting with Boscán and Navaggero in the Generalife gardens about how to write "...in Castilian, sonnets and other troubadour's arts used by the good authors from Italy..." marked the turning point in Garcilaso's poetry.

Juan Boscán Almogaver
(Barcelona, 1493 – Perpignan, 1542)

Renaissance poet and translator. Of noble family, he served in the court of the Catholic Kings and then the court of King Charles I of Spain. He introduced hendecasyllable verse and Italian stanzas, as well as poetry with blank hendecasyllables and the motifs and structures of Petrarchism, to Castilian poetry. He was persuaded to do this in a conversation with his friend, Venetian ambassador and humanist Andrea Navaggero in the gardens of the Generalife as he himself said, since the latter encouraged him to try out that poetic experience.

Charles V
(Ghent, 1500 – Yuste, Cáceres, 1558)

Charles I (1516 – 1556), the first king who united in one person the crowns of Castile and Aragon, was crowned Emperor of the Holy Roman Empire as Charles V (1519 – 1558). That same year he had a Renaissance palace built in the Alhambra (1526), establishing his residence there after his wedding in Sevilla to Isabella of Portugal. He would pick the Cuarto Dorado – previously renovated by the Catholic Monarchs – as his private chambers; they were the most comfortable quarters available in the Nasrid palaces. Their adaptation into new spaces to house the emperor as the new palace was being built was a result of the monarch's new-found tastes for Italian decorations. His sensitivity for the landscape of Granada – where he spent "the happiest hours of his existence" – and the need to modify medieval structures led to work on a tower for the Empress. It would be called the Mirador Tower, and later the Tocador or Peinador de la Reina, and is now one of the treasures of the Alhambra.

Fray Luis de Granada
(Granada, 1504 – Lisbon, 1551)

Spanish writer and Dominican friar. Orphaned at a very early age, he was taken in by the Mendoza family, the Earls of Tendilla and governors of the Alhambra, where he spent his childhood as a page for the Tendilla children until he turned nineteen, when he decided to enter the Dominican convent of Santa Cruz la Real.

Julio Aquiles and Alejandro Mayner
Sixteenth-century painters, they were followers of Raphael and Giovanni da Udine. In 1537 they decorated the Habitaciones del Emperador, known as Salas de las Frutas. Between 1539 and 1546, they decorated the frescos in the Peinador de la Reina where the conquest of Tunis by Charles V is represented in eight paintings.

Iñigo López de Mendoza y Mendoza
(?-1512, Mondéjar – Guadalajara, 1580)

Third Marquis of Mondéjar and fourth Count of Tendilla. In 1543 his father turned over the office of governor of the Alhambra to him and during his term of office the war against the Moors took place. This ended in them being expelled from Granada in 1570, after which the Albaicín was left without residents.

Philip V
(Versailles, 1683 – Madrid, 1746)

Duke of Anjou and first Bourbon king of Spain beginning in 1700, his grandfather was French King Louis XIV and his parents were the Grand Dauphin of France Louis and María Ana Victoria of Bavaria. Felipe V stripped the Marquis de Mondéjar, heir to the Count of Tendilla, of the governorship of the Alhambra. This was the beginning of a period of near total neglect of the Alhambra that lasted until the reign of Charles IV. He was the last king to live in the Alhambra.

François-René de Chateaubriand
(Saint-Malo, Brittany, 1768 – Paris, 1848)

French diplomat, politician and writer, author of Les Aventures du dernier Abencérage, he is considered to be the founder of romanticism in French literature. In 1807 he arrived in Granada, where he took notes to illustrate Voyage Picturesque by his brother Alexander, published in 1812. "You should see the Alhambra. It's like a work of faeries, magic, glory and love, unlike anything known".

Alexandre Laborde
(Paris, 1773 – Paris, 1842)

French archaeologist and politician. A great lover of the arts, he travelled throughout Europe, and while in Spain devoted himself to publishing important books. With the collaboration of Chateaubriand, he published Itinéraire descriptif de l'Espagne, the contents of which are remarkable due to the some one hundred engravings, including the baths in the Palacio de Comares and the gardens of the Generalife.

James Cavanah Murphy
(Cork, ? – London, 1814)

Irish author with some archaeological training and fond of antiques, he is representative of a group of late 18th-century British travellers who focused

their interest on the Islamic architecture of Spain, the undoubted star of which was, for them, the Alhambra. Murphy arrived in Andalusia in 1802, as he himself stated in the brief introduction to his book The Arabian Antiquities of Spain (London, 1813 – 1815) in order to correct "the interesting, but imperfect descriptions of the remains of Arab art, displayed in volumes of a modern traveller, as existing in the once renowned Mohammedan cities of Granada, Cordova and Seville." He claims to have spent seven years in Andalusia, especially in Sevilla and Granada. Despite this, his work was not received favourably by the demanding critics of the time.

Washington Irving
(Tarrytown, Westchester, New York, 1783 – Tarrytown, Westchester, New York, 1859)

American diplomat and romantic writer, several of whose government posts were in Spain. In 1828 he spent a few days in Granada, returning in the spring of the following year for a long stay. It was here that he was inspired to write Tales of the Alhambra. During his stay in the monument, he lived in Emperor Charles V's rooms.

Richard Ford
(London, 1796 – London, 1858)

Writer and artist, he came to Spain with his wife and children in 1830 because of his wife's precarious health and remained in Granada for two summers, staying in the Alhambra itself. He travelled throughout the Peninsula, studied the habits of the people and made more than five hundred drawings. On his return to England in 1833 he settled in Exeter, building a Neo-Mudéjar home that resembled the Generalife and its gardens, and where he had a large library of books in Spanish.

David Roberts
(Stockbridge, Edinburgh, 1796 – London, 1864)

Scottish romantic painter, known for his watercolours of Oriental monuments. At sixteen, he was already earning his living as a painter of circus sets. Beginning in 1824 he travelled through much of Europe painting monasteries and Gothic

cathedrals, landscapes and everything that was part of the period's artistic inventory. He arrived in Spain in October 1832 with the aim of travelling through Andalusia and drawing pictures of the most striking and interesting aspects of al-Andalus, which resulted in a Spain seen under Muslim influence and the typical 19th-century romantic stylisation. Proof of this are his engravings of the Alhambra.

Alexandre Dumas
(Villers-Cotterêts, Aisne, 1802 – Puys, 1870)

French novelist and playwright, author of The Three Musketeers and The Count of Monte Cristo. After travelling to Granada, he said: "God made the Alhambra and Granada, in case he gets tired of his own house one day."

Victor Hugo
(Besançon, 1802 – Paris, 1885)

French writer, considered the most important representative of romanticism. He was one of the first of the 19th century's enlightened travellers to visit the Alhambra, and left his signature in some location. The Alhambra inspired his book Las Orientales.

Prosper Mérimée
(Paris, 1803 – Cannes, 1870)

French writer and author of Carmen, the novel on which the opera of the same name by composer Georges Bizet is based. He travelled to Spain several times, charmed by its customs, landscapes and art, of which he left testimony in articles and letters: "I will not say anything about the Alhambra; you have it in your library but, believe me, you are not exempted from making the trip to Granada, and no book – large or small – can give you an idea of the Patio de los Leones and the Sala de los Embajadores." His name appears in the Alhambra's Visitors' Book.

Philibert Joseph Girault de Prangey
(Langres, Haute-Marne, 1804 – Courcelles, París, 1893)

French painter and designer, recognised as a rigorous expert in the vision and study of Hispano-Muslim architecture, he was in Granada in late 1832. Although his goal was to visit all of the Mediterranean basin, apparently, in the trip's first stage beginning this same year, he visited its western region: Tunisia, Algeria, Sicily and Andalusia. The Alhambra and the Generalife aroused his greatest enthusiasm, as stressed in his *Monuments Arabes et Moresques de Cordoue, Séville et Grenade* and *Choix d'ornaments Moresques de l'Alhambra*: "... these monuments imbued with the genius of a nation that has not left anywhere such brilliant remnants of its high level of civilisation ...". The drawings for this important work were done between 1832 and 1833, but would not appear until 1837 in Paris, accompanied by a descriptive text. Between 1846 and 1855 he would publish another of his most important works, *Monuments Arabes d'Egypte, de Syrie et d'Asie Mineure*.

Benjamin Disraeli
(London, 1804 – 1881)

Politician and writer, he came from a family of Spanish Jews who fled to Venice in the late 15th century due to the Inquisition. He visited Spain in 1830 en route to Jerusalem and said: "Oh wonderful Spain! Think of this romantic land cover with Moorish ruins and full of Murillo! Ah that I could describe to you the wonders of the painted temples of Seville! Ah that I could wander with you amid the fantastic and imaginative halls of the delicate Alhambra!».

John Frederick Lewis
(London, 1805 – 1876)

English painter who specialised in depicting scenes from the Orient and the Mediterranean, Lewis lived in Spain from 1832 to 1834. In Madrid, he devoted himself to copying the Prado's important paintings as watercolours. Later, he lived in Toledo and then in Granada, where he spent much of his time in the Alhambra, drawing its architecture. In 1835 *Sketches and Drawings of the Alhambra* was published in London.

Owen Jones
(London, 1809 – London, 1874)

Architect, designer and decorator, for four years he travelled throughout

Italy, Greece, Turkey, Egypt and Spain where in 1842 he conducted a special study of the Alhambra with Frenchman Jules Goury. He was also a designer and professor at the School of Design, where he experimented with, renewed and transmitted paradigms for the new stylistic and decorative applications for which his book *The Grammar of Ornament* (1856) is a universal reference.

Théophile Gautier
(Tarbes, 1811 – Paris, 1872)

French poet, critic and novelist. From 5 May to 7 October 1840, Gautier discovered Spain with his friend Eugène Piot. This six-month stay provided the material for his *Un Voyage en Espagne*, and resulted in lively impressions in his journals, characterised by the freshness of his perspective, the wonderment of his vision and the always-exaggerated desire for accuracy in his statements. A letter to his mother has been conserved and we should like to highlight the following phrase from it: "If you carry on with that attitude, I shall rent the Alhambra, furnish it with a straw mattress and a couple of cushions, and I shall not go back!"

Jean Laurent
(Garchizy, Nevers, 1816 – Spain, 1892)

French photographer who spent his professional career in Spain, where he travelled with his camera to every corner and landscape of the country. Laurent was a great innovator of photographic technique, inventing and introducing several techniques such as leptographic paper – more sensitive than that existing so far – and a new colouring system. The images taken during the different trips he made to Granada between 1856 and 1892 resulted in the album *L'Alhambra*.

José Zorrilla
(Valladolid, 1817 – Madrid, 1893)

Maximum exponent of Spanish romanticism, on 22 June 1889 he was crowned National Poet in Granada. Zorrilla lamented the fact that it was foreign writers who discovered the beauty of the Alhambra.

Charles Clifford
(Wales, 1819 – Madrid, 1863)

British photographer who, like Jean Laurent, developed his career in Spain, where he made photographic collections of almost all its cities and monuments. He accompanied Queen Elizabeth II during her trip to Andalusia in 1862. The trip was reflected in an exquisite album with about 100 photos, including several of the Alhambra.

The Contreras Family

For three generation, the Contreras family devoted itself to restoring the monument. The best known member of the family, Rafael (Granada, 1824 or 1826 – 1890), was named "restorer of ornaments" of the Alhambra in 1847 and director and curator in 1869. His most important interventions were: the replacement of the colours in the Sala de las Camas in the baths of the Comares Palace and the construction of a dome of coloured tiles – which had not originally existed – in the Patio de los Leones.

Isabella II
(Madrid, 1830 – Paris, 1904)

Queen of Spain from 1833 to 1868; in 1843, in return for its loyalty during the riots that took place the same year, she granted the city of Granada the right to add the representation of the Torre de la Vela to the standard of Granada. In 1862 she visited the Alhambra; the Paseo de los Cipreses was created to mark her visit.

Paul Gustave Doré
(Strasbourg, 1832 – Paris, 1883)

French artist, engraver and illustrator, he published his first illustration at fifteen. In 1862 he travelled throughout Spain with Baron Duvillier, and the next year they jointly published a series of articles on Valencia, Galicia, etc., which was included in the "Le Tour du Monde" collection. He lived for a few months in Barcelona. Doré was such a prolific artist that it is difficult to compile all his work.

Edgar Degas
(Paris, 1834 – 1917)

French painter and sculptor, he is known for his unique insights into the world of ballet, capturing subtle and beautiful scenes in pastels. In 1889 he travelled to Morocco and Spain with Boldini. Testimony of his stay in Granada is his signature in the Alhambra's Visitors' Book on 21 September 1889.

Manuel Gómez Moreno González
(Granada, 1834 – 1918)

Historian, archaeologist and painter, he received a pension from Granada's provincial government to go to Rome, where he would create his best historicist paintings, including the Alhambra-themed *La despedida de Boabdil*. He was a member of the German Archaeological Institute, dean of the Royal Academy of Fine Arts and professor at the School of Arts and Crafts. Author of the indispensable *Guía de Granada* (1892) and many other research-related works – among which are the noteworthy report on Sierra Elvira, near Atarfe, where many graves and remains were discovered – along with lithographs and photographs of his own drawings. He was curator of the Fine Arts Museum in Granada from 1876 to 1878. When the Special Committee of the Alhambra was created, Gómez Moreno was appointed rector of the monument. He stated that the work on the monument "must first address the ruined parts and then its restoration" at a time when, in some artistic fields, the Alhambra was not considered a Nasrid monument but rather an Orientalist idea.

Mariano Fortuny
(Reus, 1838 – Rome, 1874)

A painter, he arrived in Granada in 1870, driven by romantic ideals, together with his wife Cecilia Madrazo (daughter of one of the most respected painters of the court), and stayed in the city until 1871. The presence of the Fortuny family in the Alhambra in June 1870 is reflected in the album of famous visitors. An important legacy of pictorially and historically important drawings of Granada and the Alhambra have been conserved, with the most outstanding being that of the Palacio de Carlos V.

Ricardo Velázquez Bosco
(Burgos, 1843 – Madrid, 1923)

Spanish architect and restorer, among his extensive works are the noteworthy pavilion for the Mining Exhibition of 1883, known as the "Palace of Velázquez" in Madrid's Retiro Park (1883), along with engineer Alberto del Palacio and ceramist Daniel Zuloaga, and the Ministry of Agriculture building (1893 – 1897) whose façade is in Velázquez Bosco's characteristic style, with a portico of eight columns paired with a frieze topped by a group of sculptures. As a restorer, he worked on the Mezquita de Córdoba (the Great Mosque of Córdoba), the León Cathedral and the La Rábida Monastery, although his most important project was the 1917 General Conservation Plan for the Alhambra.

Isaac Albéniz
(Camprodón, Girona, 1860 – Cambo-les-Bains, 1909)

Composer of piano music, in 1872 at the tender age of twelve, he had his first musical contact with Granada. He returned to the city in July 1881 to give several piano recitals. He returned again and years later, in 1886, he composed his famous piano piece "Granada (Serenata)". His Granada-inspired works include "Torre Bermeja (Serenata)", "Zambra Granada" and "El Albaicín".

Santiago Rusiñol i Prats
(Barcelona, 1861 – Aranjuez, 1931)

Artist, writer and playwright, he visited Granada on several occasions between 1887 and 1922, staying at the former Siete Suelos Hotel, the palace of the Generalife and the Polinario tavern, saying of it: "The first impression one gets is amazing. It seems that one's soul enters a large bath of light, in an atmosphere of the purist beauty, where one's eyes enjoy the calmness of a gentle sensation."

Claude Debussy
(Saint-Germain, 1862 – Paris, 1918)

French composer, he – who never travelled to Spain – was inspired by a postcard sent by Manuel de Falla to compose his work La Puerta del Vino.

Joaquín Sorolla
(Valencia, 1863 – Cercedilla, Madrid, 1923)

Spanish painter, and one of the most prolific, in 1907 he began studying gardens, mainly in Andalusia. In Granada, he painted the patios and fountains of the Alhambra and Generalife from 1909 or 1910 to 1917: *Habitaciones de los Reyes Católicos en la Alhambra, El Patio de Comares, de la Alhambra de Granada.*

Angel Ganivet
(Granada, 1865 – Riga, 1898)

Spanish writer and diplomat, he was one of the Granada-born intellectuals with the most influence on the so-called Generation of '98. Ganivet was always linked to his city of Granada, where he founded the Cofradía del Avellano – richly cultural gatherings defined as a "sort of Hellenic Academy of Granada-born friends", with whom he created, among other works, *El libro de Granada*, a reference of the time that greatly influenced the intelligentsia. On 3 October 1921, the monument to Angel Ganivet was unveiled in the Alhambra Forest.

Henri Matisse
(Cateau-Cambresis, 1869 – Nice, 1954)

Avant-garde French painter, one of the great artists of 20th-century Fauvism, Matisse visited the Alhambra on 9 and 10 December 1910. His signature was registered in the visitors' book of the Nasrid monument. Some years ago the discovery of this signature led to research that discovered the purpose of Mastisse's trip to Spain, where he visitied Madrid, Sevilla, Córdoba and Granada, and the influence of this visit on his work. From his letters, we know that the Alhambra was one of the places in Spain that he found most exciting: "The Alhambra is a wonder; I've felt the greatest of pleasures there."

Manuel Gómez-Moreno Martínez
(Granada, 1870 – Madrid, 1960)

He published his first writings – dedicated to the Royal Chapel of Granada – at the age of 16, thus initiating the long list of books, pamphlets and articles that make up his bibliography. In 1889 he graduated with a degree in Liberal Arts, and a few years later he taught at the University of Sacromonte and the School of

Industrial Arts. Upon obtaining the Chair of Arabic Medieval Archaeology at the Universidad Central, he moved to Madrid in 1913, joining the most elite institutions in the capital: the Royal Academy of History, the Royal Academy of Fine Arts of San Fernando and, in 1941, the Spanish Academy. That same year, he received the doctorate "Honoris Causa" from the University of Oxford. In 1930 he accepted the Directorate-General of Fine Arts. He specialised in many fields of general knowledge, with a predominance in archaeology, history and art.

Manuel Machado
(Seville, 1874 – Madrid, 1947)

Spanish poet and Antonio Machado's brother, he was one of the most outstanding representatives of modernism in Spain. When Manuel Machado, in his poetic journey through Andalusia, sings to Granada, he hangs a resonating metaphor on her like a carnation in her hair: "hidden water that weeps …".

Manuel de Falla
(Cadiz, 1876 – Alta Gracia, Argentina, 1946)

Spanish composer, he was – along with Isaac Albéniz and Enrique Granados – one of the most important musicians of the first half of the 20th century in Spain. He lived in Granada for twenty years (1920 – 1939), but even before his arrival, he imagined it musically in the *Vida breve and En el Generalife* – composed in Paris – which make up the first part of his "Nights in the Gardens of Spain" inspired by poetry readings and reproductions of paintings of gardens by Santiago Rusiñol.

Francisco Villaespesa
(Almería, 1877 – Madrid, 1936)

Spanish Modernist poet, playwright and storyteller. He published numerous books of poetry dedicated to the Alhambra, such as *El Patio de los Arrayanes, El mirador de Lindaraxa, Los nocturnos del Generalife* and *El encanto de la Alhambra*. There is currently a plaque with a poem by Villaespesa adjacent to the Puerta de las Granadas.

Juan Ramón Jiménez
(Moguer, Huelva, 1881 – San Juan, Puerto Rico, 1958)

Spanish poet and winner of the Nobel Prize for Literature in 1956, after visiting Granada in 1924, he wrote the collection of poems *Olvidos de Granada*, where he went with Zenobia and Federico and Francisco García Lorca, as a unique traveller in search of essences. That unusual visit attracted to the poet a group of illustrious figures of the era's cultural life , among whom were Leopoldo Torres Balbás, Manuel de Falla, Miguel Cerón and Fernando de los Ríos, with his wife Gloria and daughter Laura, who would soon thereafter marry Francisco García Lorca.

Ángel Barrios Fernández
(Granada, 1882 – Madrid, 1964)

Son of Antonio Barrios Tamayo and Eloísa Fernández, he belonged to a family of great influence on the Alhambra in the late 19th and early 20th centuries. The house of Don Antonio Barrios, adjacent to the baths of the mosque, was during his time an inn, a tavern, a place for intellectuals to meet or rest and would later become the most popular place in Granada. It was visited by the most cultured and important artists, such as Palmer, Doré, Roberts and Sargent, and Spaniards like Regoyos, Rusiñol, Sorolla, Zuloaga, Baroja, Pérez Galdós, Azorín, Albéniz, Juan Ramon and Eugenio d'Ors.

Leopoldo Torres Balbás
(Madrid, 1888 – Madrid, 1960)

Precursor of scientific restoration, and architectural curator of the Alhambra and the Generalife from 1923 to 1936, the Alhambra we know today is due in great part to him. He restored the Palacio de los Leones, the Mexuar, the Patio de los Leones and the Patio de la Alberca and rebuilt the Partal Palace, among other interventions. It has always been said that the Alhambra owes him a debt that would be hard to settle. Faced with the sterile debate about his profession being that of an architect and not that of an archaeologist and whether he was more a theorist than a field professional, or if he had conflicting criteria (the intervention in the Palacio de Carlos V), he was

director of the *Crónica arqueológica de la España musulmana*, a brilliant vade mecum that appeared for decades as an insert in the journal *Al-Andalus*. His time at the Alhambra has left us what are most likely the most beautiful and valuable pages that have ever been written about it; today, they serve as essential training and consultation manuals. No one has been able to create such polytechnical and scientific, comprehensive and inclusive information about the Alhambra as did Torres Balbás. This is probably because he was one of the most genuine representatives of what is already considered a new Golden Age of Spanish culture taking place around the first third of the 20th century, a generation that emerged from the ashes of '98.

Antonio Gallego Burín
(Granada, 1895 – Madrid, 1961)

Mayor of Granada (1938 – 1951), professor of Art History at the University of Granada. His interest in culture led to important initiatives for the city, such as the recovery of the Autos Sacramentales (a form of dramatic religious literature) and the renovation of the Casa de los Tiros (House of the Shots), which became a city museum. In 1951, he was appointed Director-General of Fine Arts and created the International Festival of Music and Dance. He headed the Council of the Alhambra from 1945 to 1951, an institution with which he was connected until his death.

Federico García Lorca
(Fuente Vaqueros, 1898 – between Viznar and Alfacar, 1936)

Spanish poet, playwright and writer, he is also known for his skill in many other arts. He was part of the well-known literary movement called the Generation of '27. One of the most influential and popular poets of 20th-century Spanish literature, Lorca was executed after the military uprising of the Spanish Civil War. He travelled throughout Andalusia and Castile collecting and transcribing old popular songs and, in 1922, along with composer Manuel de Falla, he organised the First Cante Jondo Competition, held in the Plaza de los Aljibes in the Alhambra, an event attended by the best singers and guitarist players from every corner of Spain. Federico, as a good son of Granada, served as host to his friends and literary colleagues both in the city and at the Alhambra, of which he left us pages such as:

The Manolas in the Alhambra

Granada, Elvira Street, where the Manolas live,
the ones who go to the Alhambra in threes and fours,
*   alone. One is dressed in green,*
the other in mauve, the third wears a Scotch bodice
with ribbons to the train.
The two in front are herons, the one behind, a dove;
they open mysterious muslins along the tree-lined
*   avenue.*
Oh, how dark is the Alhambra! Where will
*   the Manolas go while the fountain and the rose*
*   suffer in the shade?*
Which young men are waiting for them? Under which
myrtle are they resting?
Whose hands are stealing the perfume
from their two round flowers? No one goes with them,
*   no one; two herons and a dove.*
But there are gallant young men in the world who
hide behind leaves. The cathedral has left
bronzes which the breeze takes up.
The Genil sleeps its oxen, and the Dauro its
*   butterflies. The night arrives burdened*
with its hills of shadow; one shows her shoes
between flounces of lace, the older opens her eyes,
*   and the younger half-closes hers.*
Who are they, those three,
with high breasts and long trains?
Why are they waving their kerchiefs? Where will they
*   go at these hours? Granada, Elvira Street, where*
*   the Manolas live,*
who go to the Alhambra in threes and fours, alone.

From *Doña Rosita la soltera*
o el lenguaje de las flores (1935).

Maurits Cornelis Escher
(1898 – 1972)

Dutch artist known for his engravings, woodcuts and lithographs focusing on impossible figures, tessellations and imaginary worlds. His work experiments with various methods of representing (in two- or three-dimensional drawings)

paradoxical spaces that defy the usual methods of representation. Even without being a mathematician, his works show an interest and a deep understanding of geometrical concepts, from perspective to curved spaces, including the division of the plane into equal figures. Escher travelled to Spain, and in particular to Granada, where he twice visited the Alhambra, the second time more carefully, copying many ornamental motifs. What he learned in the Alhambra would strongly influence many of his works, especially those related to the regular partition of the plane and the use of patterns that fill space without leaving any empty gaps.

José Val del Omar
(Granada, 1904 – Madrid, 1982)

Film director, he was a contemporary and friend of Lorca, Cernuda, Renau, Zambrano and other important figures in a Silver Age truncated by the Civil War. By 1928 he was already touching on some of his most characteristic techniques, such as "apanoramic overflow of the image" beyond the limits of the screen, and the concept of "tactile vision". Among his works is the outstanding Aguaespejo Granada (1953).

Francisco Prieto Moreno
(Granada, 1907 – Granada, 1985)

He served as architectural curator of the Alhambra during the period of Franco's dictatorship. Architectural curator of the Séptima Zona repair project beginning in August 1936, he was subsequently appointed Director-General of Architecture. Author of leading projects throughout the province of Granada, he was responsible for major works designed to adapt the monument to public tours and for upgrading the Jardines Nuevos del Generalife.

Jesús Bermúdez Pareja
(Granada, 1908 – Granada, 1986)

Professor of Art History at the University of Granada and member of the Organisation of Archivists, Librarians and Archaeologists, he was the first director of the Archaeological Museum of Mérida and, beginning in 1943, of the Archaeological Museum of the Alhambra, which would later become the National Museum of Hispanic-Muslim Art (1962). Linked throughout his professional life to the Alhambra, he contributed to the creation (1965) of the journal Cuadernos de la Alhambra, overseeing the section "Crónica de la Alhambra", which published his best research.

Emilio García Gómez
(Madrid, 1905 – 1995)

He studied Liberal Arts and, at twenty years of age, was assistant professor to a full professor. In 1927 he won a scholarship to study Arabic-Spanish manuscripts in Egypt, Syria and Mesopotamia. In 1935 he competed and won the Chair of Arabic Language at the University of Granada, a position he held until 4 June 1970, when he was received as a Doctor "Honoris Causa" at the same university. Together with Miguel Asín and Juan Miguel Ribera, he founded the School of Arab Studies in Granada and a similar institution in Madrid, where he founded the prestigious journal Al-Andalus. Among his many works were outstanding texts devoted to the Alhambra. García Gómez received the National History of Spain Prize (1990), the Prince of Asturias Award for Humanities and served as Director of the Royal Academy of History.

Detail of *Platform* by Ambrosio Vico (ca. 1614) in which the Alhambra and Generalife complex can be seen

Name Index

Glossary

Abencerrage member of a 15th-century family of Granada ruling as sultans, rival of the Zegris family

abocelado in a parapet, the semi-circular or oval-shaped convex moulding finish

acequia trench or canal where water is guided for irrigation and other purposes

acequiero water distributor

acropolis in Greek cities, the highest and most protected site; the highest part of a city

agronomist expert in agriculture

alacena closet, cupboard in the wall having doors or shutters

alambor 1: artificial version of stone or wood; 2: scarp or rough decline

alarife architect or master builder

albarrada wall of dry stone

alcazaba fortress, within a walled city, for the guardís refuge

alcazar 1: fortress; 2: royal home or princeís room, not necessarily fortified

aleya a verse or passage from the Koran

alfardón hexagonal, elongated tile having a rectangular centre

alfarje flat, decorated, carved wooden ceiling

alfiz Arab-style arch frame surrounding spandrels, originating either from the impost or the floor

algorfa upstairs floor or chamber

alhamí low stone bench covered in tiles

alicatado tile covering

alicer each of the individual pieces forming a border or frieze of tiles of different works; a set of these

alifato series of Arab consonants in a traditional order, the Arab alphabet

aljibe an underground water tank

aljofar seed pearl; an irregularly shaped and small-sized pearl

almatraya traditional flooring of glazed clay, typically with geometric shapes and kerb, beyond the threshold of the main rooms and areas in homes and palaces

almendrilla type of ornamental work that imitates small almonds

Almohad followers of Ibn Tumart, the 12th-century Muslim leader who unified the occidental tribes of Africa and gave rise to a new empire resulting in the downfall of the Almoravide tribe

Almoravid member of a warring tribe from the Atlas Mountains that founded a vast empire in Western Africa and conquered all of Muslim Spain from 1093 until 1148

almunia rural plot, grove or farm

alpañata very red clay earth

alquería farm workers' cottage

anastylosis the reconstruction of monuments or other structures from their broken parts

Andalusí pertaining to or relating to Al-Andalus or Muslim Spain

apoditerio hall or wardrobe of a bathroom

arrayán shrubs of the Myrtle family

arriate narrow area adorned with plants along the walls of gardens and patios

arrocabe woodwork situated on top of the walls of a building in order to link the walls together with the supported frame

artesón concave, polygonal shaped constructive element with decorations that are presented in series on the panelling

ashlar each of the processed stones typically in the shape of a cuboid rectangle, forming part of a hewn stone construction

atalaya watchtower typically located in a high position, for defending the area

atarjea brick box covering piping for its protection

ataujía precise and complex decorative work

ataurique Arab stylized plant motifs

athanor fired clay pipe for channelling water

barbican detached, separate tower used to defend ports, plazas or bridges

barrel vault a vault typically having a semi-cylindrical shape covering the space between two parallel walls

base the bottom part of a column in all classical architectural orders except in the Doric

basin stone receptacle in fountains serving for drinking, washing or other uses

bastion defensive structure that protrudes from the corner of two walls and consists of two sides forming an outward angle, two flanks that join them to the wall and an entranceway

bay space between two support walls

calahorra castle; place near a fortification

caliph title given to the Arab princes who, as successors of Mohammad, held the ultimate religious and civil powers in some Muslim territories

caliphate (Sp. *califato*) territory governed by a caliph

candilejo corn cockle (plant); a geometric decorative figure

cartouche piece of paper, wood or other material, in the form of a card, on which to draw or write

carmen house with garden or grove; vineyard

cauchil arched water distributor

celosía criss-crossed lattice arrangement of wood, gypsum or metal, placed in building windows in order to filter light and to see outwards without being seen

centring frame that supports the weight of an arch or other construction, designed to fill a space as it is not capable of supporting itself

chancellery high ranking diplomatic office in which external policy is directed

cloister vault cylindrical shaped dome

coffering ceiling, frame or dome formed by panels of wood or stone or other materials

collar beam piece or wedge of wood that is built in, in order to nail into something such as ceiling beams or window frames

conglomerate mass formed by fragments of diverse minerals joined with cement

corbel head of a beam or cantilevered piece that extends over the edge to support an eave, cover or lintel

Corinthian architectural style consisting of columns with a height of ten times their diameter, a capital decorated with acanthus leaves and spirals, and cornice with corbels

cornice upper part of an entablature

crossbeam board which supports the rafters and forms the of the backbone of the framework

cryptic dark, mysterious

cursive Arabic writing style with rounded features, resembling the typical manuscript writing

diacritic referring to an orthographic symbol that serves to give a letter or a word some distinctive meaning

dithyramb exaggerated praise, passionate hymn

diwán collection of poetry by one or various authors

Doric architectural style with columns of eight units or diameters in height, a simple capital, and a frieze decorated with metopes and triglyphs

dryland very dry place, uncultivated

dry string technique for decorating tiles consisting of tracing the design on the tile, outlining the edges with a special grease and filling each coloured area with a glaza (a type of diluted glass powder); the different parts of the drawing become a relief with a thing line incised between them

embrasure (Sp. *buhedera*) hole in a wall through which to harass the enemy

emir arab prince or leader

emirate territory ruled by an emir

empyreal pertaining to the sky or the concentric spheres in which the stars moved according to ancient beliefs

entablature set of mouldings that crown a building or mark the division of its floors

epigraphy the study and interpretation of inscriptions

escarpment flat slope that forms the wall of the main section of a fortification, from the cordon to the trench and counterscarp

eschatology set of beliefs and doctrines about the afterlife

extrados external convex surface of an arch or dome counter set against the inner curve

facing each of the two sides of a wall

Fatimid descendents of Fatima, daughter of Muhammad

fitna civil war

forum in ancient Rome, the public square where meetings and trials were held

frieze part of the entablature between the architrave and the cornice on which foliage and other decorations are typically shown

galley slave a man forced to row in the galley of a boat

gallón each of the wedge-shaped segments in certain arches and other objects with this type of finish (fountains, pillars, etc.), rounded at its widest end

gargoyle end part of a spout or gutter for draining water from roofs or fountains is drained; it typically has a striking design

grotesque whimsical decoration of insects, vermin and foliage

gypsum mineral used to make plaster

harem room in Muslim homes where women reside

hisbah set of rules governing public morality

hypocaust section of a classic or Roman bath that is heated with underground pipes and burners

impost supporting surface of the beginning point of an arch or vault

intrados lower surface of an arch or vault

Ionic architectural style having columns that are nine units or diameters in height, a capital decorated with large scrollwork and denticles in the cornice

iwan pavilion enclosed on three sides and opening into a room or patio

jaima Bedouin tent

jamb each of the two pieces that when placed vertically on the two sides of doors or windows, support the lintel or the arch

jamuga folding chair with curved legs and straps to rest the back and arms

jineta sword straight, double-edged sword with a middle groove, spindle-shaped handle and rounded knob, typical of the Nasrid culture

kasbah fortress, alcazaba

keystone stone that locks the parts of an arch or vault into place

Kufic Arabic writing style characterized by geometric features and straight lines, whose development led to ingenious decorative creations

lantern small tower with windows that tops off some domes or cupolas

latticework decoration formed with interwoven bands following a decorative pattern

lintel upper part of doors, windows and other spaces that rests on the jambs

machicolation projecting body at the top of a wall of a tower or a fortified gateway, with a parapet and with a floor with openings, used to observe and harass the enemy

madrasah Muslim school of higher studies

maqabriyya long flat stone tablet, of triangular sections, on the longitudinal axis of a tomb

maqbarat cemetery

mascarón disfigured or exaggerated face used as decoration in certain architectural works

mastaba rectangular tomb found in the interior of Muslim buildings

mawlid celebration of the birth of Mohammed

medina city; old neighbourhood of a Muslim city

metope in a Doric frieze, the space between two triglyphs

mihrab a niche or alcove located in the qibla wall in mosques and Muslim oratorios, indicating the direction for prayer

minaret mosque tower, typically tall and thin, from which the Muslim call to prayer is announced

mint factory where money is produced

mixtilinear arch an arch formed by combining straight and curved sections

mocárabe design created by combining geometrically grouped prisms, whose bottom points are cut in a concave shape, used as decoration on domes, cornices, etc. Also known as "stalactite ceilings".

mocheta niche in the doorframe or windows, where the groove is fitted

mudéjar 1: Muslim who continues living among the Christian conquerors without converting from their religion, in exchange for a tax payment; 2: architectural style that flourished in Spain from the 13th to the 16th centuries; it conserved elements of Christian art while using Arab decorative styles

muffle semi cylindrical or cup-shaped furnace that is placed within an oven in order to redirect the heat and achieve the fusion of various bodies

mullion thin column that divides a door or window into two parts

mullioned window wooden balcony with latticework shutters

muqarna mocárabe

Nasji variant of Arabic script

Nasrid descendents of Yusuf Ibn Nasr, founder of the dynasty that reigned in Granada from the 13th to the 15th centuries

parata land terraced in order to plant or grow crops

pedestal body placed under the column structure and consisting of the base and the foundation

pediment triangular shaped finish of a wall or colonnade; it also may be placed on top of doors and windows

pendentive each of the four curvilinear triangles that form the ring of the dome with the sub-arches on which they rest

plinth squared bottom section of a base

poliorcetics the art of attacking and defending strongholds

postern in fortifications, a door that is smaller than any of the main ones, and larger than an opening, found at the end or extreme of a ramp

qanat structure used to capture and channel groundwater

qasida extensive poetic genre that makes references to kings and nobility

qibla wall, generally in the front of a mosque, used to orient prayer in the direction of Mecca

quarter parcel of land enclosed for a determined purpose

qubba square room or floor covered with a wooden dome or rounded roof

quoin post board that supports and holds the doors and windows with bolts and hinges, so that they open and close when they turn

rafter each of the two wooden planks that in a timber framing form the inclination of the roof

rampart protected walkway located behind a parapet in the raised area of a wall or battlement

rawda Muslim cemetery and garden

rigattino pictorial restoration technique consisting of very thin, closely spaced coloured lines

riser slat covering a space such as a hole or the front of a doorstep

rowlock bond work consisting of bricks laid out edgewise

rustication in architecture, walls inlaid with protruding blocks having slanted or rounded edges

water bucket metal or clay container used to draw water from wells and rivers; a string of them is tied to the wheel of the noria

sebka decorative element in a rhombus, lobular or mixtilinear form that is typically presented grouped together

Serlian architectural device named after Serlio, Italian Renaissance architect and theorist

silo underground storage area for seeds, wheat and other grains

sino central piece, typically star-shaped, having a decorative geometric shape

spandrel a triangular-shaped space located between the arch frame and the arch

springer stone of a wall or pier cut at an angle from where an arch begins

squinch projecting dome outside of the facing of a wall

sultan Muslim prince or ruler

sura each of the lessons or chapters of the Qur'an

tahona home or business premise where bread is made and sold

taifa each of the reigns or sultanates into which Muslim Spain was divided after the fall of the Caliphate of Cordoba

tapia wall built of rammed earth, using a mould to contain and compact the soil

tannery leather curing industry

taqa small niche or opening in the jambs of arches or access doors, characteristic of Nasrid architecture

taujel strip of wood; construction level

toothing each of the gaps between the bricks of the horizontal edge of a wall in order to later continue its progress; one of the figures forming a geometric decoration

topiary art of decorating with plants

torus a smooth convex moulding having a semi-circular or elliptical cross-section

triglyph decoration of Doric frieze having a protruding rectangular shape and three vertical channels

trompe líoeil (Fr. "trick of the eye") artistic technique that attempts to trick the eye with perspective and other optical illusions

Umayyad descendants of the Arab leader of the same name, founders of the Caliphate of Damascus, substituted in the 8th century by the Abbasid dynasty

umbrella vault vault formed by wedge-shaped segments ("gallons") creating a circular shape at the widest end

undercarriage frame composed of two planks that are solidly joined together with crossbars and clamps attached to the wheels or the skids on which the cannon is mounted

vizier minister of a Muslim sovereign

volute a spiral-like shape in the capital

voussoir wedge-shaped stone used to form an arch or vault, the lower border of an alfarje, etc.

walí governor

wazír prime minister

zafa serving plate of various typology, including glazed, unglazed and very beautifully decorated

zafariche pool, fountain, trough or small reservoir with spouts

Ziriid Berber dynasty originating in Algeria and moving to Al-Andalus and which founded the taifa of Granada in 1013

Figure painted on one of the ceilings of the Sala de los Reyes in the Palacio de los Leones

Bibliographical Selection

General works

ARIÉ, Rachel. *El Reino nasrí de Granada: (1232-1492)*. Madrid: Mapfre, 1992.

CABANELAS RODRÍGUEZ, Darío. *Literatura, arte y religión en los palacios de la Alhambra*. Granada: Universidad de Granada, 1984.

CUADERNOS de la Alhambra. Granada: Patronato de la Alhambra y Generalife. Vols. 1-42 (1965-2007). ISSN 0590-1987.

FERNÁNDEZ PUERTAS, Antonio. «El Arte». In: JOVER ZAMORA, J.M. *Historia de España Menéndez Pidal*. Madrid: Espasa-Calpe, 2000, Vol. VIII-III.

FERNÁNDEZ PUERTAS, Antonio. *The Alhambra*. Londres: Saqi Books, 1997.

GALLEGO Y BURÍN, Antonio. *La Alhambra*. Granada: Patronato de la Alhambra y Generalife, 1963.

GRABAR, Oleg. *La Alhambra: iconografía, formas y valores*. Madrid: Alianza Editorial, 1980.

MALPICA CUELLO, Antonio. *La Alhambra de Granada, un estudio arqueológico*. Granada: Universidad de Granada, 2002.

PAVÓN MALDONADO, Basilio. *Estudios sobre la Alhambra*. Granada: Patronato de la Alhambra y Generalife, 1975-1977.

PLAN especial de protección y reforma interior de la Alhambra y Alijares. Granada: Patronato de la Alhambra y Generalife, 1986.

PUERTA VÍLCHEZ, José Miguel. *Los códigos de utopía de la Alhambra de Granada*. Granada: Diputación Provincial de Granada, 1990.

ROSENTHAL, Earl E. *El Palacio de Carlos V en Granada*. Madrid: Alianza Editorial, 1988.

SALMERÓN ESCOBAR, Pedro. *La Alhambra: estructura y paisaje*. Granada: Patronato de la Alhambra y Generalife; Jaén: Tinta Blanca; Sevilla: Almuzara, 2006.

STIERLIN, Henri. *Alhambra*. París: Imprimerie Nationale, 1991.

TORRES BALBÁS, Leopoldo. *La Alhambra y el Generalife*. Madrid: Plus Ultra, 1953.

VIGUERA MOLINS, María Jesús (coord.). «El reino nazarí de Granada (1232-1492): política, instituciones, espacio y economía». In: JOVER ZAMORA, J. M. *Historia de España Menéndez Pidal*. Madrid: Espasa-Calpe, 2000. Vol. VIII-III.

VIÑES MILLET, Cristina. *La Alhambra de Granada. Tres siglos de Historia*. Sevilla: Publicaciones del Monte de Piedad y Caja de Ahorros de Sevilla, 1982.

Specific Works

ÁLVAREZ LÓPEZ, José. *La Alhambra entre la conservación y la restauración (1905-1915)*, Cuadernos de Arte de la Universidad de Granada, 1977, vol. xv.

BARGEBUHR, Frederick P. *The Alhambra: a Cycle of Studies on the eleventh Century in Moorish Spain*. Berlin: Walter de Gruyter & Co., 1968.

BERMÚDEZ PAREJA, Jesús. *Pinturas sobre piel en la Alhambra de Granada*. Granada: Patronato de la Alhambra y Generalife, 1987.

CABANELAS RODRÍGUEZ, Darío. *El techo del Salón de Comares en la Alhambra*. Granada: Patronato de la Alhambra y Generalife, 1988.

CASTILLO BRAZALES, Juan. *Palacio de Comares. Corpus epigráfico de la Alhambra*. Granada: Patronato de la Alhambra y Generalife, 2007.

CHAMORRO MARTÍNEZ, Victoria E. *La Alhambra: el lugar y el visitante*. Granada: Patronato de la Alhambra y Generalife y Tinta Blanca Editor, 2006.

DÍEZ JORGE, Elena. *El Palacio islámico de La Alhambra: propuesta para una lectura multicultural*. Granada: Universidad de Granada, 1998.

DIWAN Ibn Zamrak al-Andalusi: Muhammad b. Yúsuf al-Sarihi. Texto editado y anotado por Muhammad Tawfiq al-Nayfar. Bayrut: Dar al-Garbí al-Islamí, 1997.

FERNÁNDEZ PUERTAS, Antonio. *La Fachada del Palacio de Comares*. Granada: Patronato de la Alhambra y Generalife, 1980.

GALERA ANDREU, Pedro. *La imagen romántica de la Alhambra*. Granada: Patronato de la Alhambra y Generalife, Madrid: El Viso, 1992.

GÁMIZ GORDO, Antonio. *Alhambra: imágenes de ciudad y paisaje (hasta 1800)*. Granada: Fundación El Legado Andalusí: Patronato de la Alhambra y Generalife, 2008.

GARCÍA GÓMEZ, Emilio. *Foco de antigua luz sobre la Alhambra: desde un texto de Ibn al-Jatib en 1362*. Madrid: Instituto Egipcio de Estudios Islámicos, 1988.

GARCÍA GÓMEZ, Emilio. *Ibn Zamrak, el poeta de la Alhambra*. Granada: Patronato de la Alhambra y Generalife, 2006.

GARCÍA GÓMEZ, Emilio. *Poemas árabes en los muros y fuentes de la Alhambra*. Madrid: Instituto Egipcio de Estudios Islámicos, 1985.

MANIFIESTO de la Alhambra. Madrid: Dirección General de Arquitectura, 1954.

ORIHUELA UZAL, Antonio. *Casas y Palacios nazaríes. Siglos XIII-XV*. Barcelona: Lunwerg, Granada: El Legado Andalusí, 1996.

RAQUEJO, Tonia. *El palacio encantado: la Alhambra en el arte británico*. Madrid: Taurus Humanidades, 1990.

RUBIERA MATA, Mª Jesús. *Ibn al-Yayyab: el otro poeta de la Alhambra*. Granada: Patronato de la Alhambra y Generalife, 1994.

SANTIAGO SIMÓN, Emilio. *La voz de la Alhambra*, Granada: Patronato de la Alhambra y Generalife y Tinta Blanca Editor, 2009.

Torre, Mª José de la. *Estudio de los materiales de construcción de la Alhambra*, Universidad de Granada, 1995.

Vilar Sánchez, J. A. *Los Reyes Católicos en la Alhambra: readaptaciones hechas por los Reyes Católicos en los palacios y murallas de la Alhambra y en las fortalezas de Granada desde enero de 1492 hasta agosto de 1500 con algunos datos hasta 1505*. Granada: Patronato de la Alhambra y Generalife, 2007.

Vílchez Vílchez, Carlos. *La Alhambra de Leopoldo Torres Balbás (obras de restauración y conservación 1923-1936)*. Granada: Comares, 1988.

Viñes Millet, Cristina. *La Alhambra que fascinó a los románticos*. Sevilla: Tinta Blanca Editor, Patronato de la Alhambra y Generalife, 2007.

Reference Works

Arié, Rachel. *España Musulmana (siglos VIII-XV)*. Barcelona: Labor, 1983.

Burckhardt, Titus. *El Arte del Islam. Lenguaje y significado*. Palma de Mallorca: José J. de Olañeta, 1999.

Creswell, K. Archibald Cameron. *Compendio de Arquitectura Paleoislámica*. Sevilla: Universidad de Sevilla, 1979.

Eguaras, Joaquina. *Ibn Luyún: tratado de Agricultura*. Granada: Patronato de la Alhambra y Generalife, 1988.

Gómez Moreno, Manuel. *Guía de Granada*. Granada: Imprenta de Indalecio Ventura, 1892.

Grabar, Oleg. *La formación del Arte islámico*. Madrid: Cátedra, 1984.

Ibn Al-Jatib. *Historia de los reyes de la Alhambra el resplandor de la luna llena (Al-Lamha al-badriyya).*

Molina López, Emilio (prel. stud.); Casciaro Ramírez, José (trans. and prol.). Granada: Universidad de Granada, 1998.

Insoll, Timothy. *The Archeology of Islam*. Oxford: Blackwell Publishers, 1999.

Les Jardins de L'Islam: 2ème Colloque International sur la Protection et la Restauration des Jardins Historiques, Grenade, du 29 octobre au 4 novembre 1973 = Islamic gardens: 2nd International Symposium on Protection and Restoration of Historical Gardens, Granada, October 29th to November 4th, 1973. París: Icomos, 1976.

Levy-Provençal, E.; García Gómez, Emilio. *El siglo XI en 1ª persona. Las memorias de Abd Allah, último rey zirí de Granada, destronado por los almorávides (1090)*. Madrid: Alianza Editorial, 1980.

Marçais, Georges. *El arte musulmán*. Madrid: Cátedra, 1983.

Pareja, Félix Mª. *Islamología*. 2 vols. Madrid, 1952-1954.

Puerta Vílchez, José Miguel. *La aventura del cálamo: historia, formas y artistas de la caligrafía árabe*. Ganada: Edilux, 2007.

Rosselló Bordoy, Guillermo. *El nombre de las casas en al-Andalus: una propuesta de terminología coránica*. Palma de Mallorca, 1991.

Rubiera Mata, Mª Jesús. *La arquitectura en la literatura árabe. Datos para una estética del placer*. Madrid: Editora Nacional, 1981.

Santiago Simón, Emilio. *Las claves del mundo islámico 622-1945*. Barcelona: Planeta, 1991.

Torres Balbás, Leopoldo. *Arte Almohade, Arte Nazarí, Arte Mudéjar*. Madrid: Plus Ultra, 1949.

Literary Works

Chateaubriand, François-René. *El último abencerraje*. Madrid: Espasa Calpe, 1979.

Espadafor Caba, Manuel. *Un siciliano en la Alhambra*. Granada: Ediciones Miguel Sánchez, 2006.

Gala, Antonio. *El Manuscrito Carmesí*. Barcelona: Planeta, 1990.

García Fresneda, Ángeles. *La fórmula*. Granada: Ediciones Miguel Sánchez, 2009.

García Gómez, Emilio. *Silla del moro y Nuevas escenas andaluzas*. Granada: Ed. Fundación Rodríguez-Acosta, 1978.

Hazm, Ibn. *El Collar de la Paloma: tratado sobre el amor y los amantes*. Traducido del árabe por Emilio García Gómez. Madrid: Alianza Editorial, 1971.

Irving, Washington. *Cuentos de la Alhambra*. Edición y prólogo de Antonio Gallego Morell. Madrid: Espasa Calpe, 1991.

Jiménez, Juan Ramón. *Olvidos de Granada*. Edición, introducción y notas de Manuel Ángel Vázquez Medel. Granada: Diputación de Granada, 2002.

Maalouf, Amin. *León el Africano*. Madrid: Alianza Editorial, 2003.

Rodríguez Almodóvar, Antonio. *El palacio de los cuatro tesoros: un cuento sobre la Alhambra*. Madrid: S.M., 2008.

Romero, Felipe. *El segundo hijo del mercader de sedas*. Granada: Editorial Comares, 2003.

Seco de Lucena Paredes, Luis. *Los Abencerrajes. Leyenda e historia*. Granada: Imp F. Román, 1960.

Tariq, Alí. *A la sombra del granado*. Madrid: Alianza Editorial, 2003.

15　Notebook